The Real
Relationship
in Psychotherapy

The Real Relationship in Psychotherapy

The Hidden Foundation of Change

Charles J. Gelso

American Psychological Association • Washington, DC

Published by
American Psychological Association
750 First Street, NE
Washington, DC 20002
www.apa.org

To order
APA Order Department
P.O. Box 92984
Washington, DC 20090-2984
Tel: (800) 374-2721; Direct: (202) 336-5510
Fax: (202) 336-5502; TDD/TTY: (202) 336-6123
Online: www.apa.org/pubs/books/
E-mail: order@apa.org

In the U.K., Europe, Africa, and the Middle East, copies may be ordered from
American Psychological Association
3 Henrietta Street
Covent Garden, London
WC2E 8LU England

Typeset in Goudy by Circle Graphics, Inc., Columbia, MD

Printer: The Maple-Vail Book Manufacturing Group, York, PA
Cover Designer: Mercury Publishing Services, Rockville, MD

The opinions and statements published are the responsibility of the authors, and such opinions and statements do not necessarily represent the policies of the American Psychological Association.

Library of Congress Cataloging-in-Publication Data

Gelso, Charles J., 1941-
  The real relationship in psychotherapy : the hidden foundation of change / Charles J. Gelso. — 1st ed.
      p. cm.
  Includes bibliographical references and index.
  ISBN-13: 978-1-4338-0867-8
  ISBN-10: 1-4338-0867-6
  ISBN-13: 978-1-4338-0868-5 (e-book)
  ISBN-10: 1-4338-0868-4 (e-book)
  1. Psychotherapist and patient. 2. Psychotherapy. I. Title.

  RC480.8.G453 2011
  616.89'14—dc22
                                    2010011129

British Library Cataloguing-in-Publication Data

A CIP record is available from the British Library.

Printed in the United States of America
First Edition

CONTENTS

PREFACE

When I first started writing about the therapeutic relationship a few decades ago, the concept of the real relationship was perplexing to me. I had a hard time grasping how it fit within the matrix of relational factors in psychotherapy, especially transference and the working alliance. Was it merely the opposite of transference? Was it any different from the working alliance? Because of my fundamental questions, when Jean Carter and I wrote our early conceptual pieces (Gelso & Carter, 1985, 1994), Jean took the lead on the sections that focused on the real relationship. She believed that the real relationship was an important and distinguishable component of the overall therapeutic relationship, and her abiding belief helped me continue forward in exploring the real relationship.

From my early questioning, and tied very much to my experiences as a practicing psychotherapist and psychotherapy supervisor, clarity began to emerge about this concept. I gradually came to see that in every psychotherapy relationship there exists a person-to-person connection that is different from the work relationship (the working alliance) as well as different from, but not merely the opposite of, the transference and countertransference relationship. This personal part is generally not at center stage, but it is a key aspect of the connection between therapist and patient. I further came to believe that this person-to-person element is more or less a part of each communication between the psychotherapy participants, especially those communications that are directly or indirectly about each other and their relationship.

The real relationship is a controversial concept. It resonates with some therapists, but others express serious misgivings. This has become very clear as my collaborators and I have presented our ideas and research findings to journal editors and at conferences. In this book, I seek to clarify the controversy as well as to clarify why the concept of real relationship is an important, perhaps vital, one in psychotherapy of every persuasion.

One of the problems with the concept of real relationship is the term itself. The term "real" implies that there must be something that is unreal, too. Indeed, in my first theoretical article about the therapeutic relationship, Carter and I (Gelso & Carter, 1985) used the term "unreal" relationship to capture the patient's transference. This was probably not a good idea. As I shall discuss in this book, everything about the relationship is real in the sense that everything exists. The term real relationship, though, seeks to capture the genuine and realistic part of the relationship and communications within it. However, because of the problems with the term real relationship, in recent years I have been using the term personal relationship in conjunction with real relationship. Students and laypersons, as well as fellow professionals, seem to more easily accept the term personal relationship. However, some take issue with that term, too, because it seems to connote a nonprofessional relationship. Other terms have been used to get at the processes that I seek to capture, for example, the new relationship, the realistic relationship, the I–thou relationship. Each is problematic. After struggling with this question of terminology for a quarter century or so, I have concluded that there is no one term that fully and satisfactorily captures the process I am seeking to capture without carrying unwanted excess baggage. I believe that we shall just have to live with this, and I suspect that we can indeed do so, while keeping mindful that the processes or substance the term depicts are far more important than the term itself!

In this book, I seek to provide a thorough treatment of the real or personal relationship, beginning with the relational context in which it is embedded and the history of the concept of real relationship (Chapter 1), and following with an exploration of its two fundamental elements, genuineness and realism (Chapters 2 and 3); the theory of the real relationship that I have framed over the years (Chapter 4); examples of the manifestation of the real relationship in the actual therapy experience (Chapter 5); the measurement and empirical study of the real relationship (Chapters 6 and 7); and a summation of some key points in the final chapter (Chapter 8). Because I want each chapter to stand mostly on its own, the reader will note more redundancy in this book than in the typical textbook. There is overlap in the content across chapters, and some case examples are repeated as they fit the material being discussed. I expect that the overlap will not detract from the process of reading the book, but of course the reader will be the final judge of that.

Although this is a scholarly work, I have also made the writing and presentation less formal than typical journal articles and books I have written. My intent is to speak to practicing psychotherapists and therapist trainees as much as to researchers and theoreticians, and it is my hope that at least some of the material dovetails with the reader's experience and thus comes to life. Because of this intent, the empirical parts of the book (especially Chapters 6 and 7) are presented in a nontechnical way, and the statistical elaborations are kept to a minimum.

I express my deep appreciation to the wonderful group of colleagues with whom I have had the good fortune to work over the years in studying the real relationship. As mentioned, Jean Carter took a major role in our early formulations of the real relationship. Jeffrey Hayes, too, contributed substantially in our book on the psychotherapy relationship (Gelso & Hayes, 1998). During the last several years, Jairo Fuertes, Frances Kelley, and Cheri Marmarosh have contributed enormously to the empirical study of the real relationship. I recall many years ago when Jairo was a graduate student in my seminar on the therapeutic relationship. His resonance to the concept of the real relationship and its importance spurred me on at a time when I had many doubts. His views influenced me more than I believe he realized. My graduate students currently and in the recent past also have been a major influence on this work, questioning in a way that has helped me stretch my thinking as well as supporting and actually conducting research on the real relationship.

I also express my gratitude to my daughter, Catherine Bayly, for her keen editorial eye and her meticulous and extremely helpful copyediting. I also thank Kalea Matsakis for her valuable feedback. APA production editor Harriet Kaplan's exceptionally careful and helpful editing of the final proofs is deeply appreciated. Finally, I extend many thanks to Susan Reynolds of the American Psychological Association for believing in this work and for guiding me through the proposal and final manuscript.

The Real
Relationship
in Psychotherapy

1

CONTEXTUALIZING THE REAL RELATIONSHIP IN PSYCHOTHERAPY AND PSYCHOANALYSIS

This book is about a concept that has been with us from the very beginnings of psychotherapy and psychoanalysis but has consistently resided in the background of our theories. Because it was so relegated, what has been termed the *real relationship* has also been poorly understood. Until recently, none of the careful definitional work that is usually devoted to scientific constructs in the behavioral sciences was afforded the real relationship; similarly, no one was studying the real relationship empirically. Many of those who did comment on the real relationship took issue with it for a variety of reasons (discussed later in this chapter). However, the concept of a real relationship in psychotherapy and psychoanalysis stayed around nonetheless, and it is my contention that it did so because practicing clinicians knew that there was something very important about this concept and the experience it implied. Indeed, my own theoretical and empirical work on the real relationship stemmed from experiences throughout my career in conducting psychotherapy, and it is those experiences that have maintained my sense of the value of the construct in the face of much dissent from both theoreticians and researchers.

In this chapter, I situate the concept of the real relationship within the broader context of the therapeutic relationship and distinguish it from other relational concepts. Then I briefly explore the history of the construct and what theoreticians of differing persuasions have had to say about it. As the reader will see, the term *real relationship* has most often been used within psychoanalytic thought, although its meanings in that context have often been highly ambiguous and varied. Despite its psychoanalytic roots, the real relationship is discussed as a vital part of all psychotherapies, and its influence exerts itself from the moment patient and therapist first encounter one another.

THE THERAPEUTIC RELATIONSHIP IN PSYCHOTHERAPY AND PSYCHOANALYSIS

The real relationship is a key part of the overall therapeutic relationship that exists between patient and therapist from their first interaction, actually from before their first meeting in the form of fantasized hopes, fears, and expectations. This overall relationship has been the topic of great attention over the years, which I shall briefly examine in the next section.

It is safe to say that there are very few generalizations one can make about psychotherapy that would receive widespread support and agreement. One such statement, however, is that the relationship that emerges between patient and therapist is very important in that it has a significant impact on the process and outcome of treatment. Even here there is disagreement about the relative impact of the therapeutic relationship in contrast to treatment techniques and methods. Just how important this relationship is, and in what ways it is seen as important, depends on who is doing the looking, and therapists from different theoretical orientations tend to have varying views about this. Still, virtually all agree that the relationship is important, and the empirical evidence surely supports this generalization (e.g., Lambert & Barley, 2002; Norcross, 2002).

The Therapeutic Relationship Defined

A remarkable fact about the theory and research that have been published on the therapeutic relationship is that so little effort has gone into defining it. When I first began to write about the therapeutic relationship, more than 2 decades ago (Gelso & Carter, 1985), I could find no definition of the phenomenon. That still seems mostly true today. Some individuals appear to have equated the relationship with the therapist-offered conditions of congruence, unconditional positive regard, and empathy as specified by client-centered therapists, in particular Carl Rogers (1957). However, such therapist-offered conditions tap aspects of the therapist's contribution to the relationship, not the relationship itself, which is immutably interactive and dyadic. Others seem to equate the relationship with the working or therapeutic alliance. This is a very narrow conception, because the working alliance captures only one component of the overall relationship, as I shall clarify later in this chapter. I should note, however, that even these apparent definitions were not offered explicitly as definitions of the therapeutic relationship.

What is the therapeutic relationship? The definition Jean Carter and I developed in 1985 seems still useful, and it was recently adopted by the Task Force on Empirically Supported Therapy Relationships sponsored by the Division of Psychotherapy of the American Psychological Association (Norcross, 2002). We defined the *therapeutic relationship* as "the feelings and attitudes that therapist and client have toward one another and the manner in which these are expressed" (Gelso & Carter, 1985, p. 159). Some have argued that this definition is too broad, and that the phrase "the manner in which they are expressed" is especially problematic. It "muddies the water and opens up the relationship to include everything" (Hill, 1994, p. 90). In contrast, I have maintained that any sound definition *must* incorporate the expression of feelings and attitudes, for without expression there can be no relationship. However, it is equally important to understand that the expression of feelings and attitudes takes on many forms, and this definition usually includes remarkably subtle variations, such as facial expressions, eye movements, and other nonverbal behaviors, as well as what are more commonly thought of as behavioral expressions.

Relationships in general, and psychotherapy relationships in particular, are complicated phenomena. Barrett-Lennard (1985) captured beautifully the complex nature of these phenomena:

> One may think of a [dyadic] relationship as being centered on the qualities and contents of experiencing of the two participating individuals with, and toward, one another. This covers a lot of territory but it does not fully encompass the ways in which the participants communicate with each other, the messages that are passed back and forth, the moment-by-moment or generalized image that A has of B's awareness of A, or of B's feeling toward A, and likewise in respect to B's image of A's interperceptions. Neither of these levels fully encompasses "a relationship" as an emergent entity that develops a life and character of its own, existing in intimate *inter*dependence with the single-person components, a "we" in the consciousness of member persons and a distinctive "you" or "they," or the like, as seen from the outside. Any of these levels of relationship can be viewed in terms of what is present or typical at a given time in the life of the relationship, or from a developmental standpoint; and interest may center on the interior process of the relationship or on the ways the relationship system maintains itself or is altered under the influence of external forces. (p. 282)

A key point made by Barrett-Lennard (1985) is that the dyadic nature of a relationship creates a "we" as well as two separate "I"s, or individuals. This "we" transcends, or at least is different from, the two "I"s, thus representing a kind of third force in any two-person relationship.

What the Relationship Is Not

For any scientific definition to be worth its salt, it must make clear what the construct it seeks to define is *not*, as much as what it is. We can usefully divide psychotherapy into a *relational aspect* and a *technical aspect*. Of course, thus far we have been talking about the relational aspect of psychotherapy. The technical aspect, the part of psychotherapy that is *not* the relationship, pertains to the techniques and methods used by therapists to bring about change, as well as the theoretically prescribed roles in which the patient and therapist engage (Gelso & Hayes, 1998). Techniques themselves may be very specific, for example, verbal techniques, such as reflection of feeling, interpretation, and open- or closed-ended questions. Techniques may also be more general, such as the gestalt two-chair technique, systematic desensitization as used by behavior therapists, or dream interpretation as used by analytic therapists. One feature of techniques, whether considered in the narrow or broad sense, is that they tend to emanate from theories of psychotherapy. Thus, the psychoanalytic, humanistic/experiential, and cognitive behavioral therapist each tends to use a set of techniques that are wedded to his or her favorite theory of therapy. The integrative therapist will use techniques tied to the theories that he or she seeks to integrate.

The roles in which therapists are involved are also prescribed by their theoretical choices, with different theories mandating differing roles for their adherents. Furthermore, theories will also suggest roles for the patients of these therapists. For example, the psychoanalytic therapist takes the role of the steady, empathic listener, who very rarely advises but who instead helps people explore their feelings, their relationships, and their histories. When the time is right, the analytic therapist will offer interpretations to help the patient gain insight. If this analytic therapist is a psychoanalyst with a classical bent, he or she will likely have the patient recline on a couch and free associate. The patient's role is to tell the therapist/analyst whatever crosses his or her mind, to not hold back thoughts or associations, and to collaborate with the therapist to gain insight into his or her conflicts. Therapists of every orientation have their roles, and they also suggest a role to which the patient must adhere if the treatment is to work.

Although the therapeutic relationship is different from the technical aspect of psychotherapy and psychoanalysis, we should not oversimplify the difference, or make it seem more than it is. In the reality of clinical practice, the relational and technical elements of psychotherapy constantly influence one another, seeming at times to even blend together.

To use interpretation as an example, the content, tone, length, and quality of a given interpretation offered by a therapist are all likely influenced by the quality of the relationship that the participants have with one another, and the relationship will affect how this interpretation is received by the patient. To continue the cycle, the quality, content, tone, length, and so on, of the interpretation will affect the relationship itself. Thus, although the technical aspects of psychotherapy are different from the relational aspects, the two are in constant synergy.

BEYOND THE GENERAL RELATIONSHIP: A TRIPARTITE MODEL

Although it is useful for the theorist and practitioner alike to think about the therapeutic relationship in general, it is not enough. To move forward, the field must become more specific than it generally has been. One way of accomplishing this greater specificity is to divide the overall relationship into components (Gelso & Carter, 1985, 1994; Gelso & Hayes, 1998). On the basis of the work of the great psychoanalyst Ralph Greenson, one of the most useful ways to divide the overall relationship is into the three components: (a) the working alliance, (b) transference–countertransference configuration, and (c) the real relationship. The stepchild in this tripartite model is clearly the real relationship, as shall be discussed in detail throughout this book. Yet the real relationship is a vitally important, perhaps the most important, component of the overall relationship. As a preface to our in-depth exploration of the real relationship, I now briefly summarize what I refer to as the *tripartite model* (Gelso & Samstag, 2008) and its components (see also, Gelso & Carter, 1985, 1994; Gelso & Hayes, 1998). My intent is to summarize the working alliance and transference–countertransference just enough to contextualize the real relationship, thus allowing an understanding of why I consider this personal relationship so vital to the overall therapeutic relationship and to the success of psychotherapy in general. Within the following summaries I provide brief definitions of the constructs.

According to the tripartite model, the working alliance, transference–countertransference, and the real relationship are present in each and every psychotherapy relationship. The extent to which one or the other is salient at a given time in the therapeutic interaction depends on many factors, for example, the particular point in treatment, treatment duration, the therapist's theoretical orientation, the personality dynamics of the patient, the patient's central problem(s), and the quality of the therapeutic relationship. Although a given component, such as transference, my be stronger and more prominent in a treatment such as psychoanalysis than in, say, cognitive behavior therapy (CBT), transference still exists in CBT and exerts an influence on the therapy.

The Working Alliance

During the past 3 decades, the working alliance has been vigorously theorized about and empirically investigated as an element that is vital to all therapies (e.g., Bordin, 1979; Horvath, 2006; Samstag, 2006). There is strong research evidence indicating that a sound working alliance contributes significantly to successful psychotherapy across the different theoretical approaches to treatment (Horvath & Bedi, 2002). The roots of this construct reside in the very beginnings of psychoanalysis. Sigmund Freud was certainly touching on something very similar to the current conception of the working alliance when he wrote about the importance of enlisting the patient as a collaborator and when he referred to the "friendly and unobjectionable transferences" that were necessary if analysis were to succeed (S. Freud, 1912/1953a). Although there were a number of key psychoanalytic papers on the alliance over the first 7 decades of the 20th century (see Gelso & Hayes, 1998), Greenson's (1965, 1967) work stands apart because, first, he theorized about a *working* alliance and, second, he sought to differentiate it from transference (and countertransference) and the real relationship. Regarding the term *working* in working alliance, this importantly signifies the purposive and collaborative effort on the part of therapist and patient in their therapeutic efforts (Gelso & Samstag, 2008; Meissner, 2000). As Greenson (1967) suggested, the working alliance is an artifact of the treatment in the sense that the sole purpose of its existence is to further the work of therapy. This relatively transference-free component emerges *from* the real relationship, which is more basic and general and, as I elaborate later in this chapter, exists any time two or more persons encounter one another.

Given these parameters, Gelso and Carter (1994) defined the *working alliance* as "the alignment or joining together of the reasonable self or ego of the client and the therapist's analyzing or 'therapizing' self or ego for the purpose of the work" (p. 297). In focusing on the reasonable side of the patient and the analyzing/therapizing side of the therapist we rely on the psychoanalytic concept of the *split* in the ego (Sterba, 1934). Thus, the ego is seen as having both reasonable/observing capacities and experiencing capacities (or sides). Although both sides are necessary for effective therapy (or living), the working alliance stems from the reasonable side, which itself allows us to stand back and reasonably observe ourselves and our experiences. The joining together of the patient and therapist's reasonable sides allows each to observe, understand, and do the work of psychotherapy in the face of the many emotional obstacles and resistances that impinge on virtually all therapies.

When this joining together occurs, the conditions for an effective working alliance described by Bordin (1979) are facilitated; that is, the patient and therapist experience a sound bond; they agree (implicitly or explicitly) on the goals of therapy and believe these are attainable, and they agree on the tasks needed to attain those goals. Along with being facilitated by a sound working alliance, these conditions also fuel the alliance.

I should say a word about the bond aspect of the working alliance, because it may seem conceptually similar to the real relationship, which certainly involves an emotional bonding. Because the working alliance focuses on the work of psychotherapy, the bond of which it is part is best thought of as a working bond, in which the participants connect around the work itself. For example, the participants feel trusting of each other that they will make the needed effort to enact their roles. The patient trusts the therapist's ability and willingness to work effectively as a therapist, and the therapist believes that the patient is willing and able to do the work of the patient, that is, in a way that is dictated by the therapist's theory of therapy. On the other hand, as I shall discuss throughout this book, the bond that is part of the real relationship is best seen as a person-to-person emotional connection that is not based on the work of therapy, although it certainly will contribute to the success or failure or that work.

Transference and Countertransference

Although transference and countertransference are constructs that very clearly originated in psychoanalysis (e.g., S. Freud, 1905/1953b, 1910/1957, 1912/1953a), and to this day are most prominently featured in the writings of psychoanalytic theorists, the phenomena they depict surely operate in every relationship. They are universals. However, the extent to which they emerge into consciousness and into the dialogue in psychotherapy will naturally depend on the theoretical inclinations of the therapist and the conditions established by the therapist, as well as by the patient and his or her problems and personality. Still, I maintain that the phenomena themselves are present in all treatments, and there is ample empirical evidence to support such a contention, as Jeff Hayes and I have elsewhere summarized (Gelso & Hayes, 1998, 2007).

Transference

Conceptions and definitions of transference have changed substantially during the past 40 years, as classical psychoanalytic theories have undergone significant changes and as self psychology, relational theories (bridging object relations theory and interpersonal theory), and intersubjective theories have gained prominence in the psychoanalytic world. As both a cause and effect of these theoretical shifts, modern psychoanalysis has at least somewhat embraced postmodern constructivism. In my work on this construct I have sought to integrate more classical thought with these currently popular conceptions. Thus, *transference* may be defined as "the client's experience of the therapist that is shaped by the client's own psychological structures and past." This experience of the therapist *"involves displacement onto the therapist of feelings, attitudes, and behaviors belonging rightfully in earlier significant relationships"* (Gelso & Hayes, 1998, p. 51).

Regarding shifting conceptions of transference in the psychoanalytic world, probably the most fundamental point of contention pertains to the extent to which transference involves distortion of the therapist by the patient. In other words, does transference involve experiencing and seeing the therapist in ways that distort the true character and experiential state of the therapist, projecting aspects of significant others in the patient's early life onto the therapist? Within classical theories, distortion has historically been seen as the heart of the process. However, in the more currently popular relational and intersubjective theories it is not. As I have studied these theories over the years, it has seemed that, really, the disagreement was about power. The relational and intersubjective schools were deeply uneasy with what they believed was the traditional view of the patient projecting onto a rather omniscient analyst who could sit back and observe objectively, offering interpretations of the patient's dynamics that were close approximations of the "real truth," if not *the* truth. In this caricature, the knowing analyst did not contribute at all to the patient's perceptions but instead was able to maintain neutrality and consistently display even-hovering attention, the analytic ideal. The relational and intersubjective analysts labeled this viewpoint a *one-person psychology*. They instead espoused a *two-person psychology* and tended to see transference as an intersubjective process to which patient and therapist each contribute and in which the therapist's job is to help the patient understand this reality that they have co-created. Despite this co-creation, it has always been understood that the patient's construction, and how he or she has experienced and perceived the therapist's contributions, is of primary interest.

Currently there appears to be an agreement among major psychoanalytic perspectives on three points: that (a) the therapist does play a role in the transference that develops; (b) the therapist or analyst cannot *not* be a contributing factor; but (c) it is still the patient's transference, and there is an important element of it, a core element, that exists across therapists. This is consistent with the definition of transference offered by intersubjectivists Stolorow and Lachmann (1984–1985) as "all the ways in which the patient's experience of the analytic relationship is shaped by his own psychological structures—by the distinctive, archaically rooted configurations of self and object that unconsciously organize his subjective universe" (p. 26) If you ponder this definition it seems clear that the patient does distort the analyst, because the patient's perceptions of the analyst are shaped by his or her own psychological structures. However, distortion should not be seen in a simple and straightforward manner, and it is not the only thing that defines transference. Distortion, in fact, is often quite subtle and complex. For example, consider idealizing transferences, as described by psychoanalytic self psychologists. Here the patient imbues the analyst with omnipotence, and self and other are partly fused; the therapist is not experienced as a fully separate person. The therapist is perceived and responded to in terms of the patient's needs and deprivations and is seen and experienced in ways that do not fit the reality of the therapist and that are not befitting the person of the therapist. Some significant distortion has taken place, but not a simple one.

In one of his earliest writings on transference, Freud (1905/1959a) actually gave us a taste of this complexity when he talked about some transferences being "revised editions." He stated that some transferences are

> ingeniously constructed; their content has been subjected to a moderating influence—to *sublimation*, as I call it—and they may even become conscious, by cleverly taking advantage of some real peculiarity in the physician's person or circumstances and attaching themselves to that. These, then, will no longer be new impressions, but revised editions. (p. 139)

Wachtel (1980) sidestepped these contentious issues around distortion by conceptualizing transference through the Piagetian terms of *assimilation* and *accommodation*. In this cognitive developmental perspective, new information that is perceived is assimilated into a preexisting mental schema, and a pre-existing schema can also be shifted to accommodate perceived information that does not fit the schemas that are already formed. Transference in this formulation may be defined as the predominance of assimilation over accommodation, whereas real relationship is seen as the predominance of accommodation over assimilation. I discuss this more fully later in this chapter.

Countertransference

Concepts and definitions of countertransference, too, have undergone considerable transformation over the past 30 years, and there are now at least four conceptions of countertransference, each with its own definition (Gelso & Hayes, 2007). Like transference, there are some basic theoretical disagreements about what constitutes countertransference. Some see it as embodied in all of the therapist's reactions to clients, whereas others require a more differentiated definition. As Jeff Hayes and I discussed in our recent book-length treatment of the topic, what is called the *totalistic conception of countertransference* (i.e., all therapist reactions are countertransference) is essentially useless from a scientific and clinical perspective, because it is so inclusive that countertransference then becomes equated with therapist reactions and loses any distinctive meaning (Gelso & Hayes, 2007). A second, more meaningful area of contention has to do with the extent to which the patient contributes to the therapist's countertransference and, indeed, co-creates it. I argue that although countertransference, like transference, is always co-created by patient and therapist, it is most fundamentally part of the therapist and has to do with the therapist's conflicts and issues. In other words, although the patient may stir the pot, it is what is in the pot to begin with that is the root cause of countertransference. Like Eagle (2000), I do not believe that the notion, popular in some quarters, that countertransference is something that is mysteriously transported into the therapist by the patient and his or her defenses (e.g., projective identification) makes good sense. Also, such a conception serves to take the responsibility for countertransference out of the therapist's hands and places it into the patient's.

Despite some areas of disagreement, there is considerable agreement in current conceptions of countertransference, and these make possible an integrative definition, as proposed by Hayes and me, as follows: "*Counter-transference is the therapist's internal or external reactions that are shaped by the therapist's past or present emotional conflicts and vulnerabilities*" (Gelso & Hayes, 2007, p. 25). Note that in this definition countertransference is rooted in the therapist's emotional conflicts or vulnerabilities, despite the inevitable stimulus from the patient. This stimulus usually serves as a trigger, which is most often a subtle or overt behavior on the part of the patient. However, the trigger may also be the general frame of the treatment. In other words:

> The patient does or says something (or more often an array of things) that connects to an area of unresolved conflict or vulnerability in the therapist. The trigger, however, may also be the therapeutic situation or frame, for example, the help-giving situation. As the trigger moves from specific patient behaviors and toward the general frame of therapy, the kind of countertransference being exhibited is more likely to be chronic. (Gelso & Hayes, 2007, p. 26)

The Real Relationship

Sitting alongside the working alliance and transference–counter-transference, and in fact commingled with them in every lived experience of psychotherapy, is what may be termed the *real relationship*. It is the transference-free element in the relationship that must be present, but one that shows itself to varying degrees in the treatment hour and even in the thoughts and fantasies of the participants outside of the session. One may also call this component the *personal relationship*, a term preferred by some (see Frank, 2006; Lipton, 1977). Following the lead of Greenson (1965, 1967), I have viewed the real relationship as consisting of two key elements: (a) genuineness and (b) realism. Thus, the real relationship may be defined as "the personal relationship existing between two or more persons as reflected in the degree to which each is genuine with the other and perceives the other in ways that befit the other." Within this conception genuineness may be viewed as being authentic or who one truly is as opposed to being phony or fake. Realism, on the other hand, is experiencing and perceiving the other in ways that befit the other rather than in ways that fit what the perceiver wishes for, needs, or fears.

Why do these two elements comprise the real relationship? It is hard to imagine a good personal relationship, one considered real by the participants, in which these two ingredients do not exist or exist only to a small extent. The inability or unwillingness to be oneself, but instead being phony, obviously does not make for a good personal or real relationship. Indeed, it is hard to feel the other is real if he is not sharing himself in ways that seem authentic. In this sense, phony and real are mutually exclusive. As for realism, a person is unlikely to feel that she is involved in anything like a real relationship if she did not feel the other was grasping her in a way that fit her but instead seemed to fit others, perhaps the perceiver, more than her. The relationship would not feel real or realistic, and would yield comments such as "Where are you coming from?" and "I just don't think you have a clue as to who I am."

These two elements of the real relationship, genuineness and realism, have been accorded different statuses in major theories. For example, historically and at present, when psychoanalytic therapists have written about the real relationship they have focused on the realism element of the real relationship. In doing so, the real relationship was used as a point of contrast to the transference relationship. The other element, genuineness, was generally not seen as important or as even a part of a real relationship. Part of the reason for this is that feelings and thoughts may be genuine but unrealistic. They may be genuinely felt and expressed but be loaded with transference, and it was transference to which real relationship was contrasted (see, e.g., A. Freud, 1954; Greenson, 1967; Meissner, 2000). Another reason for the psychoanalyst's not considering genuineness as a key part of the real relationship had to do with the analyst's general stance in analytic work. As Gelso and Hayes (1998) noted, historically, the analyst's role was so muted, his or her figure so "gray," that genuineness was not an especially meaningful concept. However, this role has changed rather dramatically as relational theories have become prominent in psychoanalysis and as the classical approaches have loosened up. As this has happened, genuineness seems to have become a more central part of theorizing about the real or personal relationship (see Frank, 2006; Wachtel, 2006).

For the humanistic/experiential therapist, for whom something like a real relationship has always been the centerpiece of psychotherapy, genuineness was the element that was attended to. Thus, for example, for Carl Rogers's client-centered or person-centered therapy, therapist genuineness or congruence was of great significance. It was one of a trio of therapist factors that were both necessary and sufficient for successful psychotherapy (the other two factors being therapist empathy and unconditional positive regard for the client; Rogers, 1957). Similarly, for the gestalt therapist, both client's and the therapist's willingness to be genuine (viz., to be real, to be truly him- or herself) is a vital part of the relationship. This authenticity allows for the development of an I–thou relationship, which is the hallmark of a good therapeutic relationship for this group of therapists. On the other hand, for therapists of this theoretical ilk, the concept of realism was never especially meaningful. This may be because humanistic approaches are deeply rooted in phenomenology, a philosophy in which the individual's perceptions are what matters. Within this philosophical framework it is not especially meaningful to think of a reality out there, for it is persons' inner reality, and the reality that they construct, that matters. Modern-day constructivism, which seems especially attractive to humanistic therapists, is closely linked to phenomenology.

Finally, for a third major cluster of theoretical approaches, the cognitive behavior theories, although the therapeutic relationship is now seen as an important part of successful treatment (see Goldfried & Davila, 2005; Holtforth & Castonguay, 2005; Lejuez, Hopko, Levine, Gholkar, & Collins, 2005), just which aspect of the real relationship is important is not differentiated. Indeed, when these theoreticians focus on the relationship, they most often seem to be referring to the working alliance and the real relationship, but the more finely grained distinctions that I think are so important as the field moves forward are not made as of yet by cognitive behavior therapists.

The Push and Pull of the Three Components

I shall have much more to say about these elements of the real relationship in subsequent chapters. For now, however, it is worth commenting on how the real relationship operates in the context of the therapeutic relationship in general and in relation to the other components of the tripartite model. The key point is that in psychotherapy, for both patients and therapists, and regardless of the therapist's theoretical orientation, the three components are far from separate but instead are constantly interacting synergistically.

During the psychotherapy hour, the therapist's job is to listen empathically and take in what the patient is communicating, verbally and nonverbally, and then respond in ways that are consistent with the therapist's implicit or explicit theory of therapy. Thus, for example, a cognitive behavior therapist may make suggestions, a person-centered therapist may reflect the patient's underlying feelings, and a psychoanalytic therapist may offer interpretations when the time is right. As this is occurring the three components are all at work simultaneously, each influencing and at times merging into the others as the treatment hour unfolds. This simultaneous and overlapping manifestation of the components is always at play, although usually implicitly. However, at times one or the other of the components moves from the background into the foreground. For example, when stressed or ruptured, or when most needed, the working alliance becomes salient.

At other times, the transference or countertransference may take center stage, and in some cases these become so salient that even therapists who do not ordinarily attend carefully to them will take notice and respond to their press. Within this context, the real or personal relationship, though always present, at times is placed in bold relief. Thus, who the participants are as human beings, how each feels toward the person of the other, and the genuineness of their interchanges become very prominent. This is especially likely to happen at the beginning of treatment and at the end of treatment. It is also likely to happen during times of stress in the relationship. For example, when the patient is experiencing transference-based negative reactions toward the therapist, the personal bond that they have, based on their reality-based feelings toward one another and their personalities, will serve to buffer the overall relationship. In this way, the real relationship and working alliance join together to allow the patient to experience reality-based, nontransferential feelings toward the therapist and to work to understand the negative reactions, to the benefit of the work. It is interesting to note that this role of the real relationship was very pronounced in the views of experienced therapists in a qualitative study of successful, long-term psychoanalytic therapy (Gelso, Hill, Mohr, Rochlen, & Zack, 1999).

As implied, one key way in which the components operate interactively is through the influence that each has on the others. Thus, the working alliance is theorized as emerging from the real relationship, and the two together will influence the extent to which the patient is able to express and gain an understanding of difficult and painful transference feelings. These transferences, in turn, affect the alliance and real relationship. Also, the countertransference is affected by the real relationship and working alliance and by transference as well. Consistent with most psychoanalytic theories, the patient may be seen as unconsciously aiming to influence the therapist through transference. Thus, the patient unconsciously wishes to create certain feelings, thoughts, and behaviors in his or her therapist, some aimed at maintaining the patient's defenses, others seeking to establish conditions for growth. Countertransference, at least as inwardly experienced by the therapist, may be seen as partly a reflection of this patient press. How countertransference is then dealt with by the therapist has major implications for the transference, working alliance, real relationship, and the treatment in general.

Throughout all of this interaction among the components of the tripartite model, the real relationship exists and is the most fundamental element. Transference would be meaningless if it were not for a real relationship, and the working alliance could not exist, either, if it did not emerge from the real relationship. Although some, myself included, have considered the working alliance to be the bedrock of the psychotherapy relationship, I have come to believe more and more in recent years that the real or personal relationship is actually the foundation of all that transpires.

A BRIEF HISTORICAL SKETCH OF THE REAL RELATIONSHIP

Despite its being in the background of clinical theory, the real or personal relationship between patient and therapist has been paid some attention since the beginnings of the talking cure.

The Psychoanalytic Roots

When writing about the psychoanalytic treatment of a colleague, Sigmund Freud (1937/1964) wrote that "Not every good relation between an analyst and his subject during and after analysis was to be regarded as transference; there were also friendly relations which were based on reality and which proved to be viable" (p. 222). Similarly, in the same article in which he presented his famous rule of abstinence, warning against supportively gratifying patients' neurotic needs, Freud (1912/1959b) stated that with the majority of his patients "now and then occasions arise in which the physician is bound to take up the position of teacher and mentor" (p. 399). It is hard to imagine the real relationship not playing a major role when one takes up the position of a mentor.

The real relationship aspect of the therapeutic relationships Freud formed with his patients is seen over and over in writings about his cases. Indeed, although he always displayed a concern about sharing too much with his patients, Freud did share aspects of himself and his life and his personality. According to Couch (1999), Freud expressed concern and warmth toward his patients. He freely communicated his reactions to their significant life events, and he revealed his own personal feelings about realistic issues. Witness this observation from one of his most famous cases, the Wolf-man:

> Once during an analytic hour Freud told me that he had just received word that his youngest son had broken his leg skiing, but that luckily it was a mild injury with no dangers of lasting damage. Freud went on to say that of his three sons the youngest was most like him in character and temperament. Freud came back to his younger son later in another connection. This was a time when I was occupied with the idea of becoming a painter. Freud advised me against this, expressing the opinion that although I probably had the ability, I would not find this profession

satisfying. He believed that the contemplative nature of the artist was not foreign to me but the rational (he once called me a "dialectician") predominated. He suggested that I should strive for a sublimation that would absorb my intellectual interest completely. It was on this occasion that he told me that his youngest son had also intended to become a painter, but had then dropped the idea and switched over to architecture. "I would have decided on painting" he told his father, "only if I were very rich or very poor." The grounds for this decision were that one should either regard painting as a luxury, pursuing it as an amateur, or else take it very seriously and achieve something really great, since to be a mediocrity in this field would give no satisfaction. Poverty and the "iron necessity" behind it would serve as a sharp spur goading one on to notable achievements. Freud welcomed his son's decision and thought his reasoning well founded. (Gardiner, 1971, pp. 144–145)

Although it is not hard to infer both transference and countertransference elements in this passage, it is also clear that Freud allowed a reality element into this relationship. This real or personal relationship element was also evidenced by the fact that Freud gave money to his financially strapped patient, Wolf-man, from time to time, and in a subsequent analysis with him offered to treat him without remuneration (Gardiner, 1971, Translator's note).

Although the real relationship was not often addressed in the early years of psychotherapy and psychoanalysis, there were some important and telling observations by leading analysts. Witness Esther Menaker's (1942) comment:

> It seems to us, however, important to distinguish between that part of the analytic experience which is relived as "real" (not to question the genuineness of this experience), and that part which is real, that is, which constitutes a direct human relationship between patient and analyst, which has an existence independent of transference, and which is the medium in which the transference reactions take place. . . . In general, it is important that the real relationship between patient and analyst have some content and substance other than that created by the analytic situation itself. This is accomplished if the analyst presents himself in a distinctly human role, unafraid to show his own personality and to function with friendly interest towards his patient, reserving his cooler objectivity for the material of the analysis. This functioning of the analyst as a real person, in the course of which he reveals something of his own ego, liberates the ego of the patient for freer functioning because the patient is able to relate himself to an image of the analyst which approximates this (the analyst's) personality rather than to one who places the analyst exclusively in the position of the authoritative, perfect parent. (pp. 172–185)

Like analysts at that time who addressed the topic, here Menaker was focusing on the realism aspect of the real relationship, and she also draws a hard line between what is realistic (the real relationship for Menaker) and what is transferential. More subtly, she also distinguishes the real relationship from the work of analysis, the working alliance, when she claimed that the real relationship has "content and substance other than that created by the analytic situation itself."

A decade or so later, Anna Freud addressed the topic and provided a critical comment on psychoanalytic practice that focused exclusively on the transference relationship. In reacting to a paper by Leo Stone (1954), she made the following statement:

> To make such a distinction [between real relationship and transference] coincides with ideas which I have always held on this subject. . . . We see the patient enter into the analysis with a reality attitude to the analyst; then the transference gains momentum until it reaches its peak in the full-blown transference neurosis, which has to be worked off analytically until the figure of the analyst emerges again, reduced to its true status. But—and this seems important to me—to the extent to which the patient has a healthy part of his personality, his real relationship to the analyst is never fully submerged. With due respect for the necessary strictest handling and interpretation of the transference, I still feel that somewhere we should leave room for the realization that patient and analyst are two real people, of equal status, in a real personal relationship to each other. I wonder whether our—at times complete—neglect of this side of the matter is not responsible for some of the hostile reactions which we get from our patients and which we are apt to ascribe to "true transferences" only. But these are technically subversive thoughts and ought to be "handled with care." (A. Freud, 1954, pp. 618–619)

In this quote Anna Freud demonstrated at once her allegiance to the classical psychoanalytic views of her times as well as what then was the heretical belief that there is much more to the therapeutic relationship than transference. She subsequently clarified her stance further in a personal communication with Greenson, making the following observation:

> I have always learned to consider transference in the light of a distortion of the real relationship of the patient to the analyst and, of course, that the type and manner of distortion showed up the contributions from the past. If there is not real relationship, this idea of the distorting influences would make no sense. (quoted in Greenson, 1978, p. 362)

Other analysts during this time period addressed the issue of real relationship in analytic work (e.g., Bibring, 1937; Gitelson, 1952, 1962; Stone, 1954, 1961; Zetzel, 1956). However, it remained for Ralph Greenson to address the topic in the most far-reaching way. Anna Freud's "technically subversive" thoughts about the analyst's neglect of the real relationship and the therapeutically disastrous consequences of such neglect (and the attribution of everything to transference) were picked up by Greenson when he and Milton Wexler made the following observation:

> It is precisely such thoughts that we propose to handle with both care and boldness, for there is a great need to explore these matters openly and in depth. It seems to us that what is technically subversive is to continue the evasion of the difficult problems posed by Anna Freud. (Greenson & Wexler, 1969, p. 29)

Greenson (1965, 1967, 1971, 1972, 1974) did indeed explore the real relationship with care and boldness. Unlike the analysts cited earlier, Greenson not only viewed the real relationship in terms of realistic perception, but he also added genuineness to his conception. The real relationship so conceptualized included the authentic being of the analyst, his or her personality and behavior. Greenson believed that this authenticity, of both being and behaving with the patient, was a key part of psychoanalysis. This view ran counter to then-prevalent belief that analysts must keep themselves hidden and remain outside of the analytic process.

In the years following Greenson's writing, a number of psychoanalysts examined the real relationship. The fundamental elements of such writings for many years were that the realistic aspects of the therapeutic relationship were important to take into account and to work with, that the genuine human encounter between analyst and patient was of great significance, and that analysts must do more than interpret and work from the transference relationship (see Couch, 1999; Lipton, 1977; Viederman, 1991). As the decades of the 20th century unfolded, psychoanalysts seemed more and more to take seriously these aspects of the therapeutic relationship. In addition, Couch (1999) made the point that two inherent parts of the real relationship must be differentiated and taken into account: (a) the *communications* between analyst and patient and (b) the *personalities* of the analyst and patient. Communications pertain to explicitly what patient and therapist say to one another, whereas their personalities reflect who the two are as people, which may be revealed in myriad ways. These two parts are considered throughout this book.

The historical discussion thus far has focused largely on what may be considered classical psychoanalysis. However, as I mentioned earlier when discussing transference, changes have occurred within the world of psychoanalysis, and these changes have great significance for what the therapeutic relationship is and should be about. Relational and intersubjective perspectives, growing respectively out of object relations/interpersonal theory and psychoanalytic self psychology, have gained much prominence. These theories tend to be described as two-person psychologies in which the therapeutic relationship and everything about it, including transference and countertransference, is co-constructed by both therapist and patient. Transference is no longer seen as distortion, at least in any simple, linear way. Generally aligning themselves with postmodernism and constructivism, such psychoanalytic theories place greater emphasis on the real relationship. However, as postmodern, constructivist theories, the very concept of "real," as well as the idea of reality itself, comes under question. Real becomes what is constructed by the perceiver for such modern-day phenomenologists, and the idea of transference as the distortion of an objective reality makes little sense. So, whereas these postmodern analysts support the concept of real relationship, they appear to be more ambivalent about the realism dimension or component of the real relationship. As Frank (2006) persuasively stated, for these analysts, "rather than non-distortion, the term 'real relationship' usually emphasizes personally significant and emotionally authentic but mutually subjective interchanges, with such interchanges being seen as a vital part of therapeutic action" (p. 17). (See Sterlin, 2006, for excellent examples of such relationally based analytic treatments.) At the same time, Frank underscored the great ambiguity in the current usage of the term *real relationship* and provided examples of this ambiguity "from the hodgepodge of interpretations I discovered during a review of the literature" (p. 17). It is interesting to note that this so-called hodgepodge seems to revolve around varying ways of talking about the concepts of realism and genuineness, or what I consider the two fundamental elements of the real relationship, as shall be elaborated in subsequent chapters.

Nonanalytic Conceptions of the Real Relationship

In addition to its roots in psychoanalytic-oriented therapy, the real relationship has been the focus of discussion in various other approaches, including humanistic/experiential therapies and CBT.

Humanistic/Experiential Therapies

Although there are many versions of humanistic psychotherapy, those that had by far the greatest influence on the general field of psychotherapy have been person-centered therapy (formerly *client-centered therapy*); gestalt therapy; and emotion-focused therapy, which is an integration of person-centered and gestalt therapies. Carl Rogers was, of course, the founder of person-centered therapy (e.g., Rogers, 1959), Fritz Perls the founder of gestalt therapy (e.g., Perls, 1969; Perls, Hefferline, & Goodman, 1951), and Leslie Greenberg the founder of emotion-focused therapy (e.g., Greenberg, 2002).

In essence, all of the major humanistic therapies are of a like mind when it comes to elements of a real or personal relationship. First, for these therapies the concept of "real" itself is questionable. Clearly rooted in phenomenology, and now constructivism, these approaches would all view reality as constructed by the observer instead of as objective fact. Because of this fundamental belief, the realism element of the real relationship is essentially not part of the humanistic therapist's concern. In other words, humanistic therapists do not attend in any central way to whether the client is experiencing and perceiving the therapist in a way that fits the therapist, and the humanistic therapist certainly does not interpret what may be considered transference distortions. Although therapists such as Rogers and Perls did acknowledge the existence of transference (see Gelso & Carter, 1985), it was never a central concept in their therapies. Similarly, the realism element of the real relationship was never central. Everything is seen as real in a certain sense because it emerges from the inner worlds of the therapist and patient. At the same time, nothing is real in the sense of an objective reality.

Whereas realism is not a meaningful construct in the humanistic therapies, the genuineness aspect of the real relationship is of great significance. In fact, it is perhaps the single most important element of the psychotherapy relationship, which itself is a vital aspect of treatment success. For example, Rogers (1957) saw therapist genuineness as one of three necessary and sufficient conditions that therapists must possess in a therapeutic relationship if client personality change is to occur (the other two being empathic understanding and unconditional positive regard). In other words, a high degree of therapist genuineness had to exist if treatment were to be successful, and for Rogers genuineness meant that within the therapeutic relationship the therapist "is freely and deeply himself, with his actual experience represented by his awareness of himself. It is the opposite of presenting a façade, either knowingly or unknowingly" (p. 97). It is important to note that for Rogers genuineness meant not that the therapist should "talk out his own feelings" (p. 97) but instead that the therapist needed to be in touch with his or her inner experiencing and not deceive the client about who the therapist is. As Rogers progressed in his career, though, he espoused great self-disclosure on the part of the therapist. In fact, when discussing his famous filmed psychotherapy session with a client, Gloria (American Psychological Association, 1965), he claimed that he wanted his clients to "see all the way through me."

For the gestaltists, although Perls himself was often criticized for being too technique oriented (see Prochaska & Norcross, 2007), there has always existed a great emphasis on the therapist and client engaging in an *I–thou relationship*, in which a premium is placed on a genuine encounter between two people in which each is honest and open with the other in the here-and-now moment. Lack of such genuineness was viewed as phony, and successful treatment could not ensue in the context of such a relationship.

For the emotion-focused therapy of Les Greenberg (e.g., Greenberg, 2002), the therapist is to be genuinely him- or herself. However, like Rogers, Greenberg distinguishes between genuineness as being congruent or in touch with one's inner experience and genuineness as expressing what one feels to the client. The former is almost invariably helpful, but the latter is more complex and needs to be considered in terms of its impact on the client. I shall have much more to say about this when exploring the concept of genuineness in depth in Chapter 2.

Cognitive Behavior Therapy

Like the humanist, the cognitive behavioral therapist rarely considers the realism element of the real relationship. It is not that the cognitive behavioral therapist is a constructivist who does not espouse a reality "out there." Instead, therapists who practice CBT are not as concerned about creating realistic perceptions in the client of the therapist as they are helping the client change behaviors and cognitions in the real world, the world outside of psychotherapy. Neither do they appear concerned about the genuineness element of the real relationship.

In seeking to promote client change in cognition and behavior in the real world, modern cognitive behavioral therapists are indeed concerned about a good helping relationship, but when they write about the therapeutic relationship they rarely differentiate its components. More simply, the cognitive behavioral therapist is interested in developing a good enough general relationship, often used synonymously with the term *rapport*, to facilitate the use of CBT techniques. When CBT authors do focus on aspects of the therapeutic relationship (e.g., Goldfried & Davila, 2005; Holtforth & Castonguay, 2005; Lejuez et al., 2005), they seem to emphasize the working alliance component. I should note, though, that although the term *real relationship* is not often used by cognitive behavioral therapists, some do indeed write about relational qualities that very much reflect a real relationship. I have more to say about this in Chapters 4 and 5.

So we see that the major theoretical orientations (psychoanalytic/ psychodynamic, humanistic/experiential, and cognitive behavioral) share, to varying degrees, the view that the therapeutic relationship in general is important to treatment success. We also see that many therapists of the analytic/ dynamic orientation tend now to hold the view that the real relationship is important, although the various theories within the broad analytic/dynamic orientation seem to emphasize the realism and genuineness elements differentially. The humanistic/experiential approaches do not write about the real relationship because the concept of real and reality are problematic for these phenomenological constructivists. However, they do place a premium on therapist genuineness. Finally, cognitive behavioral therapists rarely write about the real relationship and rarely address its elements of realism and genuineness. They instead focus on the therapeutic relationship in general and, when they get more specific, it is the working alliance they address.

CONCLUSION

We have reached a time in the history of psychotherapy during which there is general agreement that the therapeutic relationship between patient and therapist is a very important factor in the degree to which treatment succeeds or fails. I believe we are also beginning to understand that it is helpful to go beyond thinking about the therapeutic relationship in a general sense and to view it instead as an umbrella term consisting of various components. Of the components that have been considered, what may be termed the *real* or *personal relationship* between therapist and patient has received the least attention. The concept of real relationship, though, has been around from the beginnings of the talking cure, always in the background, especially in psychoanalytic thought. Aspects of it, too, have been of fundamental importance to the humanistic therapies. I have followed Ralph Greenson's lead and framed the real relationship as consisting of two basic elements: (a) genuineness and (b) realism. In the following two chapters, I discuss each of these in depth and clarify the significant place each holds within the real relationship and the psychotherapy relationship more generally.

2

GENUINENESS THROUGHOUT THE DECADES

As the real or personal relationship in psychotherapy has been here framed, genuineness is one of its two fundamental elements (the other being realism, the topic of Chapter 3 in this volume). The role of genuineness within the context of the real relationship was first described by Ralph Greenson (1967, 1978), from the perspective of classical psychoanalysis. In this chapter I examine Greenson's views and then explore the viewpoints about genuineness held by many present-day analysts. Despite the link of genuineness to psychoanalysis through the real relationship, the most influential conceptions of genuineness actually emanate from the humanistic perspective. Such conceptions are also explored in this chapter. I conclude the chapter with a research summary of the importance of genuineness to the success or failure of psychotherapy.

I should note at the outset that the literature on genuineness has largely focused on the therapist. The role of the patient is usually—and curiously— missing from such discussions. This is so because theories vary widely on the importance of therapist genuineness, whereas there does not seem to be any debate on patient genuineness. It seems that patient genuineness is either of very peripheral interest, as in cognitive behavior therapies, or that it is important but does not require in-depth analysis in, for example, humanistic/experiential and psychoanalytic/psychodynamic therapies. The patient in both humanistic and dynamic therapies is seen as moving from being defended to becoming more open to inner experience. This openness to experience is usually accompanied by a willingness to share one's once-denied feelings more and more in effective psychotherapy. Being in touch with oneself and sharing inner experience are part and parcel of genuineness. Later in this chapter I shall have more to say about patient genuineness as a desired quality within the real relationship.

Because the concept of genuineness and its meaning and role in psychotherapy are so tied to one's theory of psychotherapy, what follows immediately is an examination of the role of genuineness in the major theories that address it. I should first note, however, that common to all theories is the view that genuineness reflects one's authenticity and honesty, whereby outer behavior reflects some truly felt aspect of inner experience (Bohart, 2005). Genuineness also gets at one's intent to avoid deception, including self-deception (Frank, 2006), and the intent to be non-phony. There are many complexities surrounding the concept of genuineness, including its relation to self-disclosure. I explore these in later sections on the humanistic paradox and its resolution.

Although my focus in this chapter is on psychoanalytic and humanistic conceptions of genuineness, it is my contention that the real relationship, including its genuineness element, is a key component of all shades and brands of psychotherapy. Patient and therapist genuineness has about as much significance for the cognitive behavioral therapist as for the dynamic and experiential therapist.

GENUINENESS FROM A CLASSICAL PSYCHOANALYTIC PERSPECTIVE

Despite his view that genuineness was one of the two fundamental elements of real relationships in psychoanalysis, Greenson (1967, 1978) actually did not have a lot to say about genuineness, its definition, how it operated in and facilitated successful psychoanalysis, and how it was enacted by the analyst in contrast to the analysand. Neither did Greenson distinguish good or strong real relationships from poor or weak real relationships in terms of genuineness. He used the term *real* to refer to both the realistic and genuine relationship, but he never provided a formal definition of genuineness, simply suggesting that the word *real* (in addition to meaning "realistic and reality oriented") "may also refer to genuine, authentic, and true in contrast to artificial, synthetic, or assumed" (1967, p. 217).

Greenson's thoughts about genuineness on the part of both patient and analyst can be found only in bits and parts, because he focused explicitly on the realistic or realism aspect of real relationships. For example, when discussing the fact that patients do not run away from their analysts when the analyst makes mistakes (i.e., incorrect interpretations), Greenson claimed that the decisive factor in these patients' continuation in treatment "was the relative strength of the real relationship, the degree to which there existed not only positive transference but *genuine respect, liking, and also understanding on both sides*" (italics added; Greenson, 1978, p. 377). At another point, he stated that "Technical errors may cause pain and confusion, but they are usually repairable; *failure of humanness is much harder to remedy*" (italics added; 1978, p. 377).

Although Greenson believed that genuineness was important to successful treatment, he also believed that the analyst must maintain restraint and always keep the working alliance at the forefront of his or her attention. In other words, the preservation of a sound working alliance was seen as crucial to successful analysis, and the real relationship, including the analyst's genuine reactions to the patient, should be carefully modulated. However, unlike many analysts of his day, Greenson also believed that there were times when he needed to show what he felt to his patient. Witness the following:

> There are patients who try to isolate the psychoanalyst from real life and imagine he only exists in his office and his emotional responses are always well tempered and controlled. In such cases I have found it useful to allow myself to show the patient otherwise. Saying it in words is often not sufficient. I have permitted the patient at times to feel my disappointment in his lack of progress or to see that world events do concern me. I try to restrict the intensity of my reactions, but I do not open the door every day with the same expression on my face or close the session in the same way. I don't plan these variations. I allow myself to be flexible in such matters. I am of the opinion that it is of importance to demonstrate in certain actions and behavior that the analyst is truly a human being. This includes permitting some of his human frailties to be visible at times. . . . There is still one other area which requires an unusual amount of outspokenness on the analyst's part. I am referring to the situation which arises when the analyst detects that he and his patient are in basic disagreement on a political or social issue which is important to each of them. For example, I know from experience that I cannot work effectively with some patients who are reactionary in their political or social point of view. In such instances, I have found it advisable to tell such a patient of my feelings quite openly and as early in the treatment as possible. I suggest that he should feel free to seek another analyst if he finds my point of view too disturbing. If my own feelings on the matter are very intense and the patient's other qualities do not suffice to make him likable, I tell the patient that I am not able to work with him and insist that he find another analyst. (1978, pp. 223–224)

As you can see, for a classical analyst such as Greenson (and keeping in mind that he was writing in the 1960s and early 1970s), genuinely expressing what he felt was important. However, whether he showed certain feelings to patients depended on how strong those feelings were and whether he believed the feelings simply could not be effectively restrained. Greenson was not uniform in what he allowed his analysands to see in him. At the same time, he generally promoted analytic restraint. He believed that the real relationship was important and that genuineness was a vital part of it, yet he also maintained that the analyst's feelings should generally take a back seat (be restrained) and that the real relationship on the part of the analyst should "be permitted more leeway only in the terminal phase" (1967, p. 223). Greenson, to my knowledge, never addressed what may seem like a contradiction in these beliefs. He never explicitly examined how the analysts could keep their feelings largely to themselves and at the same time be genuine. I explore this apparent paradox later in this chapter.

Although many early analysts wrote about the real relationship (see Chapter 1 of this volume), it is difficult to find any discussion of the genuineness element other than Greenson's rather brief and sketchy comments as just described. This is likely because, until recently, psychoanalysis has been very uncomfortable with the construct of genuineness, especially as a way of being for the therapist. Consider what genuineness implies: revealing your inner feelings and thoughts, being what you feel, being who you are in the moment, and perhaps directly disclosing very delicate material to the patient. These are not qualities that were much valued in the more traditional analytic approaches, at least on the part of the analyst. Even in recent times, the more classical analysts who write about the real relationship tend not to address explicitly the genuineness component (e.g., Meissner, 2000). When it is addressed, genuineness itself is not dealt with in depth, and terms other than *genuineness* are used. Witness Couch's (1999) description below of the importance, from a classical Freudian position, of the therapist's "natural" and "human" response to the analysand. As indicated by the bracketed terms I have inserted, genuineness is more prominent in Couch's conception than is indicated by the precise words that he used:

> Any of the analyst's reactions (feelings and thoughts) are quite ordinary responses to what the patient reports about his inner and outer life. Some of these responses may be useful for an empathic understanding of the patient's character and childhood experiences and thus can become the basis for eventual interpretations; other responses may be built into clarifications, confrontations, and explanatory comments; but many of the analyst's reactions are best seen and conveyed in a clinically appropriate form as genuine reactions to important aspects of the patient's life as a fellow human being. These natural [genuine] interchanges are probably

essential for creating an analytic atmosphere of real human engagement [genuineness] in which the full personality of the patient can emerge without constriction [genuineness] and can be fully analyzed. The absence of these natural [genuine] responses by the analyst, especially when called for by actual tragedies, losses, failures, successes, disappointments, and other significant events in the patient's life, can be the cause of the most serious errors in an analysis—namely, the professionalized creation of an inhuman [disingenuous] analytic situation, divorced from real life. (p. 151)

GENUINENESS AND THE HERE AND NOW OF PSYCHOANALYTIC THOUGHT

During the latter part of the 20th century, substantial changes occurred in psychoanalysis, and a significant part of these changes pertained to the role of the analyst. Relational, interpersonal, and intersubjective theories (e.g., Mitchell & Eron, 1999; Renik, 1999; Stolorow, Brandchaft, & Atwood, 1987) became increasingly prominent. These theories, and the postmodern and social constructivist philosophies in which they are grounded, promote a much more emotionally active and involved role for the analyst or psycho-analytic therapist than does the classical view. This emotional involvement includes greater self-disclosure on the part of the analyst and, similarly, a stronger emphasis on therapist genuineness and related qualities.

Relational theorists are fond of viewing their theories as two-person theories in the sense that both therapist and patient contribute to the relation-ship and to the patient's material that is the subject of the analysis. Unlike what is viewed as the classical one-person theories that preceded them and are part of the classical view, relational theorists believe the analyst cannot be a blank screen but instead must share much more of him- or herself in the analysis and explore, at times with the patient, how his or her experiences impinge on the process and on the patient's transference. Given this very emotionally involved and expressive role, it makes sense that relational theorists would emphasize the importance of factors such as therapist or analyst genuineness. Thus, when a relational psychoanalyst writes about the real relationship (which many have), he or she is not likely to be referring to nondistortion or realism but more likely to "personally significant and emotionally authentic but mutually subjective interchanges, with such inter-changes being seen as a vital part of therapeutic action" (Frank, 2005, p. 17).

Because of their eschewal of the realism or realistic element of the real relationship promoted by classical theorists, relational/intersubjective analysts, such as Frank (2006), prefer the term *personal relationship* over *real relationship*. They tend to view this real or personal relationship as central to change and often mutative in itself. In other words, patient change, instead of occurring only through insight that is a result of analyst-offered interpretations, is seen as also occurring because of a sound personal relationship. For Frank, this personal relationship, or at least a good personal relationship, is marked by immediacy (being in the here and now), intimacy (mutual empathy and acceptance), and affective authenticity. This cluster is very similar, if not identical, to the concept of genuineness. This is especially true for affective authenticity, which Frank described as "striving to avoid deception, including self-deception, in order to foster responsive and responsible participation as an individual" (p. 39). The connection of this description to Carl Rogers's (1957) much earlier and seminal notion of congruence or genuineness is unmistakable, although Frank did not cite Rogers.

As I have mentioned, the personal relationship marked by therapist genuineness and related qualities is seen by the relational analysts as extremely important to successful treatment. In fact, this personal relationship and genuineness are often seen as themselves determining the effect of analyst technical interventions, such as interpretations. For example, Frank (2006) proposed that "the more affectively charged and truly and deeply felt—that is, the more immediately affectively authentic . . . an interpretation—the *more* likely it is to have a mutative impact" (p. 36).

So we see that within psychoanalytic thought, as theories grounded in postmodernism or social constructionism have gained ascendance, the concept of genuineness and its role in the real or personal relationship has shifted from being nonexistent or peripheral to central. Genuineness or authenticity and its correlates (immediacy and intimacy), within the real or personal relationship, indeed seem to be seen as approximately equal to the importance of technical factors in their mutative power.

GENUINENESS AS THE CENTERPIECE OF CHANGE: THE HUMANISTIC/EXPERIENTIAL THERAPIES

Whereas the concept of therapist genuineness has had to struggle to find its way into psychoanalytic therapies, it has always been vital to, perhaps the heart of, the humanistic/experiential therapies. This centrality was first seen in the seminal writings of Carl Rogers and his client-centered—and, later, person-centered—therapy. The importance of genuineness is also evident in the gestalt therapy of Fritz Perls (1969) and later proponents (see Woldt & Toman, 2005) and in the emotion-focused therapy of Leslie Greenberg (2002), which are perhaps the two most prominent humanistic/experiential psychotherapies.

In one of the most influential articles ever written about psychotherapy (Goldfried, 2007), Carl Rogers (1957) proposed certain conditions that were both necessary and sufficient for constructive personality change in psychotherapy: (a) a therapist–client relationship in which the two are in emotional contact; (b) a client who is in a state of incongruence, being vulnerable and anxious; (c) a therapist who is congruent or genuine in the relationship, (d) who experiences unconditional positive regard for the client and (e) an empathic understanding of the client's frame of reference, and (f) who communicates this regard and empathy to the client. Rogers (1957) audaciously stated that "no other conditions are necessary. If these six conditions exist, and continue over a period of time, this is sufficient. The process of constructive personality change will follow" (p. 96).

For Rogers, the therapist's *congruence* or *genuineness* was of fundamental importance. For him, these terms pertained to the therapist being aware of and in touch with his or her ongoing experience with the client as well as to the extent to which the therapist's outer behavior reflects some truly felt aspect of this inner experience (Bohart, 2005). Although for Rogers (1957) genuineness was "the opposite of presenting a façade" or "deceiving the client as to himself" (p. 97), being genuine does not imply that the therapist should self-disclose whatever is on his or her mind. Self-disclosure must always be done in the context of empathic understanding and unconditional positive regard, and it must always be used in the best interest of the client. Still, for Rogers and most humanists, a kind of controlled self-disclosure was an important part of being genuine. What was never clear in Rogers's writing was how one can be deeply genuine while holding back thoughts and feelings from the client. Certainly this is possible if the term *genuineness* is taken to mean congruence between inner experiencing, on the one hand, and self-image or representation on the other. One is then aware of what one feels. In being in touch with inner experiencing, the person is being honest with him- or herself, or integrated. However, how can the therapist be truly genuine with a client while at the same time withhold from outward expression what the therapist is experiencing in the moment?

The Humanistic Paradox: Being Genuine and Holding Back

The humanistic paradox has often been ignored in the writings on genuineness and authenticity. However, it was more recently carefully addressed by Greenberg (2002) in his writing about emotion-focused therapy. Greenberg took the earlier lead of Lietaer (1993), indicating that authenticity or congruence (terms that may be used synonymously with *genuineness*) can be divided into two components: (a) the ability to be aware of one's inner experience and (b) transparency or the willingness to explicitly communicate this inner experience to the client. Of the two, Greenberg noted that inner awareness is the most obviously beneficial. He added,

> It is always helpful for coaches [aka therapists] to be aware of their own feelings and reactions, because this awareness orients them and helps them be interpersonally clear and trustworthy. This inner awareness and contact involve being receptively open and sensitive to one's moment-by-moment, changing experience and being fully immersed in the moment. With this type of presence in the moment and emotional awareness there is less likelihood of a discrepancy between verbal and nonverbal behavior, and clients come to know that what they see is what they get. (p. 100)

To this I would add that it is also important for the therapist to understand from where his or her feelings arise, because such awareness has been theorized and empirically supported as a key element of therapists' ability to manage effectively their own countertransference to patients (Gelso & Hayes, 2007). At the same time, it is important that therapists not become preoccupied with their feelings, which would hinder their empathic immersion in the patient's experience (see the research findings of Fauth & Williams, 2005).

The second element of genuineness—*transparency*, or a willingness to communicate what the therapist thinks and feels—is much more complex and controversial. Greenberg (2002) wisely delineated certain conditions under which such self-disclosure is therapeutic. For example, as Rogers (1957) clearly stated, such communications need to be embedded within person-centered attitudes such as empathic understanding and positive regard for the patient. In addition, Greenberg advised that self-disclosures must be made in a disciplined manner; that is, therapists need to first be aware of what they deeply feel, clear on their intention of helping the patient (instead of, e.g., themselves), and sensitive to the timing of disclosures. In addition, there needs to be a meta-communication about the disclosure as well as the disclosure itself. For example, a good therapist does not simply say she feels little energy with the patient who is withholding affect from his communications with the therapist. This therapist also shares her concern about saying this to the patient and clarifies that the disclosure comes out of a wish to be helpful and improve the connection with the patient. Finally, the therapist also shares a willingness to explore with the patient how such a disclosure feels to the patient and other feelings stirred by the disclosure.

One key implication of these conditions specified by Greenberg (2002) is that the therapist should not communicate to the patient everything she or he feels. The patient's best interests must always be center stage. This makes a great deal of sense, and Greenberg's recommendations in general are very wise. However, they do not quite resolve the humanistic paradox reflected in the position that the therapist is to be genuine or congruent while at the same time holding back certain feelings and thoughts.

The Resolution

The resolution of the paradox is reflected in the idea that self-disclosure is only one element of genuineness and, I would suggest, not a necessary one at that. Thus, although genuineness is likely related to the therapist's tendency to share his or her feelings and experiencing in the moment with the patient, the relation is far from a perfect one. This implies that a therapist can be very genuine while rarely if ever being directly disclosing. *Directly* is the decisive word here, because the therapist communicates his or her being, self, and personality in myriad indirect ways. As Geller (2005) suggested, the therapist's presence itself communicates much information about him- or herself to the patient. In this respect, Geller provided the following explanation:

> By presence I mean far more than impression management. Presence has far more to do with the subtle and organic features of a person than with selling an image of oneself. The deepest sources of presence can be found in the processes that move through our bodies and take place, more or less, below the threshold of conscious awareness. Here I would include the combined effect of physical actions associated with breathing, the micromovements of the facial muscles, the pitch of voice, the stillness of posture, and temperament regulation. These action tendencies are initiated by "aliveness itself." They are a primary quality of "being in the world." (p. 475)

As for direct disclosure, patients may well experience their therapist as deeply genuine, even as therapists rarely verbalize their inner experience to the patient directly. This is especially so if the therapist shares with the patient early in the treatment why the therapist will communicate little of his or her inner experience. If such a therapist proceeds to be deeply immersed in the therapy experience, and shows the patient in numerous indirect ways that the patient is cared about and understood, and if the therapist's indirect disclosures, as well as his or her direct therapeutic responses, do not suggest any phoniness to the patient, this therapist is likely to be experienced as genuine, perhaps deeply so.

The notion that therapist self-disclosure is not a necessary part of genuineness is supported by a recent study (Ain & Gelso, 2008) in which former clients' retrospective recall of their therapists' overall amount of self-disclosure was only modestly related ($r = .33$) to these clients' ratings of the genuineness aspect of their real relationship with their therapists. In this same study, these former clients' ratings of genuineness within the real relationship were highly correlated with their evaluation of treatment outcome. Thus, the genuineness within the real relationship very much mattered to these clients, but their therapists' self-disclosure amount was not highly indicative of genuineness.

THE GENUINENESS OF THE PATIENT

Much of the focus of this chapter thus far has been on the genuineness of the therapist or analyst. However, I suggest that the concept of genuineness within the real or personal relationship is bipersonal: It pertains to both participants, as well as to their relationship, which some have referred to as the *analytic third* (e.g., Ogden, 1982).

In Carl Rogers's (1957) statement of the necessary and sufficient conditions for successful psychotherapy, the first such condition was that the client and therapist were in psychological contact. The second was that the client was incongruent; that is, there is a "discrepancy between the actual experience of the organism and the self picture of the individual insofar as it represents that experience" (Rogers, 1957, p. 96). Thus, there is a lack of some degree in the patient's awareness of his or her inner experiencing, a lack that reflects diminished genuineness. Successful treatment involves helping the patient move toward greater awareness, congruence, or genuineness. A part of this movement often involves the patient's willingness and ability not only to be aware of inner experience but also to share it with the therapist. Such sharing involves self-disclosure, and Farber (2006) recently addressed this topic in great depth. He discussed a number of positive consequences of patient self-disclosure. Most germane to this chapter is the following statement:

> Yet another consequence of sharing deeply personal aspects of self-experience is the patient's growing awareness of a greater sense of authenticity, of feeling more "real" and less fraudulent. As the space diminishes between what patients think or feel and what they say, they tend to feel far truer to themselves. At these moments they feel far more self-aware (having heightened acceptance of deeper parts of themselves) than self-conscious (painfully experiencing shameful parts of themselves) . . . Sharing intimate feelings rather than just thoughts and behaviors is an especially effective means for experiencing authenticity—and this may be even more the case when strong positive or negative feelings about the therapist are disclosed. (Farber, 2006, p. 43)

Farber went on to provide the following case example:

> Laura is a 45-year-old woman who has suffered from dysthymia for many years. The focus of her life is her work as a civil servant. She has had few

intimate relationships in her life with either men or women. She is likable and smart but is keenly aware of always feeling one step removed from others and one step removed from her own feelings. She describes them as existing outside of her. When I don't encourage Laura to speak of her feelings—toward me, toward friends in her life, toward coworkers—she is often content to relate the work-connected events of the week, filling me in on "what's new." But when I do get her to talk about her feelings, including rage toward her absent father, jealousy toward her favored brother, resentment toward her better-paid colleagues, and feelings of emotional closeness with and sexual attraction toward me—her schizoid core begins to give way and her demeanor shifts dramatically. She is there, fully in the room, aware of many of the feelings that she reflexively avoids out of discomfort and shame. She recognizes the difference between these two ways of being. For the most part, she enjoys feeling more alive and is working hard to embrace this kind of authenticity in her life outside of therapy. (pp. 44–45)

The patient's role regarding genuineness is, it would seem, far less controversial than that of the therapist. Whereas there is considerable controversy, for example, about how much and in what way the therapist should share his or her feelings and thoughts with the patient, there is general agreement that the patient is expected, at his or her own pace, to share thoughts and feelings. Although the therapist's theory will naturally influence the specifics of what is expected of the patient's self-revelations, all therapies require that patients honestly share what is on their minds; their stories; and, to one degree or another, the background of their problems. Of course, the insight therapies, and, to an extent, the humanistic/experiential therapies, in contrast to the cognitive and/or behavioral therapies, seek to establish conditions that will allow patients to go deeper and further into their internal worlds and to overcome the defensive barriers to an awareness of their inner workings. In these therapies it is expected that genuineness within the real relationship will deepen as the work progresses and as the patient continues to get more fully in touch with his or her inner experience. As more feelings come to consciousness (psychodynamic approaches) or as more inner experience comes into awareness (humanistic/experiential approaches), genuineness within the real relationship becomes itself deeper and more textured.

DOES GENUINENESS MATTER? EMPIRICAL ANSWERS

Clinically speaking, there is little doubt that patient genuineness matters, that it is a significant factor in psychotherapy. It is important in all psychotherapies. Even in therapies in which patient genuineness is not stressed (e.g., cognitive behavior therapy), it is my contention that it matters quite a bit. As for therapist genuineness, who could argue that it is okay for a psychotherapist to be phony? We would certainly find disagreement on how much and in what ways therapists should self-disclose but, as I have discussed, self-disclosure is only one part of genuineness, and not a vital part at that. How does the empirical evidence stack up against these clinically based assertions?

The Therapist's Genuineness

Over more than 4 decades it has been repeatedly demonstrated that a therapist's level of genuineness or congruence is associated with what are termed *process variables*, for example, patients' self-exploration or experiencing within the session. This seems like a self-evidently good thing, but such cannot be said, of course, until we see the relation of genuineness to the success or failure of therapy (i.e., treatment outcome).

A number of reviews of the research on therapist genuineness or congruence as related to treatment outcome have been conducted over the years. The most recent is a chapter by Klein, Kolden, Michels, and Chisholm-Stockard (2002) that sought to integrate its findings with previous reviews. All things considered, it seems likely that there is a relationship between therapist genuineness and treatment outcome. This likelihood increases when genuineness is measured from patients' perspectives, the perspective that Rogers (1957) focused on in his "conditions" article. In speculating on this conclusion, Klein et al. suggested that not only does therapist genuineness relate to treatment outcome by eliciting positive affect and promoting corrective relational experiences and attachment but that it may also be a mediator of change. For example, genuineness may mediate the effect of therapist empathy and positive regard on outcome such that these latter two qualities may influence successful treatment *through* genuineness. I think this is unlikely, although of course it needs to be studied. More likely is that genuineness is a *moderator*. The effect of qualities such as therapist empathy and positive regard on treatment outcome may well depend on how genuine the therapist is from the patient's perspective. For example, the therapist's empathy may fall on deaf ears if the patient perceives the therapist as fake, whereas the effect of empathy may be enhanced when the therapist is experienced as deeply genuine. Again, though, empirical data are needed to confirm this.

Another possibility is that therapist genuineness is especially significant when added to other variables. For example, it has been found that when genuineness is added to empathy and positive regard, the likelihood of the three predicting outcome is greater than when genuineness alone is assessed. For the purposes of this book, a key question is whether genuineness, when combined with realism within the real relationship, predicts treatment processes and outcomes. I examine this question in Chapter 7.

I have noted that therapist self-disclosure is modestly, if not strongly, indicative of genuineness. Given the link of the two (i.e., genuineness and self-disclosure), one wonders what the effect of self-disclosure is on the treatment process. Like genuineness, well-timed self-disclosures that are in the patient's best interests (instead of the therapist's) seem to have a very positive effect on patients' self-exploration within sessions and their evaluations of those sessions (Farber, 2006; Hill & Knox, 2002). It is much less clear how therapist self-disclosure affects treatment outcome, because the results are quite mixed (Hill & Knox, 2002). It does not seem as though the sheer frequency of a therapist's self-disclosures is related to treatment success. Indeed, Hill and Knox (2002) argued that therapist self-disclosures are the most beneficial when offered infrequently. In one major study (Hill, 1989), infrequent disclosures were the ones that lingered longest in patients' minds and affected them most deeply. My suspicion is that these disclosures were the ones that patients experienced as the most deeply genuine.

The Patient's Genuineness

The patient's genuineness may be thought of as both a cause and an effect of successful psychotherapy; that is, genuineness on the part of the patient has helpful effects of the treatment process and the success or failure of treatment. Patient genuineness, however, is also a result of effective psychotherapy. If one thinks of patient genuineness in the same way as therapist genuineness, then patient genuineness may be seen as having two parts: (a) awareness of internal experiencing and (b) communication of such experiencing to one's therapist. In regard to the first part, awareness of inner experiencing has always been one of the hallmarks of humanistic/experiential therapies. Also termed *emotional awareness*, this phenomenon, and the humanistic therapies to which it is wedded, has been found to be generally effective and helpful (see Elliott, Greenberg, & Lietaer, 2004; Prochaska & Norcross, 2007). In addition, patient insight, a close cousin to experiential awareness, over the years has been found to have an important positive effect on psychotherapy, according to the views expressed by 32 researchers, many of whom are leading insight researchers (Hill et al., 2008). Insight is especially close to experiential awareness when insight is considered to be an integration of intellectual and emotional understanding, or what I and a colleague have termed *integrative insight* (Gelso & Harbin, 2007).

Regarding the second element of patient genuineness, the communication of inner experiencing to one's therapist, the research literature on patient self-disclosure is directly relevant, because communication of inner experiencing is in fact one key type of self-disclosure. As I have said, from the beginning of the talking cure, the role of the patient has been to share with the therapist what is on his or her mind; to explore verbally his or her thoughts and feelings; and to examine verbally his or her background, especially as it shaped the current difficulties. Just how much of these things are called for naturally depends on the type of psychotherapy being conducted, but all therapies require at least, shall we say, a medium amount of patient self-disclosure. Farber (2006), citing Stiles (1995), stated this even more strongly: "Even therapeutic approaches that don't emphasize a disclosure–awareness–change link implicitly consider patient disclosure the core activity of psychotherapy, the center from which all therapist interventions emanate" (Farber, 2006, p. 71).

What are the empirically demonstrated effects of self-disclosure? Although the research findings tend to indicate that patient self-disclosure is positively associated with treatment outcome (Freedman & Enright, 1996; Kahn, Achter, & Shambaugh, 2001), the relationship is complex. Whether self-disclosure really helps depends on a host of factors. For example, Farber (2006) stated that existing studies have failed to differentiate disclosure that is "ruminative (going over old material the same old ways) and disclosure that leads to new ways of understanding or framing issues" (p. 76). He went on to conclude that "The former is likely to lead to no improvement or even negative therapeutic results, whereas the latter paradigm has a high probability of positive results" (p. 76). In other words, it is not the mere fact that the patient shares with the therapist that matters but instead *how* the patient shares and *what* is disclosed.

The distinction that Farber (2006) made has great significance for the concept of client genuineness. I believe that ruminative disclosure has a quality of obsessiveness and, as such, is not particularly genuine. However, disclosure that leads to new ways of understanding reflects greater genuineness on the patient's part. Remember, if the communication part of genuineness as discussed earlier indicates a communication of inner experiencing or emotional awareness, that communication is likely to be not ruminative and obsessive but a disclosure of freshly felt experience or feelings, and it is this type of genuine communication that will, although not invariably, help patients grow.

CONCLUSION

Genuineness is a fundamental element of a good personal or real relationship, because it is impossible to imagine such a relationship in the absence of genuineness, or even with low degrees of it. Therapist genuineness has always been seen as vitally important to successful treatment in the humanistic/experiential psychotherapies, and in recent years psychoanalytic therapists too have promoted the virtues of therapist genuineness. What has been missing in all theories is an understanding of genuineness as a bipersonal phenomenon, one that is formed and sustained by the therapist and the patient interactively. In part, the two participants express genuineness in their own way, in keeping with their unique roles in the therapeutic dance. In another way, the genuineness shared by each is precisely the same, in the sense that these are two human beings, partaking in an intimate personal experience at a given point in their lives. The great integrative psychotherapist Irving Yalom made the following sage comment about the shared genuineness of the therapeutic experience:

> I prefer to think of my patients and myself as *fellow travelers*, a term that abolishes the distinction between "them" (the afflicted) and "us" (the hearers). . . . We are all in this together and there is no therapist and no person immune to the inherent tragedies of existence. (Yalom, 2002, p. 8)

From the therapist's side of the relationship, genuineness, especially the part of it that reflects the therapist's communication of his or her thoughts and feelings to the patient, is a very tricky matter. On the one hand, Carl Rogers, in his comments about his treatment during a filmed session with a patient named Gloria, said that he wanted patients to "see all the way through me" (Psychological Films, 1965). Likewise, the leading relational psychoanalyst, Owen Renik (1999), in a card-playing metaphor, stated that the analyst should "play his or her cards face up" (p. 423). Yet both Rogers and his humanistic/experiential cohort, as well as the more open modern-day psychoanalysts, have always been very thoughtful and careful about what they shared their patients, exhibiting a very controlled openness. I referred to this seeming contradiction as the *humanistic paradox*, but it is really a paradox of all therapies that espouse the idea of therapists being open with their feelings. How each psychotherapist deals with this paradox will have a great deal to do with the strength of the real relationships he or she forms.

3

THE REALITY OF THE OTHER

In Chapter 2, I examined the concept of genuineness, one of the two fundamental elements of a real or personal relationship, and one of the two real-relationship elements that, to one degree or another, is involved in virtually all communications between psychotherapists and patients. In this chapter, I explore the second fundamental element of the real relationship, realism. I argue that although the therapist's and patient's perceptions of one another are crucial, there is indeed a reality of the patient and therapist, and it is extremely important for the therapist, in particular, to seek to grasp the patient's reality.

As I stated in Chapter 1 of this volume, *realism* may be defined as "perceiving and/or experiencing the other in ways that befit the other." On the low end of the realism dimension, one may badly misperceive the other, for a multitude of reasons. The perceiver may see only what he or she wishes to see, or fears to see, in the other; may be attentive only to the most obvious qualities of the other, thus missing the more nuanced reactions that incorporate subtle aspects of the other's personality; may be so self-absorbed that the other is experienced as but an extension of the perceiver (i.e., as a *self-object*, in the parlance of psychoanalytic self psychology); and/or may be misled by the other's defenses that are aimed at *not* being seen accurately. On the positive end of the realism continuum, one's experiencing of the other is in close alignment with who the other actually is, especially in terms of the other's basic self or personhood. There are few if any distortions of the other because of the needs and defenses of the perceiver, and if the other is him- or herself perceiving non-defensively then the other actually feels understood. This is the stuff (or at least one of the key ingredients) of which good relationships are made. It certainly involves empathic attunement, which of course is a key part of most, if not all, approaches to psychotherapy (e.g., Greenson, 1967; Kohut, 1977; Rogers, 1957). Later in this chapter I shall have more to say about such empathic attunement and how it is part of the therapist's management of countertransference.

Realism or realistic perception is often seen as the opposite of trans-ference. In other words, if transference is high, then realism, *ipso facto*, is low, and vice versa. On the face of it, this seems like a reasonable position, especially if transference is defined, as it was in Chapter 1, as the patient's experience of the therapist that is shaped by the patient's own psychological structures and involves displacement onto the therapist of feelings, attitudes, and behaviors belonging rightfully in earlier significant relationships. Although viewing transference, so defined, as the opposite of realism may seem sensible, I think it misses the mark in important ways. A more apt way of seeing how transference and realism interrelate is to view each as being part of the total relationship, any given treatment hour, any part of the hour, and indeed any given communication between therapist and patient. Viewed in this way, realism (and transference) may be seen as a part of all communications, perceptions, and experiences. The same may be said for countertransference. Greenson (1967) beautifully captured this interrelationship with the following remark: "There is no transference reaction, no matter how fantastic, without a germ of truth, and there is no realistic relationship without some trace of transference fantasy" (p. 219). Elsewhere (Gelso, 2009a) I provided a case vignette that exemplifies how transference and real relationship are part of a single expression:

> In my first session following rather serious surgery, my patient, John, expressed concern by asking "How are you doing, buddy?" I replied honestly, "I am doing well, thanks." As I began to pursue how some of his concern was transferentially related to the material with which we had been deal-ing, John replied. "Well, that may be so, but I also was just concerned about you as a person." As I pondered the expression of concern, it seemed clear to me that this single expression was both very rich with transference and very deeply reflective of real relationship. (p. 257)

This patient's concern for me was genuine and, more to the point of this chapter, it also reflected a reality-based interest in me as a person and a concern with understanding of each other that was not transferential. At the same time, the transference part of this communication reflected the patient's ongoing need to please and be pleasing to others, along with his abiding fear that if he were not so pleasing he would be punished and rejected, as he had been so pervasively throughout his abusive childhood.

Although I have been suggesting that realism and transference may occur simultaneously, it seems equally true that realism—or, more broadly, the realistic relationship—represents the transference-free part of every relationship, treatment hour, and communication. Thus, although transference and the real relationship are not best seen as mutually exclusive opposites, the real relationship is the part of any communication (etc.) that is free of transference, or nearly so. In essence, I am suggesting that realism and transference may be best viewed as existing on two separate continua, on which each may be high, low, and so on, within the same relationship, hour, or communication.

REALISM AND DIFFERENT THEORIES OF THERAPY

Just as the concept of transference has always been the hallmark of classical psychoanalytic theories, the concept of realistic perception has also been seen as pivotal. This is because, from the beginnings of psychoanalysis, although it was often implicit, the analysand's insight into the transference of course had to result in a more realistic perception or experience of the analyst. The interpretation of defenses and the resulting insight aimed at such realism and, eventually, its application to the analysand's world outside of analysis. The rub for many analysts came when realism or realistic perception was extended to a real relationship. For some analysts there was no such thing, because the analyst never expressed who he or she was as a person in the treatment and the analysand's transference was what the treatment was about (see Greenson & Wexler, 1969). Regarding the analyst, he or she was to maintain a kind of analytic grayness, an ambiguity as to his or her personhood. What did come through about the analyst to the analysand did so indirectly, in the analyst's nonverbal behavior, in what he or she chose to respond to in the analysand's associations, in the way the analyst dressed and his or her office décor. However, many analysts did not want to go so far as to indicate that there was a real *relationship*, or at least not one that mattered in any substantial way. As I indicated in Chapter 1 of this volume, however, some classical analysts, beginning with Freud, certainly did believe that there was a real relationship that consisted of the patient's reality-based perceptions of the analyst and the analyst's willingness to express his or her personhood. This reality-based part of the relationship coexisted with transference and was important part of the work.

These observations about the real relationship in classical psychoanalysis also apply to the modern classical analyst, although there seems to be a greater acceptance of the concept of real relationship. Although no tally that I know of has been made, on the basis of the literature (see Chapter 1) it seems to me that most classical analysts today would subscribe to the idea of a real relationship in the sense of a relationship in which the analysand and analyst perceive and experience the other as he or she truly is rather than as objects who are distorted by transference and countertransference.

Ironically, it is the relational and intersubjective psychoanalyst who will likely have the greatest trouble with the concept of realism. The irony is due to the fact that these relational and intersubjective analysts are much more focused on the actual relation between analyst and patient than are their classical counterparts. Yet relational and intersubjective analysts tend to eschew the concept of a real relationship, because to subscribe to such a concept is also to agree by implication that transference is a distortion of reality, and relational analysts tend to disagree with the idea of transference as a distortion of the analyst's (or patient's in the countertransference) true self or dynamics. For this cluster of therapists (see, e.g., Aron, 1996; Frank, 2005) there is no absolute reality of the patient but instead an image that is co-constructed by analyst and patient. Because of this belief in co-construction, the concept of distortion becomes meaningless. There is essentially no reality of the patient to distort that is independent of the image that analyst and patient co-construct.

For similar reasons, many humanistic psychotherapists do not find the concept of realism to be appealing. As modern-day phenomenologists, aka constructivists, these therapists are likely to believe that what is real is in the perceiver, not the perceived. In any event, it is the client's perceptions of reality that matter, and the therapist's job is to empathically grasp those perceptions. Ironically, the founders of the two most prominent schools of humanistic therapy, gestalt and person-centered therapy, both believed there was a reality of the client. Fritz Perls (1969) often discussed the need to actively confront transference distortions so that clients could see the therapist as the therapist is. Rogers, too, admitted that transference (qua distortion of the reality of the therapist) existed but that if the therapist provided empathy, unconditional positive regard, and congruence, these transferences would eventually dissipate without any particular effort or direct attention on the therapist's part. So, although neither Perls nor Rogers wrote about the realism part of the real relationship, they did implicitly subscribe to the notion of realism as an important part of the therapeutic relationship.

REALISM AND THE REALITY OF THE OTHER

Is there a reality of the other, or is what appears to be the other merely a construction built by both participants in the therapeutic relation? Is there a patient who has a being, a mind, and psychic reality apart from the therapist's perceptions and apart from what both participants create? The answer I shall argue for is yes, not only is there a reality of the patient, but also the absence of such a reality bespeaks severe psychopathology, and the postmodern belief in only co-construction, to the extent that it is enacted by the therapist, is likely to lead to ineffective treatment. Note that my focus in this section is on the reality of the patient, because in the therapeutic dyad it is the patient whose reality the therapists seeks to understand. However, the same fundamental points may be made for the reality, mind, and being of the therapist.

The Postmodern Fallacy

The belief that there is no mind of the patient, no internal, psychic reality of the patient that is apart from the therapist's perceptions and constructions is fundamentally postmodern (Rabin, 1995; Eagle, 2003). Stephen Mitchell (1993) captured this philosophical slant nicely:

> All the major intellectual disciplines, all knowledge, including scientific knowledge, is regarded as perspectival, not incremental; constructed, not discovered; inevitably rooted in a particular historical and cultural setting, not singular and additive; thoroughly contextual, not universal and absolute. (p. 20)

Rabin (1995) went on to clarify further:

> This constructivist metatheory in psychoanalysis assumes that there is no absolute truth. The analyst and patient together create or construct what is clinically useful for the patient's journey. Both the analyst's and the patient's subjectivities and their mutual influences are crucial to understand. (p. 468)

In his trenchant critique of the postmodern tilt in psychoanalysis, a tilt that shows itself largely through the now-popular relational/intersubjective theories, Eagle (2003) made clear that although no one could possibly now argue against the idea that patient and therapist interact and influence one another, the basis for the marriage between the relational turn in psychoanalysis and postmodernism

> resides in the claims that the analyst constitutes the patient's mind through "interpretive construction," that there is nothing corresponding to the phrase "in the patient's mind" that the patient or analyst can be right or wrong about, that the patient's mind is organized by each new intersubjective relationship (why isn't the analyst's mind also organized by each new intersubjective relationship?), and that there are no essential organized and stable properties of mind that are independent of social interaction. (p. 417)

Eagle went on to criticize what he referred to as such *new view* theorizing by offering the following observations:

> There is something disingenuous in the disjunction between, on the one hand, how new view theorists work and what they tell patients and, on the other hand, the stance they take in journal articles and books. Perhaps the disingenuousness is fortunate. For as we tried to demonstrate in our article. . . . The fact that despite the rhetoric, their conceptualization of concrete clinical material and their description of what they do is not especially different from that of any analyst. (p. 420; see also Eagle, Wolitzky, & Wakefield, 2001)

Finally, Meissner (1998) lamented this postmodern, constructivist orientation:

> It seems odd . . . that one would think of the patient, as he enters the consulting room for the first time, as without a history entirely of his own, without a developmental background, without a psychology and personality that he has acquired and developed in the course of a lifetime, all accomplished before he had any contact with the analyst. (p. 422)

Why would the postmodern therapist's enactment of the view that all reality is co-constructed lead to ineffective treatment? To the extent that this view is enacted, then the therapist is treating the patient as if the patient has no core being, no psychic reality apart from what the participants construct. The therapist is responding to the patient as if the self is nonexistent or merely a flimsy veneer that can be formed and re-formed in each encounter with another flimsily veneered other (i.e., the therapist). Similarly, the therapist is not seeking to understand the patient's inner world or self (because it really doesn't exist). It is hard to imagine effective psychotherapy proceeding with such a set of beliefs. Like Eagle, I seriously doubt that postmodern therapists and analysts treat patients in this manner. Instead, their treatment is likely quite effective. It is their philosophy—specifically, their ontology—that is flawed.

A patient who would really fit with the postmodernist's apparent view of what might be called the fully co-constructed person would be in serious trouble psychologically. Someone whose basic self or psychic reality is so readily constructed, and thus so weakly formed, would, needless to say, likely be suffering from severe psychopathology and might well be considered as having a personality disorder (e.g., borderline or narcissistic personality disorder).

Constructive Realism and the Relational Paradox

The viewpoint that I am suggesting, what I refer to as the *relational paradox*, is that, first, the therapist and patient's perceptions certainly matter and that there certainly is an intersubjective, relational influence in the sense that each party in the relationship influences the other, and both work to construct an image of the patient. However, just as certainly the patient comes to therapy with a self, with a psychic reality, and a mind that is terribly important for the therapist to try to empathically grasp in an ongoing way. This self may change, and in the best therapeutic experiences it may change in far-reaching ways. However, to say that the self may change is a far cry from the belief that the self is fully co-constructed, with the implication that it did not exist as a somewhat stable structure before the patient saw this particular therapist. For fear that the reader will think that I am reifying hypothetical constructs such as mind and self and being, I hasten to add that these are indeed hypotheticals and are really shorthand for the patient's feelings, attitudes, beliefs, defenses, and behavioral tendencies regarding and toward him- or herself and others.

Because the patient enters psychoanalysis or psychotherapy with a self or a psychic reality that is, to varying degrees, stable does not mean that this self will ever be fully grasped or understood by the therapist. Instead, the therapist seeks to grasp the patient and empathically enter his or her inner world, but he or she will succeed in this effort only to varying degrees, depending on the therapist's empathic and conceptual abilities, the patient's conscious and unconscious willingness to be known, and the complexity of this inner world of the patient. Because the therapist will never fully comprehend the patient's inner world does not mean that this inner world does not exist. All that is understood is the reality of the patient that is co-constructed by therapist and patient as the therapist seeks to grasp as deeply as possible the actual psychic reality or basic personality of the patient.

I have elsewhere (Gelso, 2009a, 2009b) used the term *constructive realism*, suggested by the cognitive psychologist Ulric Neisser (1967), to get at the idea that there is a reality of the patient (and the therapist, too) but that all the therapist can access is the reality that patient and therapist co-construct as the therapist seeks to deeply understand the patient. Donna Orange (1995, 2003), herself a leading intersubjectivist, has addressed in depth the philosophical problems therapists will encounter with alternative positions, such as objective realism, on the one hand, and postmodernism, on the other. She instead has offered a position on the reality of the patient that she refers to as *perspectival realism*, which for all intents and purposes is the same as Neisser's (1967) constructive realism. Orange (1995) stated her position the following way:

> Each participant in the inquiry has a perspective that gives access to a part or an aspect of reality. An infinite—or at least an indefinite—number of such perspectives is possible. Since none of us can entirely escape the confines of our personal perspective, our view of truth is necessarily partial, but conversation can increase our access to the whole. . . . Perspectival realism recognizes that the only truth or reality to which psychoanalysis

provides access is the subjective organization of experience understood in an intersubjective context. Such a subjective organization of experience is one perspective on a larger reality. We never fully attain or know this reality but we continually approach, apprehend, articulate, and participate in it. (pp. 61–62)

Note that for Orange, as for me, there is a reality of the patient (and, by implication, the therapist); the therapist seeks to grasp that reality through the use of his or her own reality, but he or she can only partially succeed. In sum, there must be a reality of the person, and there must be co-construction in the attempt to understand that reality. I conclude by suggesting that in more effective psychotherapies the therapist or analyst is able to empathically capture or grasp more of the patient's reality and more significant aspects of that reality.

THE THERAPIST'S GRASP OF THE PATIENT'S REALITY: AIDS AND OBSTACLES

Experience suggests that there are two general and interrelated classes of aids and obstacles to the accuracy of the therapist's grasp of the patient's reality.

The first general class of obstacles revolves around personality factors of the therapist. One need only supervise psychotherapists in training for a short time to see that, despite the fact that the people who self-select into the psychotherapy profession are more interpersonally perceptive than people in general, therapists vary rather widely in their ability to grasp the reality of the patient. Some therapist trainees seem to have a deep sense of empathy, a wonderful capacity to perceive others accurately beyond the surface. Others simply do not seem to see, except for perhaps the most behaviorally obvious. The capacity to perceive others accurately in a psychological sense is likely partly inherited and partly learned in very early experiences. However much learned or not learned, such personality factors may be an aid or an obstacle to grasping the reality of the patient.

Countertransference and Its Management

The second general class of aids and obstacles to the therapist's ability to accurately perceive patients' inner experiences and dynamics may be termed *countertransference*. It is now generally understood that countertransference can be for better or worse; it can aid the treatment, or it be an obstacle to effective psychotherapy. In terms of this chapter, what is most significant is that countertransference can interfere greatly with the accuracy of the therapist's perception of the patient, or it can aid in that accuracy. The key to which function it serves is how well the therapist manages the countertransference. Before delving into countertransference management, a few words about the concept of countertransference itself are in order. After many years of studying countertransference and observing it in clinical supervision and our own practice, Jeff Hayes and I recently wrote a book-length treatment of the topic (Gelso & Hayes, 2007); my comments here are drawn from that work.

The first thing to understand about countertransference is that, over the years, several definitions of it have been developed. These have ranged from what may be termed the *classical position* to what is usually termed the *totalistic conception*. The former equates the therapist's countertransference with the patient's transference and defines countertransference as, in essence, the therapist's transference to the patient's transference. This conception of countertransference is usually associated with more classical theories of psychoanalysis, and it is generally considered rather narrow. As partly a reaction to classical thinking and to the perceived narrowness of the classical conception of countertransference, the totalistic view emerged. Within this perspective, countertransference was seen as *all* of the therapist or analyst's feelings and reactions to the patient. Such a view is so broad that it is scientifically problematic, perhaps meaningless. If all emotional reactions are counter-transference, then there is no need for the term, or even the concept; we could simply refer to "therapist reactions." In Hayes's and my work (Gelso & Hayes, 2002, 2007; J. A. Hayes & Gelso, 2001), we have offered a conception of countertransference that integrates the various definitions. We have defined countertransference as "the therapist's internal or external reactions that are shaped by the therapist's past or present emotional conflicts and vulnerabilities." Thus, although the patient's behavior likely serves as a trigger to counter-transference reactions, for countertransference to occur the patient's material must connect to some unresolved issue or vulnerability, or what may be termed a *hook*, in the therapist. When this happens the therapist's perceptions of the patient's reality may become clouded. If this clouding occurs over a sustained period of the work, especially if it becomes acted out in the actual interactions with the patient, then the effectiveness of psychotherapy will be significantly diminished. However, if this countertransference is effectively understood, controlled, and managed, it will not hinder the work but instead will likely aid it. Among other benefits, it will help the therapist accurately grasp the patient's inner world. In the next section, I examine the elements of such countertransference management.

A Five-Factor Theory of Countertransference Management

A conception of countertransference management that has been pro-posed and studied over several years posits five key, interrelated constituents of such management (Van Wagoner, Gelso, Hayes, & Diemer, 1991; Gelso & Hayes, 2007): therapist (a) self-insight, (b) conceptualizing skills, (c) empathy, (d) self-integration, and (e) anxiety management. The interrelation of the five factors needs to be emphasized, because they generally work in concert during the treatment, even at times displaying what amounts to a statistical interaction between two of the factors (e.g., the effect of the therapist's conceptualizing ability depends on the extent of his or her self-insight). Empirical evidence gathered over several years has supported the relation of this constellation of elements to effective psychotherapeutic process and outcome (see Gelso & Hayes, 2007, Chapter 5). Let us take a look at each of these elements and how they may affect the therapist's ability to accurately perceive and understand the patient.

The first element in countertransference management is the therapist's *self-insight*. This is a fundamental element because understanding one's patients is limited by the extent to which therapists understand themselves. It is hard to imagine a therapist or analyst who can grasp the subtleties of the patient's inner world, and grasp it with some degree of accuracy, in the absence of self-understanding. This is so because the therapist inevitably perceives the patient through his or her own inner world, and if the therapist does not understand this world, then his or her understandings of the patient's inner world are bound to be less accurate. As is well known, the concept of insight and therapist self-insight is one of the foundational constructs of the talking cure. Sigmund Freud (1912/1959b), for example, claimed that no patient can develop further than his or her analyst's neuroses: "It does not suffice . . . that the physician should be of approximate normality himself; it is a justifiable requisition that he should . . . become aware of those complexes in himself which would be apt to affect his comprehension of the patient's disclosures" (p. 328).

The absence of awareness of such "complexes" in the therapist would easily allow projections onto the patient and in this sense interfere with the therapist's accurate understanding of the patient. This danger is especially likely as the patient him- or herself uses more complex and primitive defenses. For example, a patient whose defenses include projective identification stirs in the therapist the very affects that the patient unconsciously disowns. The therapist's self-insight is one of the qualities that allow him or her to grasp that the projection from the patient is just that, and not an affect that belongs in the therapist's inner world with the patient. Self-insight on the therapist's part helps the therapist not act out the patient's projection. However, like the other constituents of countertransference management, self-insight alone is often insufficient, and its effect on accurately understanding the patient depends on the other ingredients. For example, the findings of two studies (Latts & Gelso, 1995; Robbins & Jolkovski, 1987) suggest that effective countertransference management may depend on both therapists' self-insight into their countertransference feelings and their ability to conceptualize the dynamics of the treatment. In these studies, therapist trainees' awareness of countertransference feelings (self-insight) operated in concert with their use of a theory (conceptualizing skills) in controlling the acting out of countertransference reactions. Thus, those therapists who were high in both countertransference awareness and use of a theory exhibited the least countertransference behavior in a laboratory simulation of psychotherapy.

Such *conceptualizing skills*, the second countertransference management constituent, involve developing a cognitive, theoretical understanding of the patient and the dynamics of the therapeutic relationship. These entail what Annie Reich (1951) observed as a process of locating an "outside position in order to be capable of an objective evaluation of what [was] just now felt within" (p. 25). The same studies noted in the preceding paragraph suggest that when therapist trainees use their conceptualizing skills to theoretically understand patients, but at the same time have little awareness of their countertransference-based feelings, the likelihood of acting out the countertransference is greatest. Thus, theoretical understanding in the absence of self-insight can be harmful. Although these were laboratory studies conducted with trainees, I suspect they apply as well to experienced psychotherapists.

Although conceptualizing skills are most effective in conjunction with high levels of therapist self-understanding, such skills can help independently. They may help therapists prevent the acting out of their countertransference reactions because these conceptualizing skills provide a framework for understanding countertransference reactions and how to control them. This may be especially the case for patients diagnosed with certain types of pathology. For example, I have often felt that patients who have certain types of narcissistic personality disorders get unconsciously pushed out of therapy by their therapists; that is, those narcissistic patients who treat the therapist as but an object to mirror the patient's greatness, and who do not really care about their therapist as a separate person (often referred to as a *mirror transference* by psychoanalytic self-psychologists) are very difficult for most therapists to endure. To be with these patients is like not existing at all. Having a conceptual understanding for this form of narcissism tends to help the therapist, partly by letting him or her know that the patient's relational pattern is a fundamental part of his or her pathology and is not to be taken personally. Such objective understanding allows therapists to feel less pained by their personal nonexistence in the therapeutic relationship and offers the understanding that, with time, patience, and effective interventions, this will change.

The third element of countertransference management is therapist *empathy*. As is generally understood now, the therapist's empathic abilities are a significant aspect of successful psychotherapy. Defined as the therapist's partial and vicarious identification with the patient and his or her inner experience, empathy is also a key part of countertransference management. Its value in grasping the reality of the patient accurately is so obviously important that I need not devote a great amount of space to it here. In brief, the therapist's ability to climb into and emotionally as well as cognitively grasp the patient's underlying feelings, anxieties, wishes, and fears is part and parcel of perceiving the patient in ways that befit the patient, that is, that are accurate. Although the partial identification that reflects empathy is vitally important, it is equally important that the identification not be too great; that is, enough distance is needed in order to not become fused with the patient but instead to offer the patient a perspective that is different from his or her own.

The empathic process of partially and vicariously identifying with the patient without becoming fused leads to the fourth constituent of counter-transference management, therapist *self-integration*. This constituent refers to the therapist's having a relatively stable and cohesive identity and a capacity to differentiate from others, with boundaries that are neither rigid and impen-etrable nor too permeable. I have always thought of this factor as involving the therapist being able to grasp where he or she stops and the patient starts, and vice versa. On the basis of a qualitative study of countertransference management, Baehr (2004) described a case in which the issue of therapist self-integration was prominent:

> Due to her mother's reaction to having a stillborn child when the therapist was two, as well as other factors, the therapist had a history of not feeling cherished. She also felt overwhelmed by the impact of her divorce several years before. The client had a severe abuse history and resulting dissociative disorder, expressing itself in almost complete silence in therapy. Together these factors led the therapist to wish for respite and feel overwhelmed and frustrated, as well as doubting her ability to help others. The therapist . . . had some difficulty joining with the client out of fear of getting lost in a merger of her experiences and the client's. In frustration at her client's silence, the therapist would become almost punitively silent at times. This was a repetition of the perpetrator–victim relationship for the client. The therapist was struggling to stay present but really felt like sleeping. The client remained disengaged as long as she didn't feel the therapist joining her.

Given what this therapist was contending with internally, it would be hard to imagine her perceiving the patient in a way that befit her. Shaky self-integration on the therapist's part was a key element of the difficulty managing her countertransference, which in turn was partly reflected in her seeing the patient through distorting lenses.

The fifth and final constituent of countertransference management is the therapist's *anxiety management ability*. Just as the patient's anxiety is a fundamental and inextricable factor in the erection of defenses, so too is the therapist's anxiety a key part of his or her countertransference reactions. However, the most effective therapists are able to allow themselves to experience anxiety without having to erect defenses. Instead, through various means (perhaps most centrally, self-understanding) they are able to contain the anxiety and, instead of defending against it, are able to use it to help understand the patient. As the therapist comes to grips with her or his anxiety with a particular patient, he or she is better able to grasp what the patient stirs in others, and perhaps what was stirred in the patient by significant others in his or her earlier life. Of course this task of containing and understanding the anxiety is made much easier if the anxiety itself is not too intense. The existence of chronically intense anxiety and/or the inability to understand and contain this anxiety is likely to lead to poorly understanding the patient's inner world, to misperceiving the reality of the patient.

In sum, clinical and empirical evidence supports these five constructs as being basic constituents of the therapist's management of countertransference in the treatment hour. In relation to the point of this chapter, these constituents are a key to perceiving the patient and his or her inner world in ways that befit the patient.

THE PATIENT'S GRASP OF THE THERAPIST'S REALITY

The therapeutic relationship is always bipersonal, and so is the real-relationship aspect of it. Thus, the patient, as well as the therapist, contributes to the real relationship and to the part of it that pertains to perceiving the other realistically. Despite these joint contributions, the therapist and patient naturally have vastly different roles in general and roles related to perceiving realistically. A fundamental part of the therapist's role is to grasp the patient as the patient is, to comprehend him or her accurately. Although misperceptions are inevitable, and can aid the therapist's comprehension of the patient if understood and used wisely by the therapist, it is equally true that in an ongoing way the therapist seeks to understand, to have accurate empathy, and to continually refine his or her understanding of the patient.

The patient's role regarding realistic perception of the therapist is much more complicated and depends greatly on the theoretical orientation of the treatment. In all therapies, the patient has the job of communicating what is on his or her mind, sharing what he or she thinks and feels, and describing his or her main concerns. In the evocative psychotherapies (e.g., psychoanalysis and the various psychodynamic derivatives of it, as well as the humanistic/experiential treatments), the patient's feelings and reactions toward the therapist are of great interest, including the extent to which they reflect transference, that is, misperceiving the therapist in one way or another. In the analytically oriented treatments, the unfolding and working through of transferences is a key element, if not *the* key element, of successful therapy. These treatments are set up or allow transferences to come to the surface, develop, and then be understood as such and worked through. In this sense, such treatments encourage the emergence of unrealistic perceptions of the therapist so that the misperceptions can be eventually corrected.

In the humanistic/experiential treatments, on the other hand, transference distortions on the patient's part are either confronted actively (as in many gestalt therapies) or understood empathically, as are all feelings (as in person-centered therapies). In the various combinations of cognitive and behavior therapies, these transferences are likely ignored unless they create a problem for the key activities of these treatments. In sum, different theoretical approaches vary in the extent to which they establish conditions for the emergence and development of unrealistic perceptions of the therapist (aka transference), although all therapies seek ultimately the patient's seeing the therapist realistically.

At the same time, even in therapies in which transference distortions are encouraged to unfold and come to the surface it is important that there be substantial elements of a real relationship and of realistic perceptions of the therapist by the patient. Without such perceptions, the exploration and interpretation of transference would be meaningless. In addition, regardless of the theoretical orientation of the therapist, as I discuss throughout this book, a strong real relationship, marked in part of realist perceptions of the therapist, provides an invaluable aid to effective treatment.

What in the patient fosters such reality-based perceptions, and what hinders them? I would provisionally offer that the same five factors involved in countertransference management would be key patient factors that facilitate the real relationship, specifically the patient's seeing the therapist as the therapist is. Self-insight, conceptualizing skills (or what may be termed a *strong observing ego*), empathy, self-integration, and anxiety management on the part of the patient all work in tandem to foster a strong real relationship, in particular the part of the real relationship involving realism. Transference will still occur, and in the treatments for which it is central (e.g., psychoanalysis) transference is likely to occur to an even greater extent;, still, these five factors will allow a stronger real relationship alongside the transferences and will likely foster the ultimate resolution of transferences.

In a very general sense, these five factors are a reflection of psychological health and, conversely, low amounts of them bespeak psychopathology. Consider the patient who has little self-insight and empathy, who is poorly integrated psychologically (has weak boundaries and low general levels of psychological health), who has a weak ability to manage his or her anxiety, and who does not have very much skill at conceptualizing what people and relationships are about. Although it might be impossible to point to specific kinds of psychopathology tied to these ingredients, it is probably safe to say that possessing meager amounts of all of the qualities reflects severe forms of psychopathology. Thus, again in a very general sense, it is the patient's level of psychopathology that impedes perceiving and experiencing the therapists realistically. It is no accident, for example, that clinicians who work with patients diagnosed with borderline personality disorders and other severe forms of character pathology advise that therapists develop a strong real relationship with their patients.

CONCLUSION

The realism aspect has been central element of the real relationship from the earliest writings of Freud and other key psychoanalysts. In contrast to the postmodern conceptions, I have maintained that there is indeed a reality of the patient and a reality of the therapist. Each participant in psychotherapy has a separate mind, a separate being and psychic reality that exists prior to and during the treatment. Thus, there is much more to the patient and the therapist than their co-constructions of each other, as postmodernist thinking would have us believe. On the therapist's side, it is vitally important that the therapist seek to grasp empathically this reality of the patient, regardless of the therapist's theoretical orientation. However, the therapist can only partially succeed in this effort, because the reality of any other human being can never be fully understood. In his or her efforts to grasp the patient's psychic reality, the therapist has access only to the reality that therapist and patient have co-constructed. As the same time, in effective psychotherapy the therapist continually seeks to develop a clearer and more accurate understanding of the patient's reality. In sum, I have termed the *relational paradox* my proposition that there is a mind or psychic reality apart from co-construction, that the therapist can only partially succeed in grasping that mind or psychic reality but that he or she must continually seek to refine his or her comprehension of the patient's reality and that in the process all the therapist can work with is the patient's reality that therapist and patient have co-constructed. This is a position that may be termed *constructive realism*.

There are aids and impediments to perceiving the other realistically, as the other is. On the therapist's side, countertransference is a major impediment. For both patient and therapist, five elements serve as key aids to perceiving the other realistically. Self-insight, conceptualizing skills, empathy, self-integration, and anxiety management all play centrally into the realism of the therapeutic relationship.

4

A THEORY OF THE REAL RELATIONSHIP IN PSYCHOTHERAPY AND PSYCHOANALYSIS

In the previous chapters, I have provided a history and background of the concept of the real relationship from the beginnings of the talking cure, and I explored its two key elements: (a) realism and (b) genuineness. In this chapter, I articulate a theory of the real relationship and how it operates in psychotherapy in general as well as in therapies of differing orientations and durations. In presenting this theory, I incorporate some material from the earlier chapters so as to allow this chapter to stand on its own.

Let me state immediately my belief that what I term the *real* or *personal relationship* is a vital part of successful psychotherapy and psychoanalysis; that is, regardless of whether the therapist works directly with and through the real relationship, a strong real relationship is highly facilitative of successful treatment. Similarly, if the real relationship is weak or poor, it is hard to imagine treatment working well. What I mean by "working directly with and through the real relationship" and a "strong or weak real relationship" will be clarified shortly. In this chapter and throughout the book I aim also to clarify the reasoning behind my lofty assessment of the importance of the real relationship.

WHAT IS THE REAL RELATIONSHIP?

As I suggested in Chapter 1 and amplified in Chapters 2 and 3, the real relationship is theorized as consisting of two fundamental elements: (a) genuineness and (b) realism. Genuineness is seen as reflecting the ability to be who one truly is, as opposed to being phony or inauthentic. Realism, on the other hand, pertains to perceiving and experiencing the other person in ways that fit him or her—that accurately capture the reality of the other. When combining these two ingredients, genuineness and realism, the real relationship may be defined as the personal relationship existing between two or more persons as reflected in the degree to which each is genuine with the other and perceives and experiences the other in ways that befit the other. As Couch (1999) wrote, the real relationship pertains to both the personalities of therapist and patient as well to as the nature of their communication— to who the participants are, and to what and how they communicate with one another. In the strongest real relationships persons communicate genuinely with one another, are willing to let themselves be known deeply, and perceive and experience the other realistically, to an important extent.

We have seen in Chapters 2 and 3 how genuineness and realism have been differently valued in psychoanalytic/psychodynamic and humanistic/ experiential therapies. Analytic/dynamic therapists, especially those who are more classically oriented, have resonated to the concept of realism because in many ways it is seen as the other side of transference, as the twin of transference. In other words, realism involves seeing the other accurately, whereas transference entails misperceptions of the other based on unresolved conflicts from childhood. The resolution of transference involves misperceptions being replaced by accurate perceptions. In good analytic treatment, transference distortions are replaced with a real relationship. At the same time, there is always some degree of realism, or realistic perception, from the beginning of treatment onward. Although the concept of realism makes sense in more classical analytic theories, classical analysts have tended to eschew the value of genuineness because this seems to many to connote the therapist revealing too much of him- or herself and in this sense failing to maintain proper neutrality and ambiguity. This abnegation of ambiguity and neutrality then interferes with the emergence of transference and muddies the psychic waters, so to speak, so that it becomes difficult, if not impossible, for the analytic therapist to make effective interpretations of the transference. In other words, if the therapist allows a great deal of his or her feelings and views to be known, it becomes much harder to determine the extent to which most patient expressions represent transference or the real relationship.

For humanistic therapists, and what may be termed *new view* or *postmodern* psychoanalysts (see Eagle, 2003), the opposite is true. To these theorists it is vital that the therapist be who he or she truly is, to "play his or her cards face up," as Renik (1999) described it. Genuineness, at least on the part of the therapist, is viewed as one of the key ingredients of effective psychotherapy, and for many humanists it is seen as one of the necessary and sufficient conditions of successful treatment. (See Rogers's [1957] highly influential statement of the necessary and sufficient conditions of effective therapy. See also the September 2007 issue of *Psychotherapy Theory, Research, Practice, Training* [Gelso, 2007] for comments on the impact of that statement on the field over a 50-year period.) However, the notion of realism or realistic perception is often not seen as very meaningful because these therapists most often take a postmodern or constructivist position that suggests that there is no reality beyond that which the therapy participants co-construct. If there is no independent reality (no independent psychic reality of self or mind), then the concept of realism simply does not compute.

Thus, in a certain sense my dual definition of the real relationship may be unpopular with both analytic and humanistic therapists. Each group opposes one of the two elements of the real relationship. From another perspective, I have attempted to wed concepts from both theoretical camps because the constructs (realism and genuineness) both seem to me to make a great deal of sense. Indeed, it is hard to imagine anything like a sound or strong real, personal relationship in the absence of these two concepts. How could a relationship seem real or in fact feel real to the therapy participants if the participants were phony or disingenuous with one another? Similarly, it is hard to imagine something like a sound real relationship if the participants consistently misperceive or fail to grasp the reality of the other. I should reiterate here (cf. Chapter 3, this volume) that philosophically I am taking what may be termed a *constructive realist position;* that is, there is indeed a reality of the person (apart from what the two participants co-construct) to be perceived, while at the same time the way the therapist and patient see each other, or what they co-construct, is extremely important.

Whose Realism and Genuineness? A Matter of Perspective

The real relationship is a bipersonal concept inasmuch as both the therapist and the patient contribute to its development. Thus, when I discuss genuineness and realism I am not just referring, as often is the case in the literature, to the therapist's genuineness and the patient's realism. Both the patient and therapist perceive each other more or less realistically, and both behave with the other in a more or less genuine manner. Actually, there is a third perspective: that of the relationship itself. In other words, there is the patient's perspective and contribution, and the therapist's perspective and contribution, and there is the relationship between therapist and patient.

This is so in any relationship between two persons. This perspective is important in both clinical theory and research measurement.

In its bipersonal nature, a theory of the real relationship differs from some other theories about the therapeutic relationship. For example, Carl Rogers's (1957) highly influential theory of the necessary and sufficient conditions of successful therapy contained three main conditions on the part of the therapist: (a) empathic understanding, (b) unconditional positive regard, and (c) genuineness. On the patient's part, it was vital that he or she was motivated for treatment and experienced these three therapist conditions, but the patient does not contribute any active conditions of his or her own. The theory is unidirectional and reflects a kind of one-person psychology. In the theory of the real relationship as offered here, both participants are mutually and inextricably intertwined in perceiving realistically and behaving genuinely to one degree or another. The theory is bidirectional and represents a two-person psychology.

Realism and Genuineness Intertwined

Although I separate realism and genuineness for theoretical and measurement (see chap. 6, this volume) reasons, these two elements must necessarily be closely intertwined in clinical practice. As the therapist and patient interact with one another in the psychotherapy hour, the extent to which each is genuine with the other will inevitably be connected to how accurately each sees the other. That is because seeing the other as the other really is (instead of, e.g., a projection of other persons from the patient's earlier or present life) depends greatly on the other's willingness to be known, to share him- or herself honestly. As I have discussed earlier, from the therapist's side, the willingness to be known does not necessarily mean that the therapist will self-disclose a great deal. If the therapist is quiet, and spends most of his or her time listening and offering reflections, asking questions, and/or making occasional interpretations, this therapist may still be quite genuine. The therapist can be very quiet and reside anywhere on the entire continuum of genuineness or phoniness.

I have said that perceiving and experiencing the other as the other truly is requires that the other be genuine. In the same way, how genuine one is will be strongly influenced by the extent to which one feels understood accurately (i.e., realistically) by the other. This is especially true for the patient, but it also applies to the therapist to an extent.

Although the connection between realism and genuineness is very deep, as I discuss in detail in Chapter 6 of this volume, my colleagues and I have created two subscales in our measures of the real relationship, one for realism and the other for genuineness. This is because, despite their close and inevitable connection, at times the two elements may be differentially related to other processes in therapy. For example, we have found that, in therapists' views, how genuine the therapist and patient are being in their personal relationship is more closely related to the strength of the working alliance than is how realistically therapist and patient are seeing one another (Gelso et al., 2005). It may be very hard to have a good working relationship if therapist and patient are not very genuine with one another; however, not experiencing each other highly realistically may not severely damage the working alliance. In sum, despite their close link to one another, as we try to understand the network of associations of real relationship and other processes in therapy it will be useful to think of the two elements separately.

How Much and How Positive? Two Key Subelements of the Real Relationship

Several years ago, as my collaborators—Jairo Fuertes, Frances Kelley, Cheri Marmarosh—and I began our first research project aimed at developing measures of the real relationship, it became clear that the concepts of genuineness and realism were not sufficient in clarifying the nature and strength of the real relationship. Two additional concepts were needed to make good sense of real relationship: the (a) magnitude and (b) valence of the real relationship.

Magnitude pertains to how much of a real relationship (how much genuineness and realism) exists at any given point in time. The concept of magnitude stems from the idea that any relationship, treatment hour, or single communication between patient and therapist will evidence one degree or another of real or personal relationship. Consider statements such as "I have a sense of who my patient is down deep inside," or "I feel I am able to grasp who my therapist is, even though she is quiet." With such statements, we wonder *how much* of a sense the therapist has of who his patient is down deep inside, or *the extent to which* the patient is able to grasp who her quiet therapist is. These are questions of the magnitude of the real relationship, and naturally magnitude can range from high or low on a hypothetical scale.

When considering the magnitude of the real relationship, a logical question is "What magnitude is desirable for therapy to be effective?" I would offer provisionally that the greater the magnitude of realism and genuineness, the more positive the expected outcome. If the magnitude of genuineness and realism is low at the beginning of treatment, it is important that it increase as the work progresses.

From a psychoanalytic perspective, one might argue that a high magnitude of realism throughout is undesirable because, in successful analysis, the transferences must develop, emerge, and be worked through. The absence of transference throughout would not auger well for successful analysis. This argument makes sense to the extent that the real relationship is seen as the opposite of transference. However, I suggested elsewhere (Gelso, 2009a) that the real relationship is best not viewed as the opposite of transference. Instead, any given communication may consist of much transference and a high magnitude of a real relationship, a medium amount of both, a low magnitude of both, or other such combinations. I would offer that in the most successful psychoanalysis transference develops and is worked through, while the real relationship is strong throughout or strengthens as the analysis progresses. Indeed, in a qualitative study of successful, long-term dynamically oriented psychotherapy, therapists believed that strong real relationships actually facilitated the unfolding and resolution of transference (Gelso, Hill, Mohr, Rochlen, & Zack, 1999).

As for the *valence* of the real relationship, the therapists' and patients' feelings and thoughts toward one another that constitute the real relationship naturally vary on a positive–negative dimension. In other words, each participant may experience and perceive the other positively or negatively in terms of realism and genuineness. Consider qualities such as liking–disliking, caring–not caring, respecting–disrespecting, and valuing–devaluing as they might exist on a continuum. Generally speaking, the more positive the participants are toward one another in the context of the real relationship, the more effective will be the treatment. The strongest real relationships will have the most positive valences throughout or, if the valence is low at the beginning of treatment, it will improve throughout if the treatment is to be successful.

As noted elsewhere (Gelso & Hayes, 1998), therapists typically think of negative reactions on the patient's side as reflecting transference. Perhaps this reveals a natural human tendency to frame others' negative views of us as defensive, coming from some emotionally unhealthy place. In psychotherapy, negative patient perceptions of the therapist, or perceptions that the therapist is being negative toward the patient, generally are conceptualized as reflecting projections from the patient based on the patient's wishes and fears, themselves stemming from unresolved issues in the past. However, I suggest that many negative reactions on the patient's side are realistic. For example, the patient may not especially like the realistically perceived therapist, and this dislike may not represent the carryover or displacement of childhood relationships. Also, the patient may accurately perceive negative therapist reactions of which the therapist him- or herself is unaware. The point is that there indeed can be negatively valenced reactions in the context of the real relationship. At the same time, it is unlikely that treatment will succeed if there is a preponderance of negative reactions, however realistic and genuine. Greenson (1967) offered a case example that brings this point home:

> A young man, in the terminal phase of his five-year analysis, hesitates after I have made an interpretation and then tells me that he has something to say which is very difficult for him. He was about to skip over it when

he realized he had been doing just that for years, He takes a deep breath and says: "You always talk a little bit too much. You tend to exaggerate. It would be much easier for me to get mad at you and say you're cockeyed or wrong or off the point or just not answer. It's terribly hard to say what I mean because I know it will hurt your feelings."

I believe the patient has correctly perceived some traits of mine and it was somewhat painful for me to have them pointed out. I told him he was right, but I wanted to know why it was harder for him to tell it to me simply and directly as he had just done than to become enraged. He answered that he knew from experience that I would not get upset by his temper, that was obviously his neurosis and I wouldn't be touched by it. Telling me about my talking too much and exaggerating was a personal criticism and that would be hurtful. He knew I took pride in my skill as a therapist. In the past he would have been worried that I might retaliate, but he now knew it was not likely. Besides, it wouldn't kill him. (pp. 217–218)

Recently, McCullough (2009) took me to task for suggesting that good real relationships were positive:

A real relationship, by definition, should allow the freedom to confront conflicts and express negative feelings. Presumably, those feelings would be worked through until the conflict is resolved and positive feelings emerge. If this is not done, the positive valence could reflect a faked positivity. (p. 266)

As I noted in my reply to McCullough (Gelso, 2009b), I believe she is correct in this assertion, and some studies of the therapeutic relationship by my colleagues and I actually support her view (Gelso et al., 1999; Woodhouse, Schlosser, Ligiero, Crook, & Gelso, 2003). *However, the real relationship needs to be positively valenced overall, and this positive valence allows negative feelings on the patient's part to come to the surface and to be resolved.* In this sense, as suggested in Gelso et al.'s (1999) qualitative study of successful long-term dynamic therapy, the good or strong real relationship (described in the next paragraph) provides the patient with a secure base from which to explore otherwise too-threatening negative feelings, some of which are directed toward the therapist. However, again, it is important that, overall, the valence of the real relationship, from both the therapist's and the patient's side, be positive.

All things considered, *the real or personal relationship that has a high magnitude of realism and genuineness, in which there are primarily positive feelings of each participant toward the realistically perceived other, is what I would term a good or strong real relationship. It is the strength of the relationship that accounts for effective work.* Strength, as here conceptualized, must be distinguished from salience. Salience has to do with the extent to which the real relationship is in the forefront of the relationship and is a noticeable aspect of what is happening at the moment or during a particular segment of the work. The real relationship can be strong and solid but reside in the background, as happens, for example, in psychoanalytic treatments in which the work revolves around exploration of transferences, or in cognitive–behavioral work in which the focus is on therapist techniques used to resolve specific patient problems.

Locating the Real Relationship

There have been recent discussion and debate about whether the real relationship should be viewed as a component of the overall therapeutic relationship or as a quality that exists in all transactions between therapist and patient (Gelso, 2009a, 2009b; Hatcher, 2009). The *component point of view* formulates the real relationship as a component of the total relationship, and in my tripartite model the other parts are the transference–countertransference configuration and the working alliance. Each part has a certain level of salience and strength, and these will vary over the course of psychotherapy. For example, some studies have found a low–high–low pattern for transference in successful brief therapy, and a high–low–high pattern for the working alliance (Gelso, Kivlighan, Wine, Jones, & Friedman, 1997; Kivlighan & Shaughnessy, 2000; Stiles et al., 2004). The low–high–low pattern for transference indicates that the patient begins treatment with low levels of transference (especially negative transference) but that such transference builds during the middle of the work and then diminishes toward the end as the patient comes to understand and resolve key transference issues. Conversely, the high–low–high pattern for the working alliance suggests that in successful treatment a solid, positive working alliance is formed early but that, as the patient's defenses or problematic styles are confronted in the work, alliance ruptures occur, and the alliance temporarily weakens. It then is repaired and again becomes strong in the latter part of treatment. For the real relationship, I would expect a different pattern in successful therapy; that is, it is likely there would be either a consistently strong real relationship or one in which the real relationship starts at about a medium level of strength and increases steadily throughout treatment (see my discussion of research findings in chap. 7, this volume).

In contrast to the component point of view is what I have termed the *all-in-everything approach* (Gelso, 2009b). According to this view (see Frank, 2006; Hatcher, 2009; Wachtel, 2006), the real relationship is evident to varying degrees in each and every transaction between therapist and patient; so are transference and the working alliance. Greenson (1967) was getting at this all-in-everything view when he stated that "There is no transference reaction, no matter how fantastic, without a germ of truth, and there is no realistic relationship without some trace of transference fantasy" (p. 219).

Which point of view is most fruitful scientifically and meaningful clinically? Fortunately, there is no need to select one point of view over the other. Both make great sense clinically and scientifically, and both views may be implemented in research.

I view the real relationship as, in part, the transference-free element involved in every perception or experience, or interaction of and with another, more or less (Gelso, 2009a), and especially in interactions that have to do with the participants' reactions to one another and their relationship. As a psychotherapist, every interaction I have with my patient is partly indicative of our real or personal relationship and partly indicative of our alliance, the patient's transference, and my countertransference, and this part will vary in salience and strength from moment to moment. As a researcher, this is very meaningful to me, and it allows me to relate moment-to-moment expressions of the real relationship to other phenomena. However, as a researcher I am also interested in the component point of view, which will allow me to study the overall strength of the real relationship and how that relates to other relevant concepts, including treatment progress and outcome. It will also allow me to study changes in the strength of the real relationship in differing segments of the work.

At the same time, as a psychotherapist, both viewpoints are relevant. It is helpful to me to consider how various expressions by my patient and by me reflect varying degrees of the real relationship and transference or counter-transference. It also is helpful to recognize that certain actions or segments of the work are indicative of the real relationship, whereas others are suggestive of transference or my own countertransference. Finally, it helps the therapist to have a sense of the overall strength of each component of the relationship. For example, if the real relationship is strong but the working alliance is weak, knowledge of this allows me to think about what has made that happen and to realize that it is the working alliance that needs to be strengthened.

THE REAL RELATIONSHIP, THE WORKING ALLIANCE, AND THE BOND

In Chapter 1 I discussed the similarities and differences between the real relationship and the working alliance. I now elaborate further on this topic, because there is often confusion about these two key concepts.

The working alliance and the real relationship clearly are very similar. In fact, Greenson (1967) conceptualized the working alliance as emerging from the real relationship. The real or personal relationship occurs first in psychotherapy and psychoanalysis, and the alliance around doing the work of therapy develops from this personal connection. As for the real relationship, consider that all human beings inevitably have personal feelings and attitudes toward one another that are a part of their developing relationship. These exist apart from any work or job they may have to do together collaboratively, although the personal feelings and attitudes surely will influence the quality of the job they have to do and their enjoyment in doing the work. As for the psychotherapy relationship, the patient may, for example, have a feeling of liking for the therapist based on an accurate perception or sensing of the person of the therapist, and this liking will tend to have a positive effect on their work together, on the working alliance they form. Yet these personal feelings, or the personal relationship, are not the work or the working alliance.

When discussing the difference between the personal or real relationship and the working alliance I usually invite the reader or audience to consider their own experiences, and doing so helps clarify the distinctions. Ponder your own experiences as both psychotherapist and patient. As a therapist, you may notice that the working alliance with some patients you have treated is strong, but the real relationship is not so strong. You may do reasonably well at working together, but the personal connection may just not be there. There may be a sense that the two of you are just "from different tribes" as human beings. For others, it may be quite the opposite: You click just fine as persons, but perhaps your visions of the work are just too different. Also consider your experiences as a patient. Such experiences may be especially illuminating if you have had more than one therapist. I personally remember an experience as a patient in which my therapist and I had an acceptable working alliance but a rather weak personal relationship. We just seemed so different that it was hard to "take to" him, and I suspect it was hard for him to really take to me. Yet both of us were committed to the work, and I profited from it. In another personal therapy I felt both a strong personal relationship and a solid working alliance. The second therapy went better than the first, although both helped significantly. I have always thought that the second therapy was more helpful because of the stronger real relationship.

Because some major theories of the working alliance include the therapist–patient bond as part of the alliance (e.g., Bordin, 1979), there remains a question of whether the bond is part of the working alliance, the real relationship, or both. Surely the real relationship represents a bond between therapist and patient. Just as surely, though, the alliance is a bond. In a personal communication to me a number of years ago, Ed Bordin himself offered that "With regard to the real relationship, I have the distinction between bonds that are instrumental to carrying out the therapeutic work and bonds that are the resultants of the therapeutic encounter" (personal communication, May 7, 1985).

This distinction has always made a great deal of sense to me. Thus, it is useful to conceptualize the real relationship as constituting a personal bond and the working alliance as reflecting a working bond. Both serve to connect the therapist and the patient, but for different reasons. Although such distinctions are naturally fuzzy, I believe they are meaningful.

WHY AND HOW DOES THE REAL RELATIONSHIP MATTER?

What makes the real relationship important to the therapeutic enterprise? How does a strong real relationship help the patient? These questions must be answered, albeit very provisionally, if the concept of the real relationship is to be taken seriously. My answers are based partly on research and partly on clinical logic and experience.

For the patient, being seen realistically is essentially the same as being accurately understood. Such understanding from the outside, from the therapist, facilitates self-understanding. The connection of being understood to self-understanding and successful treatment of the patient has long been a topic of empirical and clinical scrutiny. The evidence for such a connection is very powerful (see Bohart, Elliott, Greenberg, & Watson, 2002).

At the same time, being in a relationship with a genuinely caring person, a person who cares about the patient for whom the patient truly is, will likely strengthen his or her sense of worth. In addition, having this strong personal connection, in which the patient feels liked and cared about for whom he or she truly is, will tend to create a sense of safety in exploring delicate and heretofore-dangerous inner feelings. The patient thus is freer to take the emotional risks of experiencing and exploring what may have been frightening transference feelings (see, e.g., Gelso et al.'s [1999] qualitative study) as well as other hidden affects.

From the standpoint of the patient's feelings toward the therapist, genuine caring for the therapist as a person deepens a sense of bond between patient and therapist. It also enhances the therapist's attractiveness to the patient, which has long been known to be influential in attitude change.

Although this discussion of how and why the real relationship helps may seem more applicable to dynamic or humanistic therapists, it is also germane to cognitive–behavior therapists. The patient's feeling that the therapist genuinely cares creates a secure base for the patient, which in turn provides encouragement to try out new behaviors. Such a relationship also makes it more likely that the patient will follow therapy instructions and assignments.

I have discussed how the patient–therapist working alliance may be conceptualized as emerging from the real relationship. As a way of summarizing why the real relationship facilitates change in the patient, it might be said that, from the patient's perspective, the strong real relationship, as I have been describing it, will tend to foster a solid working alliance.

What about the therapist's perspective? Although a competent therapist will likely work competently with patients in general, I believe we work more effectively with those patients to whom we "take," who seem to grasp who we are personally, and who respond to us in genuinely human ways. Thus, a strong real relationship enhances both the therapist's and the patient's functioning in the work, and thus it facilitates better treatment outcomes. In Chapter 7, I explore emerging research that is supportive of this assessment.

THE REAL RELATIONSHIP IN DIFFERENT THERAPIES

How does the real relationship operate in different theoretical approaches to treatment? How does it operate in brief and in long-term treatments? Apart from the theoretical differences in beliefs about realism and genuineness, what do psychodynamic, humanistic, and cognitive–behavioral therapists do differently with respect to the real relationship?

Let me first propose that although different theoretical approaches enact the real relationship differently, all therapies are benefited by a strong personal or real relationship between patient and therapist. Although I do not expect the different approaches to vary in regard to the strength of the personal relationship, they do differ in how salient the real relationship is during the work and in the extent to which the therapist works directly with and through the real relationship.

The Psychodynamic/Psychoanalytic Position on Being Real

It is impossible to talk about any one psychodynamic/psychoanalytic approach to the real relationship, because psychoanalysis is far from a monolith with respect to relational matters. The divide that may make the greatest sense is that between the more classical analytic therapists (drive, ego, and more classical object relations and self psychological therapists) and what Eagle (2003) termed the *new view* analysts (relational and intersubjective).

The Classical Position

For the classicists, although the real relationship is usually acknowledged, it is rarely brought into the work in an explicit way. Classicists who do acknowledge the real relationship and believe it is of some import still believe it is of secondary importance to the transference–countertransference configuration in the analytic work. They also tend to believe it is not as central to the effectiveness of the work as the working alliance. Meissner (2000, 2006), who has written extensively and thoughtfully about the real relationship as a component of the overall analytic relationship, made this point clearly when he stated that "the basic prerequisite for cure in analysis lies in the alliance rather than in the real relationship" (2000, p. 520). To be sure, for Meissner and many other analysts who lean toward the more classical view, the real relationship is of some importance, but its import is secondary compared with transference and the alliance.

Should an analyst or analytic therapist do anything in particular to foster the real relationship or to strengthen it? Should the therapist use the real relationship to effect change? The answer to both of these questions is a tentative "no." Probably the clearest statement of the current classical position on these matters was offered by Couch (1999), who noted that most of the time in analysis the real relation is "silently present in the background and shows itself occasionally only in those reality-oriented communications that are appropriately outside of technique" (p. 157).

Couch (1999) went on to clarify that the outer manifestations of the real relationship are most evident when the patient is not on the couch. For example, in the earliest meetings between analyst and patient, when the patient is sharing his or her reasons for seeking treatment and the analyst is clarifying the parameters of the treatment, there is a mutual assessment by each person of the other. Also, during periods of off-the-couch behavior before and right after sessions, there are reality-based interchanges (e.g., "Hello," "Goodbye," "See you tomorrow"), although some analysts tend to keep these to a minimum. Also indicative of the real relationship are times during which analysts provide information about circumstances that affect the analysis or support a conclusion the patient has reached about his or her past of present life. However, for Couch, and for many classical analysts, the most significant expressions of the real relationship

> are revealed in those rare occasions when it is vital for the analyst to acknowledge real difficulties in a patient's life, to express genuine sympathy and concern about crucial or tragic events such as illness, an accident or death in the family, and also to express congratulations for successful achievements, marriage, the birth of a baby. An initial brief acknowledgment of the reality significance of such events is clinically more important than any interpretations or silent reactions by the analyst; in fact, a persistent lack of normal responses at such times can easily destroy or sterilize an analysis. (p. 159)

Couch (1999) went on to clarify that behind the outward expressions of the real relationship are genuine and appropriate feelings of the patient and analyst toward one another as real persons, feelings that are "relatively free of transference and countertransference coloration" (p. 157).

In sum, using Meissner (2000) and Couch (1999) as representatives of the more classical position, the real relationship does exist and is of some importance for the classicist. However, it largely develops naturally, and a good analytic therapist should not seek to work with it or do analytic treatment through the real relationship. There are times when the analyst can and certainly should allow him- or herself to act within the parameters of a real person-to-person relationship, but the greatest attention is given to the transference–countertransference configuration and the working alliance.

The Relational Tilt

For relational and intersubjectivist psychoanalytic therapists the real relationship is viewed as more central to successful treatment than for classicists. Viewed more in terms of genuineness than realism (and more likely termed the *personal* or *person-to-person relationship*, as Frank [2006] argued in his important article), this aspect of the therapeutic relationship is seen as having a profound impact on the patient. Regarding genuineness (or similar terms that Frank [2006] used: *immediacy*, *authenticity*, *affectivity*, *mutual recognition*, and *intimacy*), Renik (1999) stated his belief that it is necessary for the analyst to "consistently play his or her cards face up" (p. 423). By this Renik was referring to self-disclosure and essentially doing away with the analytic concepts of ambiguity and neutrality. Thus, the analyst enacts a real relationship to an important extent through sharing his or her feelings with the patient. Such self-disclosure, however, is not a gimmick used to manipulate the patient's perceptions:

> The idea of achieving a new personal relationship is not something to go about by "acting spontaneous" or being compulsively self disclosing, for example. The new relationship [aka the personal relationship] is not possible to achieve in a deliberate way (such as Alexander and French proposed), but rather, as the result of thoroughgoing analytic work that involves our striving for openness to our own as well as our patients' experience and an authentic analytic presence. It is useful to keep the ideal of eventually achieving a new and better form of personal relatedness with one's analysand in mind, but on the back burner, as it were. (Frank, 2006, p. 50)

In sum, classical analysts and relational/intersubjective analysts have differing meanings of what constitutes the real relationship, and they have differing ideas about how it works in treatment and what the analyst should do to realize it. However, for relational/intersubjective analysts the personal relationship is of fundamental significance, perhaps as important as analytic technique in bringing about change.

Humanistic/Experiential Psychotherapy and the Art of Being Real

In many ways, it is hard to distinguish humanistic/experiential therapists from relational analysts in terms of both beliefs about the real relationship and what is done in treatment with and through the real relationship. Both camps focus more on genuineness than realism, and both believe the genuine, person-to-person relationship is a key ingredient of successful work. For person-centered humanists the treatment focus is on being genuine or congruent with oneself and with the patient, and this genuineness (along with empathic understanding of the patient and positive regard for the patient) itself will have a great impact on the patient. It will facilitate the patient's being more genuine with him- or herself and in his or her expressions to the therapist and others. Thus, change is brought about directly through the therapeutic relationship, of which genuineness is a significant part. Although for person-centered therapists genuineness is the most important aspect of the real relationship, realism also comes into play, if more indirectly. One of a therapist's basic functions is to strive to empathically understand the patient and his or her inner world. When this occurs, the therapist is grasping the reality of the patient and thus is fostering the realism aspect of the real relationship.

Despite the similarity of the various humanistic therapies regarding beliefs about the importance of therapist genuineness, just how this genuineness is revealed may differ markedly at times among theories. Such a difference is seen most vividly when one is comparing person-centered therapy and gestalt therapy, which are perhaps two most prominent of the humanistic therapies. It is true that from the 1960s onward, person-centered therapists have shared more of their own inner experiences with their patients, as long as that was done in a context of empathic understanding and positive regard for the person of the patient. At the same time, person-centered therapists have always focused mostly on empathically grasping the patient's inner experience, with self-disclosures occurring perhaps occasionally. For gestalt therapists there has always been a more radical view of genuineness. A gestalt therapist is much more likely to share his or her feelings with the patient on a moment-to-moment basis, and for these therapists this may include physical contact when it feels fitting. For example, embracing the patient as certain key moments is not at all uncommon among gestaltists, although sexual acting out is viewed, as it is in all legitimate therapies, as unethical.

Humanistic/experiential therapists also are involved in the realism aspect of the real relationship. As I have noted, for example, person-centered therapists struggle to grasp realistically the inner experience of the patient. Gestalt therapists are again more radical in fostering realism. If the patient does not seem to be perceiving the therapist accurately, the therapist is likely to state explicitly that this is happening, and at times this is done confrontationally. For example, Fritz Perls, the founder of gestalt therapy, might have told his patients that "I am not your father," or "Stop treating me as your father" (Gelso & Hayes, 1998). In other words, the therapist strives to be real and urges the patient to be real and perceive the therapist realistically. In these ways, humanistic/experiential therapies make use of the real relationship and share the belief that change comes about through such a relationship.

Cognitive–Behavioral Therapy and the Discovery of the Relationship

In the earlier days of behavior therapy and the cognitive therapies, the relationship between patient and therapist was of very minor significance.

However, it may be only a slight overstatement to say that in recent years the field of cognitive–behavioral therapy (CBT) discovered the power of the relationship. Although CBT therapists certainly continue to believe that cognitive and behavioral techniques are crucial to change, the importance of the therapeutic relationship in conjunction with techniques is becoming increasingly, albeit gradually, emphasized (see Goldfried & Davila, 2005; Holtforth & Castonguay, 2005; Lejuez, Hopko, Levine, Gholkar, & Collins, 2005).

Despite the increased attention to the therapeutic relationship, CBT therapists rarely make distinctions among the components of the overall relationship. When one reads works by such leading relationship-oriented CBT therapists as Kohlenberg and Tsai (1995); S. C. Hayes, Strosahl, and Wilson (1999); and Linehan (1993), it is clear that they are focusing on a mixture of the working alliance and the real relationship, although the term *real relationship* is not yet part of CBT language. Regarding the real relationship, its role and importance are nowhere more clearly seen than in Marsha Linehan's dialectical behavior therapy, a treatment specially tailored to patients diagnosed with borderline personality disorders (BPDs). She noted that with BPD patients who are suicidal it is the strength of the relationship that keeps the patient in therapy and that, in itself, is part of the cure (Linehan, 1993). Also, the effectiveness of dialectical behavior therapy techniques and strategies depends on a positive relationship; furthermore, a good working alliance also depends on such a relationship. For Linehan, this relationship is undoubtedly a real relationship, as she explicitly stated (p. 517). The best therapy with BPD patients involves a therapist who is genuinely compassionate, sensitive, flexible, nonjudging, accepting, and patient. In focusing on the therapist's acceptance of the patient and the relationship, Linehan explained that, most importantly, such acceptance "requires a willingness to enter into a situation and a life filled with pain, to suffer along with the patient, and to refrain from manipulating the moment to stop the pain" (p. 516). My personal work with BPD patients certainly supports this poignant statement.

Moreover, the CBT therapists who focus on what I term the *real* or *personal relationship* are very active in showing their patients that they care and in communicating understanding and caring in conjunction with the use of techniques. These therapists may also actively confront patients and honestly share more difficult feelings, but this is done in the context of a caring relationship. Because it is the CBT therapists who have come to address the importance of the relationship more recently than other approaches have, it is ironic that these therapists may be the most explicit of all in showing their patients what they feel and in actively developing a strong personal bond with their patients.

BRIEF VERSUS LONG-TERM THERAPY:
USING THE REAL RELATIONSHIP

A number of years ago, I organized a research program at the University of Maryland's counseling center that sought to understand the effectiveness of time-limited therapy and factors associated with such effectiveness (Gelso & Johnson, 1983). One of the striking findings of the research was that the personal relationship that patients felt with their therapists seemed to matter a great deal in terms of the success or failure of brief, time-limited treatments (with 8- or 16-session duration limits). In successful cases, the patients seemed to click with their therapists very early on, and they believed that their therapists were real people who actively supported them. The therapists themselves reported that they were more active and structuring than in longer term work that did not have duration limits. Since that time, it has seemed to me to be consistently true that therapists in brief therapy are more likely to work with and through the real relationship. This involves greater self-disclosure and, accordingly, less ambiguity. The therapist is more likely to tell the patient what he or she believes about the patient and the patient's life and problems. If the work is to go well, therapist and patient must click quickly, because there is less time to work through negative feelings that do emerge. This is not to say that negative feelings will not occur and be usefully addressed in brief work but instead that the real relationship needs to be generally more positive at the beginning of brief work if that work is to be successful. Along this same line, I would suggest that in brief work (in general, therapy that does not exceed 6 months), the real relationship is more in the forefront, more figure and less ground, than it is in long-term therapy or analysis.

It is tempting to conclude that the real relationship is more important, as well as more salient, in brief work than long-term work. I believe such a conclusion would be fundamentally wrong. Although the real relationship may be more ground than figure in most of a given stint of long-term therapy, it is nonetheless of great significance. For example, in a qualitative study of successful, long-term psychodynamic psychotherapy (Gelso et al., 1999), reports of the 11 therapists studied indicated that, in their view, the patients they selected to discuss formed strong real relationships with their therapists, noting that "virtually everything the therapists said implied that working alliance and real relationship (characterized especially by mutual liking) served essentially as buffers in allowing often very difficult transference feelings to come into the open and get resolved" (Gelso et al., 1999, p. 265). Similarly, a study of the psychoanalyses received by 75 psychoanalysts (Curtis, Field, Knaan-Kostman, & Mannx, 2004) found that among the top 10 most helpful behaviors exhibited by these analysts' analysts were genuineness, warmth, and emotional availability, with genuineness being at the top of the entire list. Among analyst behaviors that were most highly correlated with the analysands' change were genuineness, as well as the ability to tolerate sadness and anger between analyst and analysand. Thus, it appears that when psychoanalysts themselves receive psychoanalysis, their analysts' genuineness and other qualities that seem indicative of a strong real relationship are very important.

In sum, instead of the real relationship being more important in brief than long-term therapy I think it is more likely that the real relationship is more salient in brief work. In longer term therapy the real relationship sits more in the background but still exerts its influence, especially at certain times during which the working alliance is ruptured, transference becomes very strong, or "real life" issues show up and must be addressed. The real relationship is likely to be equally important in both brief and long-term work.

THE REAL RELATIONSHIP OVER THE COURSE OF PSYCHOTHERAPY AND PSYCHOANALYSIS

Speaking as both a psychotherapist and a trainer of psychotherapists, it seems to me that the strength and salience of the real relationship vary considerably over the course of both brief and long-term psychotherapy. In the following sections I explore how this might be so during early, middle, and ending phases of treatment. These phases are naturally simplifications, but they should prove helpful in clarifying the unfolding of the real relationship.

In the Beginning

The patient and therapist probably make their first contact through the telephone. In what may be a brief phone exchange, each gets a sense of the other and, within the context of their separate roles, each reveals parts of him- or herself. Given the incomplete data that are available in a phone exchange, the patient's perceptions are likely to be heavily influenced by what may be termed *preformed transferences*, that is, projections onto the therapist from earlier relationships. However, these early perceptions are surely partly realistic. The therapist and patient get an early and perhaps fragmentary sense of the person of the other. This sense of the other is carried with the participants until and into the first face-to-face meeting. Of course, it is now often possible to learn something about a therapist with whom one is considering working by searching the Internet. Such information, too, allows for the formation of the beginnings of a real relationship.

When the patient arrives at the therapist's office, he or she may notice the décor, including paintings or photographs on the wall, and when the actual meeting begins the patient then may see (and perceive at a less-than-conscious level) many realistic aspects of the therapist, including the therapist's appearance, attire, nonverbal expressions, posture and gestures, manner of greeting the patient and ending the session, as well as of course what the therapist says and how such verbal behavior meshes with all of these other qualities. Patients vary enormously in the extent to which they consciously notice these characteristics in their therapists. Some notice virtually everything about their therapist's behavior, as if their inner radar is constantly engaged. Others notice little. For all, however, the beginnings of a real or personal relationship are formed in this initial session and in the early part of the work in general. Although transference reactions are likely to also occur in the early meetings, the person-to-person part of the overall relationship is likely very salient in these initial sessions. What has often been referred to as "clicking" between therapist and patient, or in any relationship for that matter, is likely a reflection of a good beginning real relationship in which both participants sense that they are on the same page as persons and that they belong in the same tribe, so to speak, in ways that very much matter.

I would offer that in good real relationships there is generally an initial positive clicking between therapist and patient. Empirical data strongly support this assertion, and in Chapter 7 I shall delve into such data (e.g., Gelso et al., 2010). Furthermore, in the early work, as indicated, the real relationship is salient. It is at the forefront of the therapeutic transactions, and if it is not positive the work is unlikely to continue. The patient is likely to break off treatment, and the therapist will have less positive energy for the ensuing work, which is likely to influence the process of what is to come.

I have been focusing on the patient's reactions; however, whatever I have said about patients' formation of the real relationship applies to therapists as well. At the same time, the way in which the real relationship develops for therapists will be different from the patient's way because of the great difference in the prescribed roles of the two. Patients' roles involve sharing their stories with their therapists, including their pain, anxieties, and expectations. During this process they are consciously or unconsciously sizing up their therapist on the basis of how the therapist responds to them. The therapist, on the other hand, is involved in actively listening, trying to grasp the patient and his or her revelations while also paying attention to what he or she (the therapist) is feeling while listening. Because of these different roles, the therapist more readily senses the reality of the patient (than vice versa), and the patient more likely expresses his or her issues genuinely. So, in terms of realism and genuineness, the therapist is more likely to experience the relationship realistically, whereas the patient is more likely to share his or her feelings genuinely. Of course, these are matters of degree, because both therapist and patient are involved in a realistic and genuine encounter to one degree or another.

In sum, in the beginning stages of the treatment the real relationship is at the forefront of the overall therapeutic relationship. Patient and therapist take the crucial first steps in developing the part of their relationship that is personal and reality based. This will vary in strength; that is, it will vary from high to low in magnitude relative to the total therapeutic relationship (which also includes the working alliance, transference, and countertransference) and may vary from positive to negative in valence.

As the Work Proceeds: The Middle Phase of Treatment

If the early sessions of psychotherapy are sufficiently valuable for the patient, including if the real relationship is "good enough," the work proceeds into a middle phase, which may vary from a few sessions, in brief therapy, to several years in long-term psychotherapy or psychoanalysis. In general, during the middle phase the real relationship is mostly in the background of the work, because work on the patient's problems and conflicts take center stage. Just what constitutes such work will depend greatly on the theory of psychotherapy being implemented by the therapist.

Because the real relationship is in the background, however, does not mean it is unimportant or weak. It seems closer to the truth that the real or personal relationship serves to undergird the therapy. It, along with the working alliance, provides the patient with a solid base or perhaps a *secure base*, in attachment theory terms. This base, in turn, facilitates the difficult work of therapy. For example, if the therapist works from a psychoanalytic base, a solid real relationship will foster the expression and resolution of difficult transference feelings. If the therapist works from a cognitive–behavioral perspective, a sound personal relationship will facilitate the patient's completion of homework assignments or other tasks that there may be temptations to avoid.

Although mostly in the background, the real relationship comes to the forefront when needed during the middle phase of treatment. For example, if the therapeutic relationship is threatened by transference-based mistrust, anger, or projections onto the therapist, a sound and positive personal relationship reminds the patient of the actual reality of the therapist and helps the patient understand that the transference projections are just that and have not been earned by the therapist. Similarly, if the therapist confronts the patient with realities that are painful for the patient, this may create a rupture in the working alliance. At such points a positive personal relationship will help the patient understand that the therapist has the patient's best interests in mind while making such a confrontation.

Although these observations may be an accurate general portrayal of the real relationship during the middle phase of treatment, I must add the clinical observation that there is tremendous variability from patient to patient in regard to the development, strength, and salience of the real relationship throughout the treatment. This variability probably is related to the strengths and the degree and kind of psychopathology the patient possesses as well as individual personality differences among patients. For example, some patients may need for the real relationship to be at the forefront in general, whereas others seem to need a more muted real relationship. I have more to say about this in Chapter 5.

Realism, Genuineness, and the Ending of Treatment

During the ending phase of psychotherapy, which may last from a few sessions in brief therapy to several months in psychoanalysis, the real relationship comes to the fore again and becomes salient. The therapist who may, for theoretical or clinical reasons, have refrained from "playing his cards face up" (Renik, 1999) will often reveal more of him- or herself to the patient. Some may do so with the explicit aim of helping dissolve the transference. For others, there is likely a sense that much of the basic work has been done and that the therapist need no longer stay so much in the background in order to foster the patient's exploration. For still other therapists, becoming more open about their feelings and views may signify a wish to leave the patient with some clear messages about what the therapist believes will be important if the patient is to continue to grow. This viewpoint seems more prominent in brief therapies. Finally, many therapists share more of themselves and their feelings directly during the termination stage with the intent of facilitating the patient's internalization of the therapist as a good object (Hill et al., 2008).

As the work draws toward completion, a common experience is for the patient to become more interested in the person of the therapist and his or her life. Even in analytic therapy, in which the patient's experience and perceptions of the therapist have taken a prominent role throughout the process, perhaps reflecting a neurotic or voyeuristic interest in the therapist, the patient's interest in the therapist seems different during the termination phase of treatment. Especially when treatment has gone well, the patient displays a healthy and caring curiosity about the therapist as a person. As Charman and Graham (2004) noted, "The real relationship becomes apparent when the patient feels that he or she and the therapist are relating more like equals than at earlier times" (p. 287). On the basis of research findings, Gelso and Woodhouse (2002) noted that "in saying good-bye, the participants focus on their relationship, what it has meant, feelings surrounding its ending, and, of course, feelings surrounding the ending of treatment" (p. 363). The process of saying goodbye has a very powerful real relationship element.

STRENGTHENING THE REAL RELATIONSHIP

What can or should the therapist do to enhance the real relationship? In addressing this question we must again distinguish between the salience of the real relationship and the strength of the real relationship. Some therapists seek to keep the real relationship salient, at the center stage of the therapeutic transactions. They work with and through the real relationship. These therapists truly play their cards face up. They let the patient know in an ongoing way what they are feeling about the work and the patient. Classic examples of such therapists are Fritz Perls in his conduct of gestalt therapy (Perls, 1969) and Carl Rogers as exemplified in his famous videotaped treatment of Gloria (Psychological Films, 1965). More recently, Edward Teyber's (2006) relational approach is a clear and excellent example of working through and with the real relationship. In each of these approaches, one feature that stands out is that the therapist shares with the patient what he or she is feeling, including feelings toward the patient, in the here and now.

Playing Your Cards Face Up

The kind of response that embodies working with and through and with the real relationship has been termed *therapist immediacy* (Hill, 2004), *metacommunication* (Kiesler, 1988), and "talking in the here and now about the here and now" (Yalom, 2002).

I shall use the term *immediacy* here because it nicely captures the in-the-moment quality of such communication. Hill (2004) defined *immediacy* as comprising disclosures within the treatment hour of how the therapist is feeling about the client, him- or herself in relation to the client, or about the therapeutic relationship. This involves discussing and processing what is happening in the here-and-now client–therapist relationship (Kasper, Hill, & Kivlighan, 2008). The following is an example of immediacy taken from the 17th and final session of a relationally oriented course of psychotherapy (Hill et al., 2008, pp. 308–309). (Note that the patient is described as an articulate, bright, African American, lesbian, 29-year-old woman with long-standing symptoms of significant depression and anxiety; the therapist was a 55-year-old White heterosexual male with 30 years of clinical experience.)

Therapist:	Jo, I respect you so much.
Patient:	Do you?
Therapist:	I respect you so much. The way you go at these huge issues and face them with such courage . . . the work you've done with me since November has been so hard and so challenging and you have been so strong and capable and successful. I respect your integrity, I respect your courage.
Patient:	Thank you, but I'm glad I met *you* because there's no telling if I met with someone else. Not to say that it would have been . . . it's probably more of a feeling you know, with you than let's say somebody else who is just kind of like "so how do you feel about that?" . . . you really talk about issues and . . . It matters what we talk about in here. I always reflect back and say "Oh that makes sense" or then I'll jot it down . . .
Therapist:	You surprised me right from the get-go, Jo, you just got in the driver's seat and you put your foot on the gas pedal and you went to work. You initiated and you led me and us to such profound conversations at times. It's been a deep sharing.
Patient:	Oh yeah. It really has. (Hill et al., 2008, pp. 308–309)

In this same final session the therapist tearfully expresses a mixture of sadness at "not being able to continue with you on that and it's a loss for me that I'm not really going to be able to share all that journey, but I'm so happy to see you successfully launched on it" (Hill et al., 2008, p. 309).

It should be noted that in every measurement taken, this treatment was quite successful. Responses that might be termed *immediacy* encompassed fully 12% of the therapist's overall responses to the patient (Hill et al., 2008). Although different types of immediacy responses have been identified in the literature, the main type used in all of the studies, according to Hill et al. (2008), was encouragement by the therapist for the patient to express immediate feelings in the here and now of the therapeutic relationship. In this sense, the therapist's immediacy begets patient immediacy: The more the therapist works with and through the real relationship, the more the patient is likely to respond to the person of the therapist and express him- or herself genuinely.

The Less Disclosing Therapist

As I have said, for therapists who conduct their psychotherapy with and through the real relationship, this component of the overall relationship becomes very salient, a very clear and almost palpable part of the work. Does this lead to a stronger real relationship? Although I believe that it does, a thesis of this book is that the real relationship can be very strong without a great deal of self-disclosure on the part of the therapist. A therapist who does not self-disclose very much may still foster a strong real relationship through even infrequent disclosures, through showing his or her genuineness, through the congruence of what is said with nonverbal expressions, through a consistency in what is said to the patient, through accurately and empathically grasping the inner world of the patient, and through showing that he or she cares about the person of the patient in the myriad nonverbal ways in which a therapist may show such caring.

In addition, a therapist who exhibits limited self-disclosure may strengthen the real relationship by, in effect, respectfully disclosing why he or she does not disclose much. This allows the patient to know that there is a reason for nondisclosure and, paradoxically, that nondisclosure may reflect caring instead of indifference. In my own work, I have often used this approach. As a psycho-dynamically oriented therapist, I do not disclose a great deal, although I do believe that communication in the here and now of the therapeutic relationship is an extremely helpful, if not a necessary, condition for successful psycho-therapy. In response to patients' questions of what I feel about them, I often say, in effect: "It would be extremely easy for me to share my feelings for you, but I believe it would be more helpful in the end if we could explore what is it that makes you ask" or "What is it that is behind your question?" Of course, this works best when it is clear from everything I have done with a patient that I indeed have positive feelings for him or her. As a case example, in weekly therapy that lasted about 2 years with a college junior whom I shall call Elaine, the patient at times pressed me for what I felt about her. Indeed, I felt very caring of this young woman, who suffered from chronic depression and low self-esteem. I liked Elaine and admired her insightfulness, and I definitely felt a personal clicking with her. I looked forward to our sessions and was eager to be of help. It would have been easy to simply tell her that I had these feelings. However, the catch was that this patient deeply doubted her lovability, doubted how others felt for her, and constantly pushed for positive reactions to allay her feelings of unlovability. When receiving such reactions, she felt happy and "full" for a short while and then returned to her depressive doubting and yearning. I very much believed that sharing what I felt about her would be "more of the same" and that what was needed was a deeper exploration of what made her need the feedback so often, where it came from, and what it meant. I communicated this view to Elaine and refrained from sharing my positive feelings. I often asked what made her doubt that I cared, especially in light of my behavior with her, and we explored her feelings deeply, including her painful and depriving childhood. By any yardstick, this was a successful treatment, and I believe we had a very strong personal relationship, marked by genuineness and realism.

In sum, what strengthens the real relationship most from the therapist's side is the therapist *being* a genuine human being, actually caring and having other positive feelings toward the patient and empathically grasping the reality of the patient. Interactions in the here and now help considerably, but self-disclosures are generally more a matter of theoretical preference than a key to strengthening the real relationship. Self-disclosures foster the salience of the real relationship, to be sure, but they likely have only a modest effect on its strength.

Although I do not believe self-disclosure is the inevitable road to a strong real relationship, there certainly are times when it is not only called for but also when not doing so would be irreparably harmful to the working alliance. For example, if the therapist does not verbally or nonverbally share pleasure in a severely underachieving patient's significant accomplishment or share pain in a patient's loss of a child, the relationship will likely be harmed or even destroyed. In addition, if the patient accurately points out some behavior on the therapist's part that arises from a countertransferential place, it is wisest to simply 'fess up, and perhaps apologize, before moving forward to the exploration of the patient's feelings about the transgression.

Empathy and Strengthening the Real Relationship

I have been discussing how the therapist's genuineness, variously expressed, is a key part of strengthening the real relationship. Another key part, one that is often overlooked in discussions of the real relationship, is the therapist's empathic attunement.

As I have discussed in earlier chapters, *empathy* may be defined as the therapist's identification with the inner experience of the patient. This identification is both vicarious and partial in the sense that complete identification would result in the therapist's losing his or her own self while essentially fusing with the patient. The identification is what allows the therapist to both grasp the patient's experience intellectually and participate in the patient's emotional experience. In this sense, empathy may be both cognitive and affective.

Empathy may be exhibited in many ways. Although it is often clearly shown to the patient through accurate reflection of the patient's underlying feelings and through well-timed, accurate interpretations, it may also be demonstrated in a wide range of ways, some being highly unusual ways. For example, Bozarth (1984), a well-known person-centered therapist, presented compelling case data to demonstrate how empathy may be expressed in far different ways than the prototypic person-centered reflection of feeling. Following a session in which a very fragile client had experienced an intense and painful emotional block, she began the hour by asking Bozarth, "What have you been doing?" He responded by telling her a nearly session-long story about his car. This patient subsequently expressed appreciation that the therapist did not push her to reconfront her struggle, because what she needed then was a break from it. She also noted how the session helped her identify the core of her problems!

How does the therapist's accurate empathy foster and strengthen the real relationship? Through partially identifying with the patient's inner world and experience, the therapist moves closer to seeing the patient realistically, as he or she truly is. When one person grasps the reality of the other, the real relationship is automatically strengthened; that is, the personal bond that is part of any good real relationship becomes solidified and deepened when one person is accurately understood by another. Together with genuineness, empathy on the part of the therapist will create conditions in which the patient is more likely to be genuine and experience him or herself accurately (i.e., realistically). The therapist's empathy, in conjunction with his or her genuineness, is indeed a powerful facilitator of a strong personal relationship with the patient.

Countertransference Management and Dealing With Transference

In Chapter 3 of this volume, I discuss how the therapist's counter-transference management aids the real relationship. I shall add here only that, regardless of how countertransference is defined (and there are many definitions), it is crucial that the therapist stay tuned to his or her own inner experience, to when his or her buttons are getting pushed, and to how his or her inner experience may relate to the patient's dynamics. Staying so tuned will facilitate the therapist's genuineness in the sense that if the therapist is able to differentiate when his or her reactions are due to potential soft spots being touched by the clinical material, the therapist will likely respond to the patient in a more congruent and genuine way. The therapist's staying attuned to his or her own inner experience will also allow the therapist to see him- or herself and the patient more realistically.

With regard to transference, it is important for therapists of all persuasions to understand when the patient is misperceiving the therapist in a way that reflects that patient's unresolved issues and displacing feelings from past significant others onto the therapist. Just how the therapist works with transference will depend greatly on his or her theory of therapy. Psychoanalytic therapists, humanistic therapists, and CBT therapists, for example, will each deal with transference differently. However, it is important that therapists of all persuasions deal with distorting transferences, especially those that may be injurious to the treatment, if the real relationship is to be strong and remain strong.

CHALLENGES TO THE REAL RELATIONSHIP: WHY THEY ARE NOT PERSUASIVE

As I have said, the real relationship is a highly controversial concept in the world of psychotherapy and psychoanalysis. Some believe that it is synonymous with the working alliance or is part of the working alliance. In earlier chapters I have sought to clarify how the concepts of working alliance and real relationship are both similar and different. However, if a theoretician would prefer to view the real relationship as part of, say, the therapeutic alliance, so be it. Although I have made the case for why the real relationship is best seen as more fundamental than the working alliance, whether the alliance is seen as emerging from the real relationship or the real relationship is seen as the reality part of the therapeutic alliance may matter little. The point is that it is useful to conceptualize a real or personal relationship as part of each and every treatment, to one degree or another, and of every segment of therapy, every hour, and every response that therapist and patient make to one another.

It seems to me that there have been three major challenges to the viability and value of the real relationship (see Gelso, 2002, 2009a, 2009b). The first challenge goes something like this: "Because everything in the therapeutic relationship is real, the concept of a real relationship seems redundant and superfluous." In response to this challenge I offer that, although everything in the relationship is surely real in the sense that all feelings, attitudes, and actions do exist, the concept of a real relationship addresses meanings that go well beyond the mere existence of such feelings, actions, and attitudes. The concept of the real relationship as I have described it incorporates both realism of perception/experience and genuineness of expression. It must be remembered in this respect that the concept of *real*, as it was developed in psychoanalysis, meant "realistic," which in turn was contrasted to unrealistic or transferential. In any event, the real relationship is also not redundant or superfluous because it captures aspects of the therapeutic relationship that are not captured by other existing concepts, such as the working alliance and transference (see chap. 1, this volume).

A second challenge is reflected in the following question: "Who is it who knows what is real, or who is the so-called arbiter of reality?" As we shall see in subsequent chapters of this volume, this question has a more political than theoretical flavor to it. The criticism behind the question is that the very concept of a real relationship presumes that someone within the relationship knows what is real and what is not real, and it is almost always the therapist who is seen as the knowing one. Seeing the therapist as the arbiter of reality places the therapist in an omniscient position and the patient in an inferior role. As I noted elsewhere (Gelso, 2009), hidden within this criticism is an attack on classical psychoanalysis because this theory seemed to its critics to place the analyst in such an all-powerful place. It was as though the analyst had the market on truth, and if the patient had a different perception, then such a difference must have emerged from resistance and defense. My rebuttal to this criticism is that one need not (and should not) presume that either member of the psychotherapy dyad is the total arbiter of reality in order for the concept of the real relationship to be viable and valid. Both the therapist and the patient have a view, to which each certainly is entitled. This position is part of the constructive realism that I advocated in Chapter 3. Thus, there is indeed a reality of the patient and a reality of the therapist, but both participants have perceptions and constructions of these realities that are extremely important, even when (or perhaps especially when) they are in disagreement.

The third challenge may be stated this way: "Even if there is a reality, it can never be fully known. Thus, the concept of real relationship has little merit." Refutation of such an argument is rather easy. Not being able to fully know reality in no way negates the merits or validity of a real relationship as I have described it. It is highly doubtful that we can fully know anything in the behavioral sciences. All we can hope to do is keep improving our approximation of an ever-changing reality. Still, our partial knowing of the reality of the therapist and the patient can help us greatly in our quest to understand and improve psychotherapy.

CONCLUSION

The real or personal relationship shows itself in every therapy, every segment of therapy, every session, and every interaction. Still, the real relationship varies considerably in strength from therapist to therapist and patient to patient. I have theorized that the strength of the real relationship, more than its salience, has much to do with how well or poorly treatment goes. If treatment is to be effective, it helps considerably for the patient and therapist have an initial clicking and that the real relationship be strong throughout. If the real relationship is not strong at the beginning, it will likely need to strengthen over the course of the therapy if the treatment is to reach its potential.

In this chapter, I have discussed how the real relationship is addressed differently in the major theoretical approaches to therapy; how the real relationship shows itself differently during the early, middle, and termination stages of treatment; and what the therapist can do to strengthen the real relationship. Simply disclosing more about oneself is insufficient and itself may be harmful to the real relationship, depending on how, what, and when the therapist discloses. Yet the real relationship may be very strong, if not salient, for a minimally disclosing therapist.

In the following chapters I examine the real relationship more fully in terms of its manifestation in the psychotherapy hour, and then I look into the emerging research on this construct. Although in this chapter I have sought to explore the real relationship theoretically, these theoretical explorations shall be more fully operationalized in Chapter 8, the final chapter. There I shall translate this theory and the clinical and research findings about the real relationship into a series of theoretical propositions that are capable of clinical and empirical scrutiny.

5

THE REAL RELATIONSHIP WITHIN THE PSYCHOTHERAPY HOUR

When discussing the real relationship with practicing therapists, researchers, and graduate students, I am usually asked to clarify how this aspect of the overall therapeutic relationship manifests itself in the clinical hour. What does it look like in treatment? What are examples of a real relationship? These are the questions most often asked, and in this chapter I seek to address them, exploring how the real or personal relationship reveals itself in psychotherapy sessions. I use case examples and vignettes to pinpoint what is and what is not the real relationship as well as how this relationship affects and is affected by the psychotherapy process. I provide examples from the major theoretical systems to demonstrate how the real relationship operates in diverse treatments. Some of these examples are from the work of my graduate students in an advanced psychotherapy practicum I teach. As part of students' assignments in this course, they read about and discuss aspects of the therapeutic relationship, including the real relationship. Although varying theories are discussed and used in the practicum, the course has a decidedly psychodynamic/psychoanalytic emphasis. Other examples are drawn from my own clinical work, as well as that of experienced colleagues and from the published literature. Some of the case examples have appeared in earlier chapters in this book. I repeat them because they nicely exemplify a given point and further my intent in this chapter of clarifying how the real or personal relationship shows itself in therapy.

Despite the fact that the real relationship will show itself somewhat differently in different theoretically based approaches to psychotherapy, it is important to note that, regardless of the therapist's theoretical orientation, the real relationship will be expressed at each of three levels. From both clinical and a scientific perspectives, it is useful to examine the real or personal relationship during the psychotherapy hour from each of these three levels.

1. First, the real relationship most often exists in the background of the psychotherapy transactions. It shows itself through the participants' ongoing sensing and understanding of one another and in their feelings toward each other. In this way, the real relationship is manifested inwardly, in therapists' and patients' feelings, understanding, and sensing. These inner states simply exist as the therapist and patient explore the patient's inner conflicts and outward behavior about matters other than their relationship. However, the real relationship comes into the foreground when it is needed, usually when there is some rupture in one or more parts of the relationship, when difficult transference feelings surface, or during particularly stressful times when the patient needs the support of a strong real relationship to move forward.

2. At a second level, the real relationship will show itself either saliently or subtly in the actions of both participants that reflect genuineness and realism, as well as the valence of these. Examples of these actions are provided in this chapter.

3. Although the real relationship will be a prominent part of some of the participants' inner states and outer behavior toward one another, at another level the real relationship is part of each and every communication between the participants, to one degree or another. In keeping with Greenson's (1967) formulations, there is a real relationship element in all communications, no matter how fantastical they are. By the same token, there is a transference element in every transaction, regardless of how reality based that transaction may be.

Throughout this chapter, I present examples of the real relationship from the therapist's perspective and the patient's perspective. I highlight key ways in which the real relationship is exemplified in treatment.

THE THERAPIST'S EXPRESSION OF THE REAL RELATIONSHIP

The therapist's expression of the real relationship with a patient can take many forms, including not only the physical surroundings of his or her office but also the extent to which he or she self-discloses and whether he or she responds to patients with immediacy.

Physical Surroundings and the Context of Psychotherapy

The vehicle through which the therapist or analyst will initially express his or her personhood is the physical environment that is created. When, for example, one of my patients somewhat humorously expressed a kind of fondness for the "professorial shabbiness" of my office some years ago, the patient was picking up on something about me, because this professorial shabbiness is indeed a part of who I am. Similarly, when my patients or students enter my current office, they face directly a wall full of books. Although this appearance will stir transference feelings in many, it also is a reflection of who I am, because I place a very high value on books and being around books, even those I don't read!

Office decor says a good bit about who the therapist is as a person, and such décor includes the paintings he or she has on the wall, the diplomas he or she does or does not display, the furniture and colors, and so on. Similarly, the therapist's attire presents the patient with a sense of that therapist's personhood. Even dressing in a subdued fashion in order to not contaminate the transference will communicate something important about the therapist. So too will the therapist's general appearance, both obvious features (e.g., heavy or slender, race and skin color, more or less attractive) and the more subtle expressions and posture that are part of the person of the therapist.

The therapist's manner of greeting the patient, ranging from a warm handshake to a more remote "Hello," says much about that therapist, both as a person and as a professional, and the extent to which he or she is willing to participate in a strong real relationship and allow that relationship to be salient. I want to communicate to my patients that I am pleased to see them (when this is true), and I wish to make them feel warmly received by me on a personal level. This reality of expression establishes a caring human context in which psychoanalytic therapy (or therapy of any orientation) can proceed effectively, including the analysis and working through of transference feelings when this is deemed appropriate. By contrast, Greenson (1967) lamented what he called the "affective atherosclerosis" that affected so many analysts of his day. I suggest that a tepid, neutral greeting is often part of that ailment.

At times the patient will *not* see an obvious aspect of the physical environment or the therapist, and I believe this reveals important information about the real relationship. For example, following my divorce after a long marriage, I discontinued wearing a wedding ring. Some patients noticed this immediately, and others never noticed. Although transference was no doubt at work in what and how these patients did or did not notice, so was their willingness to notice me as a real person with a life outside of the psychotherapy hour. Similarly, changes in what the patient sees are important. Greenson (1978) provided an example of a patient who, in the fourth year of analysis, suddenly asked as he entered his analyst's office, "Is that a new chair?" Greenson went on to say that "That chair was there, unchanged, from the first day he came to see me. What changed was something in his awareness of me and of himself as real persons" (p. 438).

Self-Disclosure, Immediacy, and the Real Relationship

In a certain sense, much of what was discussed in the prior section reflects therapists' self-disclosures, because the physical context and the therapist nonverbal behavior that has been described are a kind of self-disclosure. More direct self-disclosures may pertain to factual information about the therapist (e.g., does the therapist have children, where therapist did his or her graduate work, in what field the therapist studied, and what the therapist's approach to therapy is). Disclosures of this sort of information certainly communicate important data about the reality of the therapist. Answering questions about such things, or providing the information even if not asked, makes the real relationship more salient, although not necessarily stronger. Although patients are entitled to certain kinds of information about their therapists, in my view it is unwise to simply provide the information without being curious about why the patient is asking. Questions about the therapist say a lot about the patient and often are a gateway to important transference material. The main point, however, is that what information the therapist reveals about him- or herself, whether or not in response to patients' questions, says much about how salient will be the real relationship (from the therapist's side) and whether the therapist will be doing the therapy primarily through the real relationship.

An example of a therapist who places the real relationship at center stage would be a cognitive–behavioral therapist who readily shares information about himself. This therapist may, for example, see patients in his home office, and to reach this office patients might have to walk through the therapist's home. At times, the therapist's wife and other relatives might be in the house as patients walk to the office. This therapist makes clear who he is and how he feels about the patient. He is highly supportive as he works with his patients, although he certainly can also be challenging of self-defeating thoughts and behaviors. He is especially expert in therapy with anxiety disorders.

Immediacy, as discussed in previous chapters, is a kind of self-disclosure that goes beyond factual information. As Hill (2004) noted, immediacy is seen as self-disclosure within the psychotherapy hour of how the therapist is feeling about the patient, about him- or herself in relation to the patient, or about the therapist–patient relationship. Such immediacy involves the therapist sharing his or her experience and feelings in the here and now, instead of past feelings. Although such feelings may be driven by countertransference-based conflicts—that is, by the therapist's unresolved conflicts and vulnerabilities— they do reflect the reality of the therapist, and they also usually imply genuineness on the part of the therapist. (Note that immediacy may also be seen as exploration of the patient's feelings in the moment toward the therapist and the relationship; see Kasper, Hill, & Kivlighan, 2008.) The therapist's use of immediacy in the hour serves to make the real relationship salient and is a primary way of working with and through the real relationship.

Two intensive case studies by Hill and her colleagues provide very clear examples of therapist immediacy and thus of working through and with the real relationship (Hill et al., 2008; Kasper et al., 2008). In one of these studies (Kasper et al., 2008), a very experienced, interpersonally oriented 51-year-old male therapist (Dr. N) worked with a 24-year-old White female (Lily) who sought treatment for problems in relationships. In the course of this 12-session time-limited therapy the therapist expressed a range of feelings in the moment that were directly relevant to the patient and the work. These included feelings of sadness, hurt, disappointment, caring, closeness, connection, and pride in the work and the patient. For example, in the eighth session Dr. N addressed Lily's seemingly indifferent reaction to their termination of therapy a few weeks hence by stating "Last week when we were talking about when we're gonna end and how long we're gonna go . . . I was sort of wondering what's going on that it doesn't seem like it matters to you one way or the other how long we [meet]." Lily replied "No; actually, the truth of the matter is, like I mean I think I mentioned to you that I would like to go on more than 12." She continued by saying that she felt it would be selfish to tell him that she would prefer to have more sessions. Dr. N stated, "So you didn't in some ways wanna hurt me or upset me," and then "For me it hurt, that it felt like it didn't matter [to you] how long we [met]." In an interchange that was part of the research study, Lily made the following statement:

> This was really an incredible session and I really feel much closer and more attached to Dr. N. It was knowing how disappointed he seemed at the thought of my distance (over discussing our ending) and I never would have realized this if he hadn't brought it up . . . It's amazing to know what a strong effect I can have on someone. . . . This led to a very

valuable discussion of how I relate to people and the negative effects of this. (Kasper et al., 2008, p. 289)

This vignette shows the therapist sharing what he genuinely felt in a way that was clinically sensitive. Whether he was realistically grasping the patient's inner world we cannot determine fully, but from the patient's reaction it is clear that she felt understood. This seems very clearly like a demonstration of the real relationship, and I suspect that the therapist's behavior served to strengthen the existing real relationship.

A second example comes from the qualitative study conducted by Hill et al. (2008) that was presented in Chapter 4 of this volume. Here the patient (Jo) was described by the research team as an "articulate, bright, African-American, lesbian, 29-year old woman with long-standing symptoms of significant depression and anxiety" (p. 299). The therapist (Dr. W) was a highly experienced 55-year-old White man who was interpersonally oriented and who drew from family systems theory and attachment theory. The treatment lasted for 17 sessions.

On the basis of Jo's communications after the interchange presented in Chapter 4, along with her written comments to the researchers after the session, the researchers concluded that this immediacy on the part of the therapist helped Jo open up as she discussed her experience of having been molested and raped and how these assaults had affected her. The patient clarified that she had never before shared these experiences with anyone and that she wanted to stop ignoring them. The researchers concluded that Dr. W's validation of Jo's strengths facilitated her courage to talk about difficult topics:

> Dr. W's expression of his faith in Jo's capacity for self-healing was a way of reparenting her and suggesting how she could come to parent herself . . . . His acceptance of her also seemed to allow her to accept herself and not blame herself quite so much for the terrible things she had experienced (e.g., sexual assault, abandonment). (Hill et al., 2008, p. 309)

As I reflected on this material from my own more conservative position, I wondered whether the therapist's intense expression of respect might have felt invasive to the patient at some level, as her subsequent discussion of being sexually assaulted could have symbolized. It has always seemed important to me to be mindful of the fact that intense self-revelations on the part of the therapist likely provoke reactions in the patient at many levels and that overt expressions by the patient may not match less conscious experience. Still, this case example very clearly demonstrates how a therapist may place the real relationship at center stage, making it the most salient aspect of the overall relationship at that point in time. Responding to patients with immediacy tends to foster such salience.

Facilitating the Patient's Direct Experience of the Real Relationship

At times, a therapist may deliberately seek to foster the patient's experience of the realistic aspect of the relationship. This is most likely to be effective when the therapist is aware that the patient, for one reason or another, is muting the reality of the therapist when at the same time the therapist believes that perceiving that reality is both possible for the patient (i.e., the patient is capable of seeing and experiencing the reality of the therapist without undue anxiety) and helpful. This can be done quite directly, as in the following case material, which was provided by Patrice Duquette (personal communication, May 2009), a highly experienced psychodynamically oriented psychotherapist who has written about the importance of the real relationship (e.g., Duquette, 1997):

> Pam was a patient in weekly individual and group psychotherapy for several years. She was 36, married, and the mother of a two year old; and she had gone back to school for six years before successfully completing a [certified public accountant] program. The economy had turned more quickly than usual, and her original plan of part-time work after a second child had to be changed. Pam became distraught over issues such as her family's economic situation, her current difficulty getting pregnant again, and relationship troubles with her husband. She often brought her anxieties to her therapy and would consciously make an effort to separate out what was her characteristic response to the situation and what was the husband's part in the mix.
>
> In the midst of a session in which Pam was describing her employment seeking and concerns of how to network to find better opportunities, she noted how "tight" she was, using that term to describe her physical and emotional experience. From past experience in her therapy, she knew that a sensation of muscle tightness was often the first clue to a rigidity in her thinking and a lack of being able to openly consider any issue in front of her. [Note that the comments about the actual therapy transactions are made by Dr. Duquette and are in parentheses.]
>
> | | |
> |---|---|
> | *Pam (P):* | I can hear myself being tight. I don't want to really feel, don't want to have those feelings. But I don't want to be like this either. (Her mouth is set tight, her forehead is raised and eyes tightened, her voice is very tight and has a cry in it.) |
> | *Dr. Duquette (T):* | Can you feel your throat at all? |
> | P: | Not really. Can't feel it separate from all the other tightness. Not quite. Don't want to almost. Feels like I can't feel or think, like my brain has just stopped. |

T: Try a bit. Can you feel anything? Can you direct your energy, to feel where you are? Can you look at me?

P: A little bit. (Tears well up obviously in her eyes, her mouth twists more, her eyes go to an almost vacant look, with her eye contact less intensely focused.) Now I just . . . just . . . it just feels like there is a big gaping hole. (Silence, and she continues looking, but is appearing more frightened by the second.)

T: Stay here. Can you look at me? At me . . . here?

P: A little . . . (More tears, eyes are still looking vague and fading.)

T: What do you see? Here? Are you alone?

P: I see you.

T: (Nods and gestures as if to say "More.")

P: I can see you (mouth still twisting, patient is limiting her verbal output).

T: What do you see in me? Can you see my eyes? What do you see?

P: That you are present.

T: Who is, who am I?

P: Double D. (Patient chuckles, as if it were a private joke. Therapist recalls that this is how the patient writes her name in her appointment book and smiles slightly in recognition.) Dr. Duquette, that's who you are. (She says this in a firmer voice, with a moment of eye contact. Such moments had come up before in group situations, when I had directed her and others to use my full name by way of fuller recognition of me and our relationships in a given moment.)

T: And so?

P: That you see me, care about me, are listening. And that as you see me you are like 99.9% accurate about what you see. (Her voice is settling, she speaks more spontaneously, her eye contact is more directed. But then a shift occurs.)

T: What just happened there?

P: Just fell into a vacuum, couldn't think, couldn't find anything. (Her voice is stronger, but now more guarded.)

T: It seemed to change pretty quickly for you at some point.

P: Yeah, that was about it. I just lost what I could do. It seemed suddenly so scary. Too vulnerable.

T: (Talks about some of the possibilities of the experience from some sense she has about the patient's coming out into the world, using historical data talked about over the years.)

P: (Interrupts somewhat) Yeah, it is some of that. Somehow I am having a hard time following you. I keep on thinking about what happened with my daughter and me yesterday. I don't know if it is because I am trying to distract myself or if it matters. I think it is because it matters, not just distract myself.

T: Tell me about it.

P: I met my friend and her 5 yr old daughter at the Rainforest Cafe for lunch. (She asks if I had ever been there and we discuss briefly how dark and loud it is, as there are moving statues and a "rainstorm" that happens every half hour as an experience for the kids. I acknowledge having been there but only infrequently as I find it too much effort with all the noise and the lack of a comfortable ambience. She describes being angry at first where they were sat [sic], but then realized it was the brightest and most quiet area of the restaurant which was easier for her and her friend with their girls.) Alexis had to hug me more at first, then she ended up in my lap. Not the easiest way to eat lunch but it was OK. She asked me to put my arms around her when the noises were too loud, and even said, no—put your hand right here on my belly and keep it. (Patient tears up.)

T: It was as if you were containing all the noise and dark and helping her stay OK with it by your presence. Literally offering her that as you ate and she responded, too.

P: She did. We ate lunch and later on we went to the play area and she climbed up on a statue and then began yelling for me to come and get her off. I went over there and first talked to her, then helped her sit down, then slide off. I knew it was important somehow to tell her to sit down and to find a way off without just picking her up.

T: Again, you directed the energy, contained it and showed her how to move through that scary experience up on the statue.

P: Yeah, I did. (Face screws up again, mouth gets tight.)

T: Now what? What is it now?

P: Don't know. It feels OK, but scary somehow.

T: I would say something about the statement "directing the energy" or about your energy seems to start this then and now.

P: Yeah! Yeah. That seems scary somehow.

T: Talk about that more.

(Patient talks about some of the experience, seems too powerful, capable, she can't or shouldn't do whatever.)

T: Your face looks like you are waiting for something to slam you right now. Feel anything?

P: Well, yeah, somehow that should happen. I can't tell why but know that I am just getting tighter again.

T: I would have to say we are seeing you caught between your mother and your father. The "vacuum" or the "slammer."

P: Yeah!! It is like that. Like I shouldn't do that, shouldn't move out into the world, he always would find a way to slam me down. And she was just such a vacuum. Right now as I think about that time when I couldn't talk either, it is like the white room I used to work in with the photographer. It was a room without a real corner between the floor and the wall, it just kind of had a curve there. But it was big and white, and felt like an emptiness.

This is what Duquette had to say about this interaction and her attempt to bring her (the therapist's) own reality and personhood to the fore:

In the midst of working to contain her experience, Pam was able to glimpse the relationship through a small window at first. When she attempted to move out from her inner turmoil, the experience of vulnerability caused her to withdraw again. As her experience became emotionally overwhelming, she not only withdrew from emotional contact to regroup, she was able to recognize a significant loss of functional ability in the moment. She was able to note how she couldn't "feel or think," and as the therapist encouraged her to try to re-engage with her inner experience and express it, the patient found herself further withdrawing, but could not note that verbally. The therapist made note of the further withdrawal with the invitation to look inward, and then the therapist shifted her efforts to further the establishment of a sense of the therapist's presence, both current and past and thus help the patient regain her footing and continue interacting in the moment. Through the contact with the therapist she was able to stretch her developmental repertoire slowly but surely. The therapist used the real element of their relationship, first the experience of her physical presence, through eye contact, then through what seems to be a trivial element, the naming of her. When the patient makes a slight joke at first, then names her in accordance with the prior contact they have had, the referencing moves from the personal to the interpersonal, signaling an intent to re-engage in the relationship, to which the therapist responded and the pair moved on into a more involved mutual interaction. (P. Duquette, personal communication, May 2009)

In this clinical example the therapist sensitively pushed the patient to see the reality of the therapist, and it seemed to me that this facilitated the patient's centering herself so she could then face further internal resistances and move through them. Some therapists would be more insistent on the patient's responding to the person of the therapist instead of to the therapist as a transference figure. For example, Yalom (2002) told of his work with a patient in which he and she exchanged impressionistic summaries of each therapy session:

> This format was also a challenging exercise in therapist transparency. The patient had so idealized me, had placed me on such an elevated pedestal, that a true meeting between us was not possible. Therefore, in my notes I deliberately attempted to reveal the very human feelings and experiences I had: my frustrations, my irritations, my insomnia, my vanity. This exercise, done early in my career, facilitated therapy and liberated me a good deal in subsequent work. (pp. 80–81)

In this treatment, Yalom made his reality so salient to the patient that she had to respond to him as a person. She could not lapse into transference distortions, at least not for long.

The Growth and Unfolding of the Real Relationship

At times, the real relationship is strong from the very beginning of treatment. Therapist and patient click as persons in the first meeting, and their personal relationship is strong throughout. It may deepen further over the course of the work, as the two individuals come to know each other more fully and as their intimacy level increases with the emergence of more personal, difficult material from the patient. The therapist's manner of responding to such material and adding his or her own feelings and thoughts to the mix are a big part of this deepening of the real relationship.

In other cases, the real relationship may not be strong initially but improves over the course of the work. Such was the case in a therapy offered by one of my supervisees. This student, whom I shall call Jack, was in the 4th year of his doctoral training, and in terms of race/ethnicity he was European American. At the time of our work, Jack was 30 years old and had a training background of supervised humanistic and psychodynamic therapy as well as intensive training in therapeutic verbal techniques, often referred to as *helping skills* (e.g., reflection of feeling, open question, interpretation, confrontation; see Hill, 2009). Jack was working with me in supervision on conducting psychodynamically oriented therapy. We met weekly, and before our meetings I listened to all or a portion of the audiotape from his previous sessions. For his level of training and experience, Jack was highly skilled and had all the makings of a gifted therapist.

The patient, Maria, was a 21-year-old college junior. She was a tall, heavyset Hispanic woman (racially a combination of Black and Native South American) who came from a highly educated and financially well-to-do family. The treatment lasted for 26 weekly sessions over two semesters. Maria had sought therapy because she chronically experienced an emotional numbness, carried with her a sense of emptiness, and felt very distant from others, although behaviorally she gave outsiders the impression of being very friendly and happy go lucky. As implied, she suffered from a moderate level of dysthymia; the term "smiling depressive" seemed to fit Maria well.

One of Jack's difficulties as a budding therapist was a tendency to be too supportive in an effort to win patients over (i.e., to develop a working alliance). It was hard for Jack simply to hear and comment on the patient's underlying pain without putting a positive spin on it, and if his patients experienced painful emotions in response to a comment of his, Jack tended to feel badly about himself. Thus, after the third session with Maria, Jack wrote the following in his process notes:

> My expectations about the process of our therapy have been skewed. I envisioned our therapy as a corrective experience that would allow some victorious catharsis for Maria, where her in-session experience of pain and negative affect was welcomed, positively spun as progress. My expectations conflict with Maria's central issue, such that Maria's experience of feelings will come with a great deal of pain and discomfort. Whereas I felt abusive and responsible for Maria's touching on some actual emotion in this session, I realize that Maria's discomfort is necessary and will actually facilitate our work.

During the early part of the work Jack felt distant from Maria, and he did not feel very genuine. Indeed, he had trouble being genuine, and his experience of Maria in the moment also lacked realism; that is, he had trouble openly grasping her painful experience. Thus, Jack's way of being with Maria did not reflect a strong real relationship. For her part, Maria had great difficulty experiencing and expressing what she felt in the moment. Her talk in therapy seemed far removed from what she really felt, although all the words were right. She was clearly low in genuineness, and she did not seem to perceive/experience Jack very clearly or realistically. In fact, each of the participants had trouble perceiving/experiencing the other as they truly were (low realism), mainly because each seemed to hide significant aspects of themselves. Because Maria was a highly motivated patient and Jack a highly motivated therapist with considerable skill, the working alliance seemed to develop well, but the real relationship was very weak.

This was a therapy in which the real relationship seemed to strengthen gradually. It strengthened slowly and seemed to especially strengthen during the final six or seven sessions. For instance, in the 25th session Jack recorded the following in his process notes:

> It was nice to reflect with Maria on her experience of our work together. I think Maria has maintained some positive transference toward me, but I also see that our real relationship has improved over the course of the work. For a number of sessions, it was hard to build a relationship with Maria, because there was little true self offered. As she became more honest and vulnerable in our work together, I came to know Maria as she truly is and not as a fictitious portrayal of herself. I like Maria, I have enjoyed our work together, and I've learned a good deal in working with her.

As for the therapist's contribution to the real relationship, after one of these later sessions he made the following comment:

> I felt very close to Maria throughout this session. Toward the end of the session, as we spoke about Maria's projections onto me, I made a self-disclosure. . . . We also spoke with immediacy about our intense session a few weeks back. Maria asked me about[,] and I disclosed about[,] my experience during the session. After listening to the session, I am not disappointed or regretful of my self-disclosure during the session, but it is interesting that I disclosed twice and that I've never self-disclosed within a session with a client an any of my doctoral training.

In listening to the session tapes there was little doubt in my mind that the real relationship had strengthened substantially over the course of this therapy. Jack's occasional self-disclosures were quite appropriate, and he was more often being truly himself in the sessions. He was also allowing—indeed, facilitating—Maria's experience of her innermost feelings. Maria, too, had changed from being an emotionally remote person with an "as if" quality to someone who shared at least a good part of what she felt in a way that beautifully fit Rogers's (1957) notion of congruence or genuineness. As I listened to tapes and worked weekly with Jack in supervision, it seemed to me that the growing strength of the real relationship between Jack and Maria was a result of their working alliance and their positive intentions around the work as well as a cause of further movement and growth.

The Real Relationship at the End of Treatment

Earlier in this chapter I noted that the real relationship is often salient at the beginning of treatment, when patient and therapist are getting acquainted with each other. So too is it in the forefront during the termination stage, as the participants are preparing to end the work. Some therapists believe that the termination phase is the time to explicitly dissolve the transference relationship by being more direct about who they are and their feelings around the work and the patient. Others may have been more open throughout, adhering to Renik's (1999) suggestion that the therapist or analyst ought to "play his or her cards face up" (p. 423). Even these more self-revealing therapists, however, go a step or so further in their self-revelations during the termination phase. They, too, become even more the human being than the working, "in role" therapist during this ending period.

Why does the real relationship come more to the foreground during the ending part of treatment? The explicit ending of a good relationship almost requires us to come forth with each other as human beings. After all, although the psychotherapy participants have played out their roles as therapist and patient throughout treatment, they are indeed two human beings whose engagement in those roles is coming to an end. Indelibly left are their humanness and their human experience of the ending of their relationship.

In the latter part of an advanced psychotherapy practicum that I teach, my graduate students each provided a brief example of the real relationship in their work. Three of these examples pertained to the termination session of therapy with a 12-session limit. What follows are the unedited summaries, followed by my comment.

An Ending Hug

The therapist who wrote the following excerpt was a 26-year-old female doctoral student with a humanistic theoretical orientation.

> The client had 12 sessions with me in which she talked about painful feelings that she was never good enough to be loved. She had turned very critical on herself because she had been criticized a lot as a child. Through our work she started to see patterns in her life, and she had a lot of emotional sessions. In the last session she confessed she had thought

about dropping out because it had been so painful to talk about these things, but that she was glad she had stayed. She felt it was a relief to confront things she had been avoiding, and that now she understood herself better. She thanked me for working with her and asked if it would be OK for us to hug as we were walking out of the room. I said yes and hugged her, and it felt really genuine and not related to transference. This is the first time I had hugged a client but it seemed appropriate to me. I felt like we had deeply connected throughout work together and I was happy for her that she was able to make progress.

Although the use of touch in psychotherapy remains a controversial topic (Bonitz, 2008), in this case is seemed a very natural and positive consequence of the real relationship. Although I have no doubt that the patient's request had transference elements, as did the therapist's response, it also seemed clear that the real relationship element was a stronger part of this physical contact.

You Have Mattered

The therapist who recorded the following notes was a 31-year-old male doctoral student with an integrative–humanistic perspective.

> During the termination stage . . . my client asked me about my progression in my graduate program. He had not asked me about my studies since our first session, when I informed him of my supervision. I told him that I was in the middle of my second year and that I had three more years to go. He commented that his father (a psychologist) had several years of school as well, and it sounded like a lot of work. I interpreted his inquiry as a genuine interest and liking for me, so I wanted to share more with him. I stated that "School IS a lot of work, but I am able to establish meaningful relationships in my clinical work, which makes it worth it . . . for example, my relationship with you." At this statement, he smiled and made a small fist pump gesture in the air, acknowledging that the sentiment was shared. Part of me wondered if my disclosure was more for my benefit or his. Also, part of me worried that I was gratifying or reinforcing his need for admiration. However, I felt compelled to share with him in words that I enjoyed his company. It was true that during this semester, I had enjoyed my work with this client most (of my four clients), and my supervisor commented on this as well.

The reality of the therapist's and patient's caring for the person of the other is very clear in this vignette. Their interchange, although not dramatic, is a rather poignant example of a deep connection within a real relationship. At the same time, based on the therapist's case presentation in our practicum class, it was also clear that there was a transference and countertransference enactment in this interchange. The vignette vividly demonstrates how the real relationship and transference are displayed in a single interchange, even as the real relationship is in the foreground during this termination session.

Mutuality and Crisis

The therapist who recorded the following notes was a 27-year-old female doctoral student with a psychodynamic orientation. She recalled a therapeutic encounter from her first psychotherapy practicum:

> My client had suffered from depression. . . . She came to therapy with everything bottled up, having shared very little, if anything, with others regarding what she thought and felt. This became apparent as it was obviously difficult for her to talk about feeling sadness, and she hated that she cried so easily. She arrived late for the first three sessions but from the fourth session on, arrived on time, even though she had shared with me that she was struggling to commit to therapy. By the fifth or sixth session, I felt very connected to my client and it was clear that she too felt connected to me, easily willing to reschedule a session that she had missed and consistently completing the few homework assignments that I had suggested, knowing well that she often struggled to juggle too many assignments. Around this time, she started to allude to a traumatic event which I believed to be sexual . . . yet she did not feel ready to talk about it yet. I assured her that she could talk about it if and when she felt comfortable. A few sessions later, around the ninth or tenth session, she shared with me that she had been raped over winter break and had not told anyone about it. In that moment, I feel like our real relationship emerged and stayed apparent for the rest of our time together. I was able to feel her sadness and pain, and express empathy toward her in a natural and understanding way and in return, she opened up, lowered her resistance and allowed herself to let me into her world, through expression of her thoughts and feelings. She was able to appreciate my role as a therapist and as an understanding and compassionate person with whom she could share what she had been keeping to herself, and I was able to appreciate the difficulty she had with opening up and the hard work she had dedicated to being able to finally open up. Our last session together was wonderful, during which we both shared how much the other had helped us grow and experience the gifts that we both had to offer each other. We thanked each other for providing a wonderful learning opportunity and for creating an open and honest environment in which we both felt like we could be open and honest with each other.

Here one can see the real relationship developing gradually in the early part of brief therapy but accelerating when the patient shared a traumatic experience that had been previously suppressed. As I have written earlier in this book, personal crises often call the real relationship to the forefront of the relationship, whereas it had previously been much more in the background. The degree of mutuality in this treatment was notable, perhaps too much for the more cautious therapist. However, this therapist and patient were involved in a therapeutic relationship as, to use Yalom's (2002) term, *fellow travelers*. Here is what Yalom had to say about this concept:

> Though there are many phrases for the therapeutic relationship (patient/ therapist, client/counselor, analysand/analyst, client/facilitator, and the latest—and, by far, the most repulsive—user/provider), none of these phrases accurately convey my sense of the therapeutic relationship. Instead, I prefer to think of my patients and myself as *fellow travelers*, a term that abolishes the distinctions between "them" (the afflicted) and "us" (the healers). During my training I was often exposed to the idea of the fully analyzed therapist, but as I have progressed through life, formed intimate relationships with a good many of my therapist colleagues, met the senior figures in the field, been called upon to render help to my former therapists and teachers, and myself become a teacher and an elder, I have come to realize the mythic nature of this idea. We are all in this together and there is no therapist and no person immune to the inherent tragedies of existence. (pp. 7–8)

Throughout his book, *The Gift of Therapy: An Open Letter to New Generations of Therapists and Their Patients* (2002), Yalom described in a very personal manner the myriad ways in which he engages in a mutual, real relationship with his patients, ways in which he helpfully becomes a fellow traveler with them. The young therapist trainee in the last vignette, too, displayed this nicely with her patient at the end of treatment.

A FEW MORE WORDS ABOUT THE THERAPIST'S EXPRESSION OF THE REAL RELATIONSHIP

Most of the examples provided thus far have been of the therapist sharing aspects of him- or herself—the therapist's physical surroundings and appearance, verbal self-disclosures, and the use of immediacy—and how these may be enacted at different points in treatment. As such, most examples have pertained to the genuineness aspect of the real relationship as offered by the therapist. The focus has been on genuineness rather than realism because the therapist's ongoing experience of the patient involves seeking to understand the patient as the patient is. Thus, the realism element of the real relationship from the therapist's side entails the accurate perception/experience of the patient, and this hardly requires case examples. It is what we as therapists seek to be about. The opposite, the lack of accurate perceptions, may best be seen in the literature on countertransference because, as I discussed in Chapter 3, countertransference is the greatest impediment to the realism portion of the real relationship from the therapist's side.

A second, perhaps more important point about the material presented thus far in this chapter is that the focus has been on salient examples of the real relationship. It bears repeating that salience does not equal strength. Patient and therapist may have a very strong real relationship, but it may reside in the background of the work, having its effects in "quieter," less obvious ways. Similarly, there is a real relationship element in everything that transpires between therapist and patient, although that element is often less obvious or salient.

The examples of therapist-offered expressions of the real relationship also do not capture the strength of the real relationship in therapists who do not self-disclose. As I have maintained throughout this book, nondisclosing therapists may be highly genuine and be perceived and experienced as such by their patients. The perception of genuineness may well be driven by the congruence between verbal and nonverbal behavior and by the consistency of the therapist's expressions. For example, a therapist who consistently responds to his or her patient with empathic kindness will be experienced as genuine; so too will a therapist whose facial expressions match what he or she actually says to the patient. A therapist who warmly receives the patient and listens attentively and compassionately, and who actually feels warm and compassionate, is very likely to communicate these feelings and to come across as genuine. A therapist who does not self-disclose in response to the patient's questions about his or her feelings may still be experienced as genuine if this therapist gives believable, sensible, and honest reasons for not disclosing. An example of providing such a reason rather than disclosing was given in Chapter 4, when I described the case of Elaine, a patient of mine for whom I felt that disclosures about my caring would not be helpful, because they would avoid addressing the emptiness and unlovability Elaine felt that drove her to seek such reassurances in all of her relationships. I am certain that Elaine and I had a very strong real relationship even though direct self-disclosures on my part were very minimal. A minimally self-disclosing therapist may still be truly him- or herself and be experienced as such, as genuine, by the patient.

THE PATIENT'S EXPRESSION OF THE REAL RELATIONSHIP

The real relationship is a two-way street. Because of this, it is important to provide examples of the patient's contribution to this key element of the overall work.

You Talk Too Much

A number of years ago, Greenson (1967) provided a classic example of a patient-expressed real relationship:

> A young man, in the terminal phase of his five-year analysis, hesitates after I have made an interpretation and then tells me that he has something to say which is very difficult for him. He was about to skip over it when he realized he had been doing just that for years. He takes a deep breath and says: "You always talk a little bit too much. You tend to exaggerate. It would be much easier for me to get mad at you and say you're cockeyed or wrong or off the point or just not answer. It's terribly hard to say what I mean because I know it will hurt your feelings."
>
> I believe the patient has correctly perceived some traits of mine and it was somewhat painful for me to have them pointed out. I told him he was right, but I wanted to know why it was harder for him to tell it to me simply and directly as he had just done than to become enraged. He answered that he knew from experience that I would not get upset by his temper. Telling me about my talking too much and exaggerating was a personal criticism and that would be hurtful. He knew I took pride in my skill as a therapist. In the past he would have been worried that I might retaliate, but he now knew it was not likely. Besides, it wouldn't kill him. (pp. 217–218)

In this example, the patient is experiencing the therapist accurately and sharing his perception in a very personal and genuine manner. The analyst, too, responds genuinely by confirming the patient's criticism while at the same time seeking analytic exploration.

Please Don't Project Your Stuff Onto Me

An example of the patient's perceiving a therapist's errant behavior accurately, and sharing that perception, comes from my work with a 35-year-old woman who, at the time of the interaction, had been in twice-a-week analytically oriented psychotherapy for 2 years. This was a treatment in which the patient and I had a very sound working alliance and a strong real relationship.

The patient had become increasingly troubled by a particular reaction of mine. Each time she expressed her difficulties with her children, I seemed to respond unempathically, often offering unneeded suggestions and at times even appearing critical. The patient perceived these reactions realistically and responded with realistic hurt and frustration. This had been going on intermittently for some time, and during a particular session she finally expressed her feelings to me, including her impressions of my reactions as perhaps reflecting my own issues. In response to her comments, I became aware that, in fact, my conflicts surrounding my own parenting were impeding my empathy with this patient when she discussed certain issues with her children. Once these countertransference conflicts were grasped, I was able to regain my empathic stance when the patient explored her parenting.

As with Greenson's (1967) patient, it was difficult for my patient to point out my ineffective behavior. However, her experience of me was accurate and her expression of that experience quite genuine. For my part, it seemed clear that, as I discussed in Chapter 3, countertransference conflicts were impeding my experiencing the patient realistically, and the patient's real relationship response to me helped me get back on track in terms of my contribution to our real relationship (i.e., accurately understanding her). I believe this is a good example of how a solid working alliance and an already-strong real relationship facilitated the patient's expression of real and genuine feelings toward her therapist and helped the therapist further strengthen his contribution to the real relationship.

THE REAL RELATIONSHIP AND TRANSFERENCE IN THE SAME EXPRESSION

The patient's expression (and the therapist's, too) of the real relationship, as I have said, is not an all-or-nothing thing. Any given expression likely reflects degrees of both transference and real relationship. An example I provided in Chapter 3 seems apt.

I Care About You; Please Care About Me

> In my first session following rather serious surgery, my patient, John, expressed concern by asking "How are you doing buddy?" I replied honestly, "I am doing well, thanks." As I began to pursue how some of his concern was transferentially related to the material with which we had been dealing, John replied, "Well, that may be so, but I also was just concerned about you as a person." As I pondered the expression of concern, it seemed clear to me that this single expression was both very rich with transference and very deeply reflective of real relationship. (Gelso, 2009a, p. 257)

This single reaction, it seemed to me, reflected John's genuine caring for me personally. We had worked together on two occasions that summed to more than 6 years. So, despite what I would describe as my rather conservative approach to psychodynamic work, including limited self-disclosure, we knew each other well and genuinely cared for each other. Yet, on the basis of the material that we had explored in recent months, I knew that John's expression reflected his ongoing need to please and be pleasing to others and his fear that if he were not so pleasing he would be cast aside or even abused, as he had been throughout his childhood.

Hold My Hand

In the following excerpt from a very long-term treatment (lasting over a decade), the patient and I had a sound working alliance, which helped her explore threatening and painful conflicts:

> The client is a 41-year-old woman in long-term psychoanalytically based therapy. During the hour, she is exploring her need to separate emotionally from her father and her brother if she is to be able to truly enjoy sexual intimacy with her husband. But the thought of this necessary separation is frightening and saddening. She expresses the wish that I figuratively hold her hand in the process, and she realizes that in one way, her hand-holding maintains her disruptive connection to father—I become the provocative and untrustworthy father in the transference. Another way allows me, as a real person, to join with her as the adult she has become in helping her cope with the loss involved in this necessary separation. (adapted from Gelso & Hayes, 1998, p. 135)

Here we see wishes that are at once transference based and real relationship based. All three key components of the psychotherapy relationship, as described in Chapter 1, are present and salient.

CONCLUSION

The real or personal relationship shows itself in myriad ways within the psychotherapy hour. In this chapter I have provided examples of clinical manifestations of the real relationship. However, it must be remembered that what has been exemplified are instances in which the real relationship is salient. From the therapist's side, the examples have tended to focus on therapist self-disclosure and immediacy. What has not been exemplified, and perhaps cannot be exemplified, is the often-hidden real relationship. This is represented by the ongoing feelings and perceptions of the participants toward one another that are based in reality (the realism element) as well as the genuine expression of self that seems an ordinary part of the relationship but may in fact be the foundation. Having presented a theory of the real relationship (see Chapter 4, this volume) and a number of examples of its manifestation during the psychotherapy hour (the present chapter), in the next two chapters I describe how this elusive concept may be measured (Chapter 6, this volume) and the research evidence that has been gathered in its relation to other key concepts and to treatment process and outcome (Chapter 7, this volume).

6

MEASURING THE REAL RELATIONSHIP

Few things stir the minds and hearts of psychological researchers like a measure that is at once reliable, valid, and economical to use. Especially when such a measure is accompanied by or derived from sound theory, it can have an enormous impact on research on a given topic. An impact of this magnitude has occurred over the past 20 or so years in the area of the working alliance. Bordin (1979) offered a theory of the working alliance that was pantheoretical and integrative. He clearly articulated three fundamental aspects of the alliance: (a) the bond between therapist and patient, (b) the extent to which they agree on the goals of treatment, and (c) the extent to which they agree on the tasks needed to attain those goals. His theory also had great heuristic value. Perhaps because of these qualities, Adam Horvath (1982; Horvath & Greenberg, 1989) was able to develop from Bordin's theory a measure of the working alliance that displayed sound psychometric qualities and was economical to use in psychotherapy research. Although other measures of alliance were developed during this same time period, I do not believe any possessed these important qualities to the extent that Horvath's (1982) Working Alliance Inventory (WAI) did. The initial 36-item version was made even more convenient to use when Tracey and Kokotovic (1989) created a shortened 12-item version (the WAI–S) that seemed to possess equally sound psychometric features as the WAI (Busseri & Tyler, 2003). These measures have been used in numerous studies of the working alliance.

Over this same time period or before, there had been no equivalent development in the area of the real relationship. Greenson's (1967; Greenson & Wexler, 1969) early theoretical statements, along with those of others cited in chapter 1, did provide a theoretical basis for research, but these theoretical statements possessed considerable ambiguity. They did not lend themselves readily to the development of measuring devices or, for that matter, to the development of theoretical hypotheses that could be investigated in controlled research.

In my early work with Jean Carter and subsequent writing with Jeff Hayes, we sought to organize and refine a series of theoretical propositions about how the real relationship works in both brief and long-term psychotherapy (Gelso & Carter, 1985, 1994; Gelso & Hayes, 1998). These statements facilitated the development of paper-and-pencil measures of the real relationship that I describe and discuss in this chapter. Three such measures have been created. The first measure was constructed by Eugster and Wampold (1996), and the other two were created more recently by my research collaborators and me (Gelso et al., 2005; Kelley, Gelso, Fuertes, Marmarosh, & Lanier, in press). In addition to such measures to be used in quantitative research, questions have been developed for use in qualitative research. In this chapter, I focus primarily on the quantitative measures, along with the research studies that have validated them. I also discuss measurement issues and offer suggestions for future research aimed at developing and refining measures of the real relationship. My aim in this chapter is to provide, in one place, the measures of the real relationship, the supportive data for these measures, and direction that future measurement research on the topic of the real relationship might take. I have sought to present this material in a nontechnical way so that it is readily accessible to practicing therapists as well as researchers. The more technical material (e.g., confirmatory factor analyses [CFAs]) are presented in the journal articles on with this chapter is based (viz., Eugster & Wampold, 1996; Gelso et al., 2005; Kelley et al., in press).

BEGINNING MEASUREMENT EFFORTS

The first measure of the real relationship was presented as part of a battery of measures. The battery was used to predict the evaluation of psychotherapy sessions from the vantage points of patients and therapists (Eugster & Wampold, 1996). The researchers selected nine constructs that appeared to be important in treatment success. Among these constructs was the real relationship, which was operationalized by eight items rated by the therapist and eight items rated by the patient. Both therapist and patient made ratings of therapist- and patient-offered real relationship; in other words, each participant rated the quality of the real relationship as offered by him- or herself and by the other person in the dyad. This allowed for four scores. In Tables 6.1 and 6.2 are presented two of these measures, those completed by the patient. For the two measures that are completed by the therapist, the content is identical except for the vantage point (therapist instead of patient) to which the item refers. Note that participants were asked to rate the real relationship on a 6-point Likert scale, with ratings ranging from 1 (*strongly disagree*) to 6 (*strongly agree*); specifically, participants are asked to "please circle the number that best represents your level of agreement with each statement in terms of your experience and your perceptions about your therapist (or your client) during the last session." Although Eugster and Wampold (1996) had participants make ratings for a given session, it seems a viable item to ask for any time period that fits a given study. For example, in a study my colleagues and I conducted (Kelley et al., in press), we had patients make ratings on the Eugster and Wampold measure for the last five sessions combined.

Although Eugster and Wampold (1996) tailored their measures after the theoretical formulations offered by Gelso and Carter (1994), inspection of the self items (patient's ratings of themselves) indicates that these items revolve around the patient's feelings of liking and caring for the therapist (five items) and patients' genuineness (two items), and the therapist's realistic perception of the patient (one item). The patient-rated therapist measure contains five items focused on therapist genuineness and three items around liking. No items pertain to realism. Thus, it appears that although the Eugster and Wampold scales were based on Gelso and Carter's theory, these scales did not focus on the realism construct but instead tended to load heavily on genuineness and liking or caring about the other.

TABLE 6.1
Patient Real Relationship Scale (Assessed by Patient)

Item	Scale[a]					
1. I did not like my therapist in these sessions.	1	2	3	4	5	6
2. I was honest and open with my therapist in these sessions.	1	2	3	4	5	6
3. In these sessions, I felt caring toward my therapist as a person.	1	2	3	4	5	6
4. I did not enjoy seeing my therapist in these sessions.	1	2	3	4	5	6
5. In these sessions, I felt close to my therapist.	1	2	3	4	5	6
6. In these sessions, I felt connected to my therapist only as his/her patient.	1	2	3	4	5	6
7. In these sessions, I related to my therapist with genuine feeling.	1	2	3	4	5	6
8. In these sessions, my therapist did not see me as I really am.	1	2	3	4	5	6

Note. Measures from *Systematic Effects of Participant Role on the Evaluation of the Psychotherapy Session*, by S. L. Eugster, 1995. Unpublished doctoral dissertation, University of Wisconsin–Madison. Used with permission of the author. See also Eugster and Wampold (1996).
[a]1 = *strongly disagree*, 6 = *strongly agree*.

TABLE 6.2
Therapist Real Relationship Scale (Assessed by Patient)

Item	Scale[a]					
1. In these sessions, my therapist really cared about me as a person.	1	2	3	4	5	6
2. In these sessions, my therapist did not share any personal information with me.	1	2	3	4	5	6
3. My therapist was honest and open with me in these sessions.	1	2	3	4	5	6
4. In these sessions, my therapist did not like me.	1	2	3	4	5	6
5. My therapist remained in a formal therapist role throughout these sessions.	1	2	3	4	5	6
6. In these sessions, my therapist revealed something of what s/he is really like as a person.	1	2	3	4	5	6
7. My therapist interacted with me in a casual or spontaneous manner in these sessions.	1	2	3	4	5	6
8. My therapist did not enjoy seeing me in these sessions.	1	2	3	4	5	6

Note. Measures from *Systematic Effects of Participant Role on the Evaluation of the Psychotherapy Session*, by S. L. Eugster, 1995. Unpublished doctoral dissertation, University of Wisconsin–Madison. Used with permission of the author. See also Eugster and Wampold (1996).
[a]1 = *strongly disagree*, 6 = *strongly agree*.

A study of 114 highly experienced therapists and 119 patients of these therapists found that Eugster and Wampold's (1996) measures possessed what might be termed minimally acceptable reliability. The measures completed by the patients had Cronbach's alpha coefficients of .66 for their rating of the therapist-offered real relationship and .72 for their self-ratings of the real relationship. For the therapist-rated version the coefficients were .73 when rating the patient and .63 when rating the self. In a subsequent study conducted by Kelley et al. (in press), only patients' reports were examined; the alpha coefficient for patients' self-ratings of the real relationship was .64, and for patients' ratings of the real relationship offered by their therapists it was .81.

Although I could find no validation study per se on this measure, its association with patients' and therapists' session evaluation in Eugster and Wampold's (1996) study serves as an initial validation of sorts. That study found that therapists' ratings of patients' real relationships correlated moderately with these therapists' evaluations of a session that had just been completed ($r = .53$); however, these same therapists' ratings of the real relationship they offered to their patients correlated more modestly with their evaluations of the session ($r = .28$). In regard to patients' ratings, it was found that patients' evaluations of the real relationship offered by their therapists and enacted by themselves both correlated substantially with their evaluation of a given psychotherapy session ($rs = .60$ and .64, respectively). In sum, the simple bivariate correlations indicate that therapists' and patients' evaluations of the real relationship offered by themselves and the other person in the dyad are significantly associated with their session evaluations, although the correlation of therapists' ratings of their own real relationships with their patients and session evaluation is rather unimpressive.

Additional findings were that both the therapist-rated relationship and patient-rated real relationship as enacted by self and other in the therapeutic dyad (four ratings) were significantly ($p < .05$) associated with therapist and patient self- and other ratings of patient involvement, therapist involvement, patient comfort, therapist comfort (not significant for therapist ratings of the real relationship and their own comfort), patient progress, therapist expertness, and therapist interpersonal style (e.g., warmth, friendliness, empathy). Because the connection of the real relationship with each of these other variables is theoretically sensible and predictable, the correlations that were found do lend some support for the convergent and construct validity of Eugster and Wampold's (1996) measure of real relationship.

After scrutinizing this complicated study (which also included complex regression analyses that I discuss in Chapter 7, this volume), it seems to me that Eugster and Wampold's (1996) measure, while possessing serious limitations (e.g., shaky reliability, no evidence regarding discriminant validity), may be a viable brief measure of the real relationship as long as the researcher remains cognizant of the conception of the real relationship that is portrayed by the items of this measure; that is, on the positive end, the items reflect the real relationship as characterized by genuineness and authenticity of the participants with each other, and by liking and caring. There is nearly no attention given to the realistic, nontransferential element of the real relationship that is one of the two key elements of the theory I have presented.

Eugster and Wampold's (1996) study informed the measure-development research that my collaborators and I conducted. We developed measures of the real relationship from the vantage point of the therapist and the patient, and these are presented in some detail later in this chapter. I should note that Jairo Fuertes, Cheri Marmarosh, and Frances Kelley have been major collaborators in each of the two measure-development studies described herein, and they have been key investigators in subsequent research on the real relationship.

THE REAL RELATIONSHIP INVENTORIES

When my collaborators and I began our program of research on the real relationship it seemed clear to us that the first step needed to be the development of measures. Eugster and Wampold's (1996) measures were available, but these had not been validated, and from our vantage point they possessed theoretical limitations, as noted earlier. So we set about the task developing psychometrically sound and theoretically rooted measures from both the therapist's and the patient's perspective. From the outset, we were committed to developing measures that would be relatively brief, so that they indeed would get used; that would be applicable across theories and did not possess theoretical jargon; and that were derived from a theory of the real relationship. Regarding this last point, we organized theory-based subscales for the two key elements of the real relationship: (a) genuineness and (b) realism. For each of these two elements, it further seemed important to measure magnitude (how much of the element is present) and valence (how positive vs. negative are the perceptions/evaluations). Finally, it seemed clear to us that, for both the therapist and patient forms, we must develop items that tapped each member of the psychotherapy dyad's perceptions of self, of other, and of their relationship.

The daunting nature of the task becomes apparent when one considers that each of our two measures was organized to tap realism and genuineness and, within these, magnitude and valence, from the vantage points of self, other, and relationship. Thus, for each measure (therapist and patient) we needed to write items within each of 12 cells ($2 \times 2 \times 3$, or realism–genuineness, magnitude–valence, and self–other relationship). Such a measure could easily become so lengthy that it would not often be used. In the end, we decided on two 24-item scales, one for therapist and one for patient, each containing two subscales (Genuineness and Realism). The specifics of each measure are presented in subsequent sections, along with the measure itself. Note that our intent from the beginning was to develop measures of the real relationship that reflected what might be termed the *strength* of the real relationship, where strength is a function of the participants' genuineness and realism and the magnitude and valence of each of these qualities.

THE THERAPIST VERSION OF THE REAL RELATIONSHIP INVENTORY

The first step in creating the therapist version of the Real Relationship Inventory (RRI-T)[1] was to write items based on the theoretical conceptions of Gelso and Carter (1985, 1994) and Gelso and Hayes (1998). Six of the members of our research team wrote items that sought to be free of theoretical jargon and not linked to any particular theory. Items were written to reflect realism and genuineness primarily. Then, within these two basic elements, we framed the items to tap magnitude and valence, with the reference points being the therapist, the patient, and their relationship. Thus, whereas all items

---

[1]Much of the material presented on the RRI-T is based on Gelso et al.'s (2005) study. See that article for more details on the measure and its development.

were rated by the therapist, the focal point of the item could be the therapist, the patient, or their relationship. At the time of the item writing our team consisted of three doctoral-level psychologists with postdoctoral experience ranging from 6 to 30 years and three doctoral students who had already received their master's degrees.

As indicated, we had agreed to develop 24-item measures, and we further decided on two 12-item subscales, one for realism and one for genuineness. To an extent, this is similar to the question of how many angels are on the head of a pin: The answer is inevitably arbitrary. However, from our vantage point this number, along with the number of items per subscale, allowed for a measure that would be economical while also being long enough to be reliable (see Ponterotto & Ruckdeschel, 2007) and to possess content validity.

Item Development and Selection

Our initial item writing resulted in 130 items. Four of our research team members then worked to eliminate items that were repetitive, not consistent with the aforementioned theory of the real relationship, or too linked with one or more of the existing theories of personality and psychotherapy. Items that had potential but possessed one of these problems were at times rewritten. This paring resulted in 99 items, still far too many. These same four members then classified each item into 1 of 12 cells determined by realism–genuineness, magnitude–valence, and self–other relationship, as described earlier. The remaining two members, blind to the ratings of the first subgroup, classified each item as reflecting genuineness or realism and, within these, magnitude or valence. If the two subgroups agreed on the classification of items into the categories of genuineness or realism, the items were maintained. On the basis of this procedure, along with an additional elimination because of redundancy, we reduced the measure to 44 items (23 genuineness items and 21 realism items).

Next, we created an item development sample by sending our 44-item measure to 200 randomly selected members of Divisions 29 (Psychotherapy) and 42 (Independent Practice) of the American Psychological Association. After two mailings and a postcard reminder, we received usable returns from 80 psychologists; these participants completed our measure in reference to a patient they had seen in therapy during the last week and with whom they had had at least five sessions. Items were responded to on a 5-point Likert scale on which 5 = *strongly agree* and 1 = *strongly disagree*.

The responses of the item development sample were used to further reduce our measure to the 24-item limit we had preestablished, with 12 items for the two subscales of Genuineness and Realism. The three general guidelines we followed to so reduce the measure were as follows: (a) no item–total correlation within a subscale could be less than .40, (b) alpha reliability coefficients that were not reduced when a given item was deleted would result in elimination of that item, and (c) items with the highest item–total correlation would be maintained as long as there was at least one item in the six cells for a given subscale (determined by magnitude and valence × self, other, and relationship). Other steps included a back-translation, deletion and addition of two items to allow for at least one item in each of the six aforementioned cells, and further efforts to reduce redundancy (see Gelso et al., 2005, for further details).

The Measure

On the basis of the responses of the item development sample, the internal consistency of the final 24 items was highly satisfactory, with alpha coefficients for the Realism subscale, Genuineness subscale, and total score being .89, .87, and .93, respectively. The correlation between the two subscales was .75, indicating that realism and genuineness are highly overlapping constructs. The RRI-T is presented in Exhibit 6.1.

Inspection of the items in the RRI-T indicates that 6 items tap the therapist's self-perception, 11 tap their ratings of the patient's reaction, and 7 tap their ratings of the therapist–patient relationship. The means for each item were clearly on the high side, with the overall item mean being 3.75 on our 5-point scale. Means that are this high present the researcher with a dilemma. On the one hand, from a psychometric viewpoint, the overall mean ought to be very close to the scale midpoint of 3.0 to maximize measurement. On the other hand, from a clinical perspective, there is an abundance of evidence indicating that therapeutic relationships are positive on the whole, reflecting a higher rating. We maintained the current items and the 5-point scale ranging from *strongly agree* to *strongly disagree* because of a belief that in the final analysis it was best to match the reality of the clinical situation. I have more to say about measurement and measurement issues in the latter part of this chapter.

Validation of the Real Relationship Inventory, Therapist Version

Validation involved first rechecking the reliability of the RRI-T and, second, determining whether our measure correlated with other measures to which it theoretically should correlate as well as measures to which it theoretically should not correlate. The former is termed *convergent validity* and the latter *discriminant validity*.

Given the conceptualization and definition of the real relationship provided in earlier chapters, it made sense that the real relationship should

EXHIBIT 6.1
The Real Relationship Inventory, Therapist Form

Please complete the items below in terms of your relationship with your client or patient. Use the following 1–5 scale in rating each item, placing your rating in the space adjacent to the item.

Strongly Agree	Agree	Neutral	Disagree	Strongly Disagree
5	4	3	2	1

_____ 1. My client is able to see me as a real person separate from my role as a therapist.

_____ 2. My client and I are able to be genuine in our relationship.

_____ 3. My client feels liking for the "real me."

_____ 4. My client genuinely expresses his/her positive feelings toward me.

_____ 5. I am able to realistically respond to my client.

_____ 6. I hold back significant parts of myself.

_____ 7. I feel there is a "real" relationship between us aside from the professional relationship.

_____ 8. My client and I are honest in our relationship.

_____ 9. My client has little caring for who I "truly am."

_____10. We feel a deep and genuine caring for one another.

_____11. My client holds back significant parts of him/herself.

_____12. My client has respect for me as a person.

_____13. There is no genuinely positive connection between us.

_____14. My client's feelings toward me seem to fit who I am as a person.

_____15. I do not like my client as a person.

_____16. I value the honesty of our relationship.

_____17. The relationship between my client and me is strengthened by our understanding of one another.

_____18. It is difficult for me to express what I truly feel about my client.

_____19. My client has unrealistic perceptions of me.

_____20. My client and I have difficulty accepting each other as we really are.

_____21. My client distorts the therapy relationship.

_____22. I have difficulty being honest with my client.

_____23. My client shares with me the most vulnerable parts of him/herself.

_____24. My client genuinely expresses a connection to me.

Note. Realism subscale items are Nos. 1, 3, 5, 7, 9, 12, 14, 15, 17, 19, 20, 21; Genuineness subscale items are Nos. 2, 4, 6, 8, 10, 11, 13, 16, 18, 22, 23, 24. Reverse-scored items are Nos. 6, 9, 11, 13, 15, 18, 19, 20, 21, and 22. From "Measuring the Real Relationship in Psychotherapy: Initial Validation of the Therapist Form," by C. J. Gelso, F. A. Kelley, J. N. Fuertes, C. Marmarosh, S. E. Holmes, C. Costa, and G. R. Hancock, 2005, _Journal of Counseling Psychology, 52_, p. 649. Copyright 2005 by the American Psychological Association.

positively and rather strongly relate to the working alliance (Horvath & Greenberg, 1989). It also should relate positively to therapist-perceived depth and smoothness of sessions (Stiles & Snow, 1984), as well as both intellectual, and especially emotional, insight (Gelso, Kivlighan, Wine, Jones, & Friedman, 1997). On the other hand, theoretically, the stronger the real relationship, the less negative transference would be expected (Gelso et al., 1997), because the real relationship reflects, in part, the nontransference element of the overall relationship. Finally, for a measure such as the RRI-T to be considered valid it should not relate to the participant's wish to look good, that is, to make socially desirable responses (Reynolds, 1982). We used established measures for each of these constructs, and again all measures were completed by the therapists in regard to the last patient they had seen during the past week. The measures, including reliability and validity data on them, were detailed by Gelso et al. (2005).

To recheck reliability and test for validity, we sent the 44-item measure to a second sample of 200 psychologists who were members of Divisions 29 and 42 of the American Psychological Association, as well as to 73 graduate students enrolled in counseling and psychotherapy practica. All of these potential participants were asked to complete the 44-item measure, along with other measures. After two mailings and a postcard reminder, 79 members of the professional sample and 51 of the graduate students completed usable measures. Reliability in the form of internal consistency was again quite satisfactory for this sample, with coefficient alphas being .79 for the Realism subscale, .83 for the Genuineness subscale, and .89 for the total score. The professional and graduate student samples did not differ, except that the alpha coefficients were higher for Realism in the professional sample than in the graduate student sample (.81 vs. .72).

The validity analysis is presented in Table 6.3 in the form of Pearson product–moment correlation coefficients. All correlations are based on the final 24 items of the RRI-T. These coefficients are presented for the two subscales of the RRI-T and the total score.

As can be seen in Table 6.1, the relationship of the RRI-T to the working alliance, session quality (depth and smoothness of the session), intellectual and emotional insight, and negative transference are all in the theoretically predicted direction, thus supporting the convergent validity of the RRI-T. Furthermore, discriminant validity is supported in that the RRI-T is not correlated with social desirability. It is noteworthy that there is not a significant relation between the RRI-T and positive transference. On the basis of past research on positive transference, we had not expected such a relation. Thus, the lack of a relation does not disconfirm the validity of the RRI-T. Overall, these correlations strongly support the validity of the RRI-T.

TABLE 6.3

Pearson Product–Moment Correlations of the Real Relationship Inventory, Therapist Version (RRI-T; Realism, Genuineness, and Total) With Validation Measures

Measure	RRI-T Scale		
	Realism	Genuineness	Total
Working Alliance Inventory[a]	.32**	.55**	.47**
Session Evaluation Questionnaire—Depth[b]	.30**	.38**	.36**
Session Evaluation Questionnaire—Smoothness[b]	.42**	.40**	.43**
Emotional insight[c]	.21*	.31**	.28**
Intellectual insight[c]	.18*	.20*	.21*
Negative transference, last session[d]	−.27**	−.26**	−.29**
Negative transference, last 5 sessions[d]	−.16	−.21*	−.20*
Positive transference, last session[d]	.13	.09	.12
Positive transference, last 5 sessions[d]	.09	.05	.08
Social Desirability Scale[e]	.06	.10	.08

Note. From "Measuring the Real Relationship in Psychotherapy: Initial Validation of the Therapist Form," by C. J. Gelso, F. A. Kelley, J. N. Fuertes, C. Marmarosh, S. E. Holmes, C. Costa, and G. R. Hancock, 2005, *Journal of Counseling Psychology, 52,* p. 645. Copyright 2005 by the American Psychological Association. [a]Short Form (Tracey & Kokotovic, 1989). [b]Stiles and Snow (1984). [c]From Gelso, Kivlighan, Wine, Jones, and Friedman (1997). [d]From Graff and Luborsky (1977). [e]Marlowe–Crowne Social Desirability Scale—Short Form (Reynolds, 1982).
*p < .05. **p < .01.

An additional index of validity pertains to whether the two subscales of the RRI are sufficiently different from one another to be considered reflective of two different constructs. A way of testing for this is through CFA. In comparing our two-factor model with a one-factor model, it was clear that the one-factor model represented the best fit to the data. This of course brings into question the value of two subscales representing separate constructs (realism and genuineness). Despite this finding, it seems to me that it is premature to eliminate the subscale analysis (see also McCullough, 2009). First, the subscales are based on a theory of the real relationship. Second, and perhaps more important, it is easy to foresee situations in which realism and genuineness correlate differently with certain phenomena. An example of this actually occurred in the present study, whereby the correlation of RRI Genuineness with the working alliance ($r = .55$) was significantly different, $t(89) = 5.13$, $p < .01$, than the correlation of RRI Realism with the working alliance ($r = .32$). This indicates that the therapist's perception of genuineness within the real relationship was more related to the working alliance than was the therapist's perception of realism. Theoretically, this suggests the possibility that genuineness contributes more to a sound working alliance than does realism. Findings such as this suggest some tantalizing food for thought clinically, and they support the idea that the two subscales of the RRI-T ought to be maintained, at least for the time being.

THE CLIENT VERSION OF THE REAL RELATIONSHIP INVENTORY

We next set out to develop a client version of the RRI, the RRI-C.[2]

Item Development and Validation

In developing the RRI-C, we used the same item creation and reduction procedures as when we developed the RRI-T. From the outset, we aimed to develop a 24-item theoretically driven measure containing two subscales, Realism and Genuineness. Our team for this study consisted of five members, three with doctorates and postdoctoral experience ranging from 7 to 31 years, and two post–master's-level doctoral students. Our intent again was to write items that were pantheoretical and free of theoretical jargon; tapped the realism and genuineness elements, and within those, magnitude and valence; and pertained to self, other, and their relationship.

Four of our team members initially wrote 180 items. Through three series of iterations involving the eliminating of redundant items (as much as possible) and two back-translations, the measure was reduced to 40 items (19 for realism and 21 for genuineness). At this point, one of our team members, Frances Kelley, used the 40-item version to conduct a further item-reduction study and a validation study that constituted her doctoral dissertation (Kelley, 2002).

Getting a sufficiently large sample of patients involved in psychotherapy to conduct measure development research is no small feat. In seeking to obtain such a sample, we decided to take a multipronged approach. We distributed 543 survey packets to waiting rooms of therapists in private practice, waiting rooms at two university counseling centers and a university psychology clinic, mailboxes of psychology graduate students and students enrolled in a therapy practicum, and graduate students in professional counseling classes. Participants were asked to complete the measure if they had had at least eight sessions with their current therapist. In all, we received 187 usable packets. Sixty-one of these participants completed a retest 2 weeks after finishing the first testing, and 48 of these packets were usable.

Our procedures for item reduction on a subsample of 94 participants were the same as those used in the development of the RRI-T. Through these item reduction procedures, the 40-item scale was reduced to the desired 24 items, 12 for each subscale.

---

[2]Much of the material presented on the RRI-C is based on research presented by Kelley et al. (in press).

The Measure

Internal consistency, based on the responses of the 94 participants, was highly satisfactory. Cronbach's alpha was .90 for the Realism subscale, .91 for the Genuineness subscale, and .95 for the total score. The Realism and Genuineness subscales were highly correlated ($r = .80$), indicating much overlap, as was the case with the RRI-T. Retest reliability was also very strong: The coefficients of stability were .84 for Realism, .88 for Genuineness, and .87 for the total score. As with the RRI-T, the means were quite high on the RRI-C, with the average item score being 4.16. This is slightly higher than the mean for the RRI-T, but it is consistent with the almost-universal pattern of patients making more favorable evaluations of their therapy than their therapists make. The RRI-C is presented in Exhibit 6.2.

Validation of the RRI-C

As with the RRI-T, we sought to validate the RRI-C against measures to which it theoretically would be expected to positively relate, negatively relate, and not relate. To the extent that the theorized relations were substantiated, the validity of our measure would be supported. In seeking such validation measures it was very clear that the working alliance ought to be substantially, positively related to the real relationship. In addition, the RRI-T certainly should relate positively to Eugster and Wampold's (1996) measures of the real relationship presented in Tables 6.1 and 6.2 of this chapter, because theoretically the RRI-C and Eugster and Wampold's measures assess the same construct. In this same sense, our measure ought to be strongly correlated with the Genuineness subscale of the Barrett-Lennard Relationship Inventory (BLRI; Barrett-Lennard, 1964), a well-established measure of Carl Rogers's (1957) necessary and sufficient conditions of successful psychotherapy. Positive relations between the RRI-C and Eugster and Wampold's measures of the real relationship, as well as the Genuineness subscale, would be considered support for the concurrent validity of our measure.

The ability to form a real relationship would seem to depend on one's capacity to observe oneself and to have an understanding of the self based on this observing capacity. Thus, we theorized that the RRI-C should relate to a measure of the strength of the patient's observing ego. Furthermore, because part of what the RRI-C seeks to assess is the patient's genuineness in the therapeutic relationship, we expected our measure to be negatively related to a measure of *other-directedness*, the tendency to hide one's true feelings and behave in a way that is expected by others. Similarly, we expected the RRI-C to be negatively related to a measure of the patient's tendency to attend to his or her inner thoughts and feelings, or what is termed *private self-consciousness*.

EXHIBIT 6.2
The Real Relationship Inventory, Client Form

Please complete the items below in terms of your relationship with your therapist. Use the following 1–5 scale in rating each item, placing your rating in the space adjacent to the item.

Strongly Agree	Agree	Neutral	Disagree	Strongly Disagree
5	4	3	2	1

_____ 1. I was able to be myself with my therapist.

_____ 2. My therapist and I had a realistic perception of our relationship.

_____ 3. I was holding back significant parts of myself.

_____ 4. I appreciated being able to express my feelings in therapy.

_____ 5. My therapist liked the real me.

_____ 6. It was difficult to accept who my therapist really is.

_____ 7. I was open and honest with my therapist.

_____ 8. My therapist's perceptions of me seem colored by his or her own issues.

_____ 9. The relationship between my therapist and me was strengthened by our understanding of one another.

_____ 10. My therapist seemed genuinely connected to me.

_____ 11. I was able to communicate my moment-to-moment inner experience to my therapist.

_____ 12. My therapist was holding back his/her genuine self.

_____ 13. I appreciated my therapist's limitations and strengths.

_____ 14. We do not really know each other realistically.

_____ 15. My therapist and I were able to be authentic in our relationship.

_____ 16. I was able to see myself realistically in therapy.

_____ 17. My therapist and I had an honest relationship.

_____ 18. I was able to separate out my realistic perceptions of my therapist from my unrealistic perceptions.

_____ 19. My therapist and I expressed a deep and genuine caring for one another.

_____ 20. I had a realistic understanding of my therapist as a person.

_____ 21. My therapist did not see me as I really am.

_____ 22. I felt there was a significant holding back in our relationship.

_____ 23. My therapist's perceptions of me were accurate.

_____ 24. It was difficult for me to express what I truly felt about my therapist.

Note. Genuineness items are Nos. 1, 3, 4, 7, 10, 11, 12, 15, 17, 19, 22, 24; Realism items are Nos. 2, 5, 6, 8, 9, 13, 14, 16, 18, 20, 21, 23. Reverse-scored items are Nos. 3, 6, 8, 12, 14, 21, 22, and 24. From "The Real Relationship Inventory: Development and Psychometric Investigation of the Client Form," by F. Kelley, C. Gelso, J. Fuertes, C. Marmarosh, and S. Lanier, in press, *Psychotherapy Theory, Research, Practice, Training.* Copyright by the American Psychological Association.

Finally, we hoped our measure would not be affected by patients' tendencies to give socially desirable responses.

The correlations of the RRI-C with measures of each of the just-mentioned constructs are presented in Table 6.4. As can be seen, the RRI-C is highly related to the working alliance, to Eugster and Wampold's (1996) measures of the real relationship, and to the Genuineness subscale of the BLRI. It is also significantly positively related to strength of observing ego and negatively related to other-directedness. However, in contrast to our expectations, it is unrelated to private self-consciousness. Support for discriminant validity is provided in the near-zero relationship between the RRI-C and a measure of socially desirable responding.

In addition to the validation research presented in Table 6.4, we conducted a CFA to determine whether the two-factor solution (Realism and Genuineness factors) represented the best fit to the data. Although the subscales of Realism and Genuineness are highly intercorrelated, the CFA did support the two-factor solution. The details of this analysis were presented by Kelley et al. (in press).

The pattern of correlations in Table 6.4 provides strong support for the validity of the RRI-C; however, three issues deserve some discussion. First, we observed positive relations of the RRI-C with measures of the same or highly similar constructs, which provides support for the concurrent validity of our measure. However, correlations of such a magnitude also lead to the

TABLE 6.4
Pearson Product–Moment Correlations of the Real Relationship
Inventory, Client Version (RRI-C; Realism, Genuineness, and Total)
With Validation Measures

Measure	RRI-C Scale		
	Realism	Genuineness	Total
Working Alliance Inventory[a]	.76**	.74**	.79**
Patient real relationship[b]	.63**	.64**	.67**
Therapist real relationship[b]	.65**	.48**	.60**
Therapist genuineness[c]	.69**	.65**	.71**
Observing ego strength[c]	.35**	.26*	.33**
Other-Directedness Scale[c]	−.20	−.25*	−.24*
Private Self-Consciousness Scale[c]	.20	.10	.16
Social Desirability Scale[d]	.03	.07	.05

Note. From "The Real Relationship Inventory: Development and Psychometric Investigation of the Client Form," by F. Kelley , C. Gelso, J. Fuertes, C. Marmarosh, and S. Lanier, in press, *Psychotherapy Theory, Research, Practice, Training*. Copyright by the American Psychological Association.
[a]Short Form (Tracey & Kokotovic, 1989). [b]From Eugster and Wampold (1996). [c]From the Barrett-Lennard Relationship Inventory (Barrett-Lennard, 1964). [d]Marlowe–Crowne Social Desirability Scale—Short Form (Reynolds, 1982)
*p < .05. **p < . 01.

question of the need for a new measure. In response, although the RRI-C and Eugster and Wampold's (1996) measures of the real relationship, as well as the Genuineness subscale of the BLRI, are highly correlated, our measure has certain advantages over the other ones. The RRI-C contains balanced sub-scales for Realism and Genuineness; contains items deliberately written to get at the magnitude and valence of genuineness and realism; and contains items that tap the patient's perception of self, therapist, and their relationship. It also possesses sound reliability. Eugster and Wampold's measures do not have these features. Regarding genuineness, the BLRI taps only the patient's perception of the therapist's genuineness, whereas our scale represents a more bipersonal view. As such, the Genuineness subscale of the RRI-C assesses the patient's perception of the self, the therapist, and their relationship.

A second issue that warrants discussion is the very high correlation between the RRI-C and the WAI–S (Tracey & Kokotovic, 1989). Indeed, this cor-relation is so high ($r = .79$) that one must question whether the patient-rated real relationship is the same construct as patient-rated working alliance. To discuss this point, I must note that the WAI measures three components of the working alliance: (a) therapist–patient agreement on the goals of treatment, (b) agreement on the tasks that will facilitate the attainment of these goals, and (c) the personal bond. Theoretically, the similarity of the two constructs is especially striking for the bond component of the WAI. Earlier, I con-ceptualized the bond that is part of the real relationship as a personal bond, whereas the bond that is part of the working alliance was seen as a working bond. However, when patients are asked to rate these constructs they may not make such a fine distinction. Inspection of the RRI-C correlations with the three components of the WAI supports such a contention. The goal and task components were highly correlated with the RRI-C, but the coefficients were not so high as to suggest that the two constructs were the same ($rs = .66$ and $.65$ for the Goal and Task subscales of the WAI–S, respectively). The correlation of RRI-C with the WAI Bond subscale, however, was .81. Thus, it does appear that the WAI Bond subscale and the RRI-C are close to the same construct.

Because of this extremely high correlation, we inspected the items on the Bond subscale of the WAI–S. Of the four items of that subscale, only one pertains to the collaborative relationship that seems to define a working alliance. Three items clearly pertain to the personal bond that is inherent in a real relationship. Thus, it may be that the Bond subscale of the WAI–S is actually a measure of the real relationship. The question for future research is how the performance of this four-item subscale compares with that of the RRI-C in capturing aspects of the real relationship and its correlates.

A final issue has to do with the one instance in which the RRI-C did not correlate in the theoretically expected way. Our measure was unrelated to a measure of what is termed *personal self-consciousness*. A post hoc inspection of this measure suggests that the private mulling over of the self that is a key part of this construct bespeaks a rather anxious attention to one's inner world and has little to do with the strength of real, personal relationships formed by the patient. It should also be noted that the reliability of the measure we used for private self-consciousness was low ($\alpha = .61$) and thus makes the validity of the measure suspect.

MEASURING THE REAL RELATIONSHIP: ISSUES AND FUTURE DIRECTIONS

The measures that have been developed to assess the strength of the real relationship are promising. They clearly are highly reliable, and the beginning evidence for their validity is strong. The measures are sufficiently validated to allow for research use, and indeed they have been used in a series of studies that are summarized in chapter 7.

At the same time, I want to emphasize that these measures are only a beginning, and further research aimed at measure refinement, and perhaps the development of additional measures of the real relationship, is needed (see Gelso, 2009a, 2009b). An example of such refinement is the research conducted by Hatcher and Gillaspy (2006) on the WAI and the WAI–S. These researchers subjected the WAI to analysis from an item response theory perspective and produced a psychometrically superior version. Such a revision would help solve the measurement problem created by high mean scores on both forms of the RRI.

A second measurement issue pertains to the very high intercorrelation between the Realism and Genuineness subscales of both the RRI-T and RRI-C. Despite the fact that the CFA supported the two factors in the RRI-C, the very high intercorrelations may be problematic. Assuming that the two elements are indeed separable, it may be useful to work on a measure explicitly aimed at generating two distinct factors. When our research teams wrote items we did not seek to do so in a way that would clearly separate realism from genuineness. Such an approach can indeed be taken, although one must then wonder whether explicitly writing items to separate two constructs actually captures or negates the very reality we seek to understand. If realism and genuineness are indeed highly correlated in the real world, then our measures of them ought to be likewise. This is a measurement conundrum worth pondering.

Given the current measures and the possibility that realism and genuineness in reality are highly interrelated, should we even pay attention to subscale scores, or instead should we use only the total score in the RRI measures? I agree with Hatcher (2009) and McCullough (2009) that at this point it makes the greatest sense to maintain and use the subscale scores as well as the total score. As I mentioned earlier in this chapter, some highly interesting findings have emerged in research involving the differential predictions allowed for by the two subscales, and it is easy to conjure research questions for which realism and genuineness ought to behave differently.

It would be helpful to develop methods of assessing the real relationship through the use of outside observers and behavioral markers. Rating scales used by observers, as well as behavioral markers, would allow us to pinpoint when the real relationship is strong and weak in sessions and the precise indicators of strong versus weak real relationships. Similarly, it would be valuable to be able to rate the real-relationship element at the response level, similar to ratings that may be made of many key psychotherapy constructs. In other words, each therapist or patient response could be rated on a real-relationship scale to determine its strength. This approach could be a useful supplement to the kinds of measures that our research teams have developed.

It would be beneficial to develop a measure of the working alliance bond that pertains only to the collaborative aspect of the bond (see Hatcher & Barends, 2006). This would facilitate the separation of the real relationship and working alliance so that they are two distinct but interrelated constructs. That is what Bordin's (1979) conceptualization suggests (Hatcher & Barends, 2006), and reducing the great overlap between the RRI-C and the Bond subscale of the WAI would be theoretically consistent and heuristically valuable.

CONCLUSION

Several years ago, Jean Carter and I (Gelso & Carter, 1994) wrote an article in which we presented theoretical propositions about how the different components of the overall therapeutic relationships (working alliance, real relationship, and transference–countertransference configuration) interrelate with one another and how each unfolds over the course of brief and long-term psychotherapy. In response to the propositions pertaining specifically to the real relationship, Greenberg (1994), a leading and highly influential psychotherapy researcher, commented on the great complexity of this construct and stated that "To measure the real relationship as a structural component, which combines both genuineness and the quality of being realistic, seems impossible" (p. 308). At the time, I believed Greenberg was correct. However, as my collaborators and I continued to refine our ideas about the real relationship, we have been able to develop the measures presented in this chapter. These measures are certainly not without their problems. For example, one may certainly raise the question about whether realism can be measured at all from the perspective of the patient, given the inevitable misperceptions of their therapists that patients experience. Furthermore, postmodern critics certainly may eschew the idea of a measureable reality to begin with. However, from the beginning we have taken the position that, although the complex reality of any person or relationship may never be fully known, it is valuable to assess the views of the real relationship, including the realism dimension, from the perspective of the patient and the therapist. The measures presented in this chapter are a clear step in this direction. They are a start, and my hope is that they will allow for research that begins to illuminate the role of the real relationship in the overall matrix of qualities that makes for more and less effective psychotherapy.

7

EMERGING RESEARCH FINDINGS ABOUT THE REAL RELATIONSHIP IN THE PROCESS AND OUTCOME OF PSYCHOTHERAPY

There have been many differing ideas presented over the years about the real relationship and its role in psychotherapy and psychoanalysis. These ideas, usually offered by psychoanalysts, were grounded in clinical experience and case material. They had little, if any, connection to empirical research. This has posed a major problem in the area of the real relationship. As Joseph Masling (2003) wrote in his critique of the antiempirical attitude evident in the work of Stephen Mitchell and many psychoanalysts,

> However meritorious the clinical method, and no matter what rich clinical insights are derived from it, fool's gold looks genuine until subjected to careful examination. Adding empirical data to clinical data can only enrich the mixture and help detect base elements. (p. 604)

This chapter reflects my bow to Masling's wisdom and my belief that empirical research is fundamentally important in advancing knowledge in psychotherapy in general and in the area of the real relationship in particular.

In this chapter, I describe what is known about the real relationship on the basis of empirical research. I begin by exploring the interrelation of the real relationship to the other components of the tripartite model of the therapeutic relationship (Gelso & Samstag, 2008) described in Chapter 1. I then examine the connection of the real relationship to a construct that has received much attention in recent years: attachment styles or patterns. I focus on the association of the strength of the real relationship to the therapy participants' attachment patterns in both relationships in general as well as the psychotherapy relationship. I also examine how the real relationship relates to other patient and the therapist qualities, in addition to its role in the process and outcome of psychotherapy. I conclude the chapter with suggestions about future directions for research on the real relationship.

Given the paucity of empirical research on the real relationship throughout the 20th century, it is remarkable that a chapter on the topic is even possible. Indeed, I could locate only one empirical investigation that was conducted during the last century that explicitly studied the real relationship: Eugster and Wampold's (1996) study, which was one of the key empirical foundations for the research program my collaborators and I developed.

At this point, a number of studies have been published that either explicitly focus on the real relationship or have a great bearing on it. Several studies are now in various stages of publication but not yet published. Some have only been presented at professional conferences. To give the reader a full picture of what we are in the process of learning empirically about the real relationship, I shall include these not-yet-published findings in this chapter. My aim is to present an empirically based, nontechnical portrait of the real relationship, a portrait that has heuristic value to scientists and is clinically meaningful to practitioners. To aid the reader in integrating the findings, the essential conclusions at which I have arrived after summarizing a series of studies are presented in italics.

THE REAL RELATIONSHIP AND THE TRIPARTITE MODEL

As I described in Chapter 1, for a number of years I have theorized about and empirically studied a model of the psychotherapy relationship that included three fundamental components: (a) a working alliance, (b) a transference–countertransference configuration, and (c) a real relationship (Gelso & Carter, 1985, 1994; Gelso & Hayes, 1998; Gelso & Samstag, 2008). In Chapter 1 I also discussed how these components ought to relate to each other in the clinical hour. What has been found empirically about how the real relationship relates to the other components?

The Real Relationship and the Working Alliance

Theoretically, I have followed Greenson's (1967) lead and suggested an inherent link between the real relationship and the working alliance; that is, the working alliance is theorized to emerge from the real relationship. The real relationship is the more fundamental of the two, existing in any and all relationships. The working alliance, on the other hand, develops only when there is work to be done. Thus, it is the alliance that exists for the purpose of getting the work of therapy accomplished, whereas the real relationship has no explicit intent. It simply exists, and it must exist, to varying degrees and at varying strengths. Given this inherent connection, one would certainly expect a close empirical relationship between the working alliance and the real relationship. That is precisely what my colleagues and I have found in four qualitative studies: that therapists' ratings of the strength of their real relationship with their patients relate moderately to strongly to these therapists' ratings of their working alliances (Fuertes et al., 2007; Gelso et al., 2005; LoCoco, Prestano, Gullo, & Gelso, 2009; Marmarosh et al., 2009). The range of overlap in the real relationship and the working alliance in these therapist ratings has ranged from 22% to 43%. This represents a very clear-cut relationship between the two constructs while at the same time indicating that they are separate variables. In other words, the real relationship and the working alliance are distinguishable by therapists, but they are very clearly connected. This quantitative finding is supported by a qualitative study that revealed that psychodynamically oriented therapists thought of the real relationship and the working alliance as functioning in tandem to foster the exploration and resolution of difficult transference feelings in their patients (Gelso, Hill, Mohr, Rochlen, & Zack, 1999).

For patients' ratings, the picture is somewhat different in that the connection between the real relationship and working alliance seems even stronger. In four studies (Fuertes et al., 2007; Kelley et al., in press; LoCoco et al., 2009; Marmarosh et al., 2009) the overlap in the variables was up to 62%. If this figure (i.e., equivalent to a correlation coefficient of .79) is corrected for the inevitable unreliability of such estimates, then it begins to look like the two constructs may not be separated in patients' minds. Kelley et al.'s (in press) study sheds light on this overlap. These investigators found that the correlation of the strength of the real relationship was significantly higher with the Bond subscale of the Working Alliance Inventory (WAI; Horvath, 1982; Horvath & Greenberg, 1989), which measures the emotional bond between therapist and client, than with the subscales of the WAI that measure therapist and client agreement on the goals of treatment and the tasks that will be helpful in attaining those goals. An inspection of the Bond subscale of the WAI form that we used in our studies revealed that three of the four items tap the personal feelings that the therapist perceives the patient and he or she have for one another, whereas only one item assesses the therapist–patient collaboration in the work. Thus, the Bond subscale of the WAI seems to be a mixture of items pertaining to the work of therapy and the personal relationship. In any event, for patients, the working alliance and the real relationship, although distinguishable, seem even more closely related than for therapists.

One additional finding about the connection of the patient-rated real relationship to the working alliance should be noted. LoCoco et al. (2009) unexpectedly discovered that the correlation of patient-rated real relationship and working alliance appeared to be stronger after eight sessions than after the third session of brief therapy ($rs = .50$ after three sessions and .73 after eight sessions). This pattern also occurred for therapist-rated real relationship and working alliance, but it was not as pronounced ($rs = .67$ after the third session and .80 after the eighth session). Thus, it appears that very early in therapy the working alliance and real relationship are moderately related, but as therapy progresses the two components of the overall relationship become more intertwined, especially in patients' ratings. This may imply that, as therapy unfolds, patients and therapists move toward experiencing these different elements of the therapeutic relationship as all of a piece, that is, as very highly interrelated. Alternatively, it could be that the same patients for whom the working alliance and real relationship are not highly related early in the work are more likely to discontinue treatment. Perhaps in such cases one or the other of the real relationship and working alliance is weak, and when either is weak, treatment is less likely to continue. These are ideas that are worth testing in future studies.

In sum, the theory suggesting a close connection between the real relationship and the working alliance is very clearly supported by the data. In the eyes of both therapists and patients, the two are moderately to very strongly interrelated, although they are also distinguishable, especially in the eyes of therapists.

Transference and the Real Relationship

The real relationship is usually seen as, in part, the transference-free element of, first, the overall therapeutic relationship and, second, every perception or experience of the other person in that relationship (Gelso, 2009a). Because of this idea, one would expect that transference and the real relationship would be negatively related to one another. Because the real relationship is more than the transference-free part of the relationship or any given interaction (because it includes genuineness as well as realism), one would not expect this negative relation to be as pronounced.

Two studies have tested the relation between the strength of the real relationship and the amount of transference in psychotherapy. In the first study, Gelso et al. (2005) queried 79 practicing psychotherapists and 51 graduate student therapists. These participants were asked to consider their relationship with the last client they had seen during the past week with whom they had conducted at least five psychotherapy sessions. The therapists made ratings of the strength of the real relationship with these clients, as well as the transference the clients had exhibited in their work. Transference was defined as the degree to which the material provided by the client was overtly or covertly related to the therapist and was a manifestation or displacement from early important relationship(s). Ratings were made of transference during the last session and last five sessions. Transference ratings were made for positive and negative transference. As predicted, the strength of the real relationship was modestly and negatively related to negative transference for the last session ($r = -.29$, $p < .01$) and last five sessions combined ($r = -.20$, $p < .05$). In other words, the stronger the real relationship in the treatment, the less negative transference that emerged during these sessions.

This finding of an inverse relation between the strength of the real relationship and the amount of negative transference was replicated in a study of 31 therapist–patient dyads at a university counseling center (Marmarosh et al., 2009). Therapists' ratings of transference (defined the same as in Gelso et al.'s [2005] study) after the third therapy session were correlated with therapists' and patients' ratings of the strength of the real relationship after the third session. Therapists' ratings of the real relationship were again found to relate negatively to their perceptions of negative transference ($r = -.50$, $p < .001$); however, patients' ratings of the real relationship were not related to their therapists' perceptions of negative transference ($r = -.10$, $p > .05$).

In putting together the findings from Marmarosh et al. (2009) and Gelso et al. (2005), it appears that *the stronger the real relationship in therapists' eyes, the less negative transference they see in their patients but, for patients, their therapists' perceptions of the negative transference they exhibit have little or nothing to do with these patients' perceptions of the real relationship.* The relation of negative transference to the real relationship should not be taken to mean that when the real relationship is strong there is no negative transference; instead, I believe it more likely hints that when the real relationship is strong it is unlikely that the patient will exhibit very substantial negative transference, that is, to a degree that would seriously hinder treatment. The reader should stay mindful of the fact that negative transference and a strong real relationship can surely coexist, as negative correlation coefficients in the range of .20 to .50 indicate.

Whereas the real relationship and negative transference were negatively related in therapists' ratings, the real relationship was unrelated to positive transference. I should note that a relationship was not expected between the real relationship and positive transference because the latter concept has proven so ambiguous and elusive to measure. Positive transference may easily be confused with the working alliance and real relationship, or in any event not be seen as transference at all. Perhaps because of such ambiguity, in all of the research emanating from the Maryland Psychotherapy Relationship

Research Program (i.e., that my colleagues and I have conducted) positive transference is much more weakly related to other relevant variables than is negative transference.

The final variable in the tripartite model is countertransference. Despite a fairly sizable number of studies on this topic (see Gelso & Hayes, 2007), no work to date has examined the relation of the real relationship to therapist countertransference. Theoretically, one would expect a negative relation, at least to countertransference behavior (i.e., acted-out countertransference), and both laboratory and field research is now underway to test this expectation.

ATTACHMENT IN GENERAL AND ATTACHMENT TO ONE'S PSYCHOTHERAPIST

One of most fertile areas of research in all of psychology in recent years has been that of infant attachment and its ramifications in adult relationships, including the psychotherapy relationship (see Cassidy, 2000; Cassidy & Shaver, 2008; Wallin, 2007). Springing from the theoretical work of John Bowlby (1973, 1969/1982, 1988), and receiving impetus from the seminal studies of Marie Ainsworth and her collaborators (e.g., Ainsworth, Blehar, Waters, & Wall, 1978), discoveries about attachment and its role in the lives and relationships of people have burgeoned over the past two decades.

Attachment theory and research have great implications for work on the real relationship in psychotherapy. A fundamental thesis that may be drawn from attachment theory is that the patient forms an emotional attachment with his or her therapist, and through this attachment the therapist becomes a secure base from which the patient may venture out (or, perhaps more aptly, venture inward) to explore feelings that are otherwise too threatening. This implies that the attachment to one's therapist is very influential. However, even more fundamental are patients' attachment tendencies or styles, learned very early in life through their relationships with primary caregivers and carried on into adult relationships. Bowlby (1973, 1969/1982), for example, has postulated that, on the basis of early attachment relationships with primary caregivers, people form *working models* (or mental representations) of themselves as worthy or not worthy of care and of others as trustworthy (or not) to provide care and responsiveness to one's needs. It is these working models that are carried into adult life and relationships, including the psychotherapy relationship.

The specifics of these working models may be evidenced in people's attachment styles or tendencies. For example, if one is securely attached, he or she is likely to form appropriately trusting adult relationships and be comfortable with both intimacy and autonomy. On the other hand, individuals who form anxious attachments tend to be preoccupied with relationships and worry excessively about being abandoned. *Avoidant attachment,* another pattern, is quite different from, say, *anxious attachment* in that avoidant attachment leads people to be uncomfortable with closeness or dependency and to mute their emotional lives in relationships. These different patterns would seem to have great implications for the real relationship that is formed with one's therapist.

In addition to the basic attachment patterns just noted, in recent years Mallinckrodt and his collaborators have developed a measure of clients' attachment to their therapist (Mallinckrodt, 2000; Mallinckrodt, Gantt, & Coble, 1995). This measure taps the extent to which patients' attachments to their therapists are secure, are indicative of being preoccupied and wishing to merge, or are fearful and avoidant. Obviously, there are close connections between the basic tendencies toward secure, anxious, and avoidant attachments and relationships with therapists that represent secure attachments, preoccupied–merging attachments, and fearful–avoidant attachments. Like the more basic attachment patterns, attachment-to-therapist patterns would seem to have a great bearing on the real relationship that is formed.

Basic Attachment

Three investigations from the Maryland research program have addressed the connection of the real relationship to basic attachment patterns (Fuertes et al., 2007; Marmarosh et al., 2009; Moore & Gelso, 2009). In these studies, my colleagues and I have used the Experience in Close Relationships Scale (Brennan, Clarke, & Shaver, 1998) to examine clients' tendencies toward secure attachments, anxious attachments, and avoidant attachments.

In a study of college students' recollections of the psychotherapy they had received, Moore and Gelso (2009) found that, as predicted, secure attachment tendencies were positively related to the strength of the real relationship. Also as predicted, the tendency toward avoidant attachments was connected to weaker real relationships. This retrospective finding was replicated in an actual treatment study (Marmarosh et al., 2009) in which the attachment patterns of 31 patients were assessed prior to therapy, and the strength of their real relationship with their therapist was assessed after the third session of treatment. It was found again the avoidant attachment tendencies on the part of the patient were negatively related to the strength of their real relationships with their therapists.

It appears that therapists' own attachment patterns, too, relate to the strength of the real relationships they form; specifically, Fuertes et al. (2007) found that therapists' attachment avoidance was also negatively related to their ratings of the real relationship. *Thus, we can tentatively suggest two* things: that (a) patients' secure attachment tendencies make for stronger real relationships with their therapists and (b) both patients' and therapists' attachment avoidance appears to make for weaker real relationships. These findings make good clinical sense. If the patient has a tendency toward secure attachments (i.e., forms trusting relationships and is comfortable with both intimacy and autonomy), he or she is likely to form a good real relationship. Similarly, if patients or therapists are attachment avoidant (i.e., are uncomfortable with close relationships and with normal dependency and avoid emotions in relationships), it is hard to imagine them readily forming strong real relationships in psychotherapy.

What my colleagues and I have not found in our studies is a relationship between attachment anxiety and the real relationship. Apparently, high attachment anxiety may lead to either strong or weak real relationships. On the one hand, such styles may push patients to want to engulf the therapist and idealize the real relationship, whereas on the other hand anxious attachment may impel the patient to fearfully misinterpret the therapist's therapeutic intentions and stance.

Attachment to the Therapist

Using a sample of 59 patients currently in individual psychotherapy, Fuertes et al. (2007) found that patients' security of attachment to their therapists was positively related to these patients' ratings of the strength of the real relationship. Moore and Gelso (2009) replicated this finding with a sample of 108 college students who had had at least five therapy sessions and had completed therapy within the last 3 years. In addition, both Fuertes et al. and Moore and Gelso discovered that when patients had fearful–avoidant attachments to their therapists, they viewed the real relationship as weaker. In both these studies, patients' tendencies toward what was termed *preoccupied–merger attachments* to their therapists were unrelated to the real relationship.

These findings about attachment to the therapist seem to closely mirror findings on patients' general attachment patterns as they relate to the real relationship. In sum, *the more secure are patients' basic attachment patterns, the more secure will be their attachments to their therapists, and the stronger will be their real relationships. At the same time, the greater the attachment avoidance the patient carries with him or her, the more likely he or she is to form a fearful–avoidant attachment to his or her therapist, and the weaker will be their real relationship.* It is interesting that in Moore and Gelso's (2009) study there is support for a mediating role of the real relationship in those cases in which patients had more avoidant attachment. The mediation went like this: Greater attachment avoidance seems to promote a weaker real relationship, which in turn stimulates more fearful and avoidant patient attachments to their therapists. In a clinical sense, these findings raise the question of how to best work with patients who are avoidantly attached. What techniques and what relationship ingredients can foster better real relationships with these patients? This seems important, because if real relationships are strengthened, then it appears likely that patients will form less fearful and avoidant attachments with their therapists.

PATIENT FACTORS IN THE FORMATION OF STRONG REAL RELATIONSHIPS

What patient factors, in addition to attachment tendencies, are related to the strength of the real relationship that patients have with their therapists? This question allows one to begin to clarify the nomonological network of associations between the real relationship and other key variables. Despite the very early stage of real-relationship research, my colleagues and I have studied the connection of the real relationship to a few patient variables (in addition to the working alliance, transference, and attachment, as reported earlier in this chapter).

Research has found that *a cluster of patient variables appears to relate to the strength of the real relationship patients form with their psychotherapists. The variables in this cluster are patients' observing egos* (Clarke, 1996), *insight during treatment* (Graff & Luborsky, 1977), *and the tendency to attend to one's inner feelings* (Fenigstein, Scheier, & Buss, 1975). The first of these, patients' observing egos, reflects the capacity to stand back and observe one's self, with the implication that this capacity leads to accurate self-observations. Theoretically, the strength of the observing ego is closely related to patients' tendency to attend to their inner feelings, as well as their level of insight, or the ability to understand oneself, one's motives, and one's behavior. Kelley et al. (in press) found that patients' self-ratings of their observing egos and their tendency to attend to their inner thoughts and feelings related to their perception of the strength of the real relationship. In a second study, therapists' ratings of their patients' insight were related to these therapists' evaluations of the real relationship (Gelso et al., 2005).

These findings seem plausible from a clinical perspective. The real relationships that patients form with their therapists would be expected to be strengthened when patients attend to their inner thoughts and feelings, observe these accurately, and gain insight into their therapy. In terms of the two elements of the real relationship, clinically speaking, the three patient variables being discussed would seem to clearly influence the tendency to perceive the therapist realistically as well as the tendency to behave genuinely.

A fourth patient variable, the tendency to hide one's true feelings and to conform to others' expectations, also was found to relate inversely to real relationship

(Kelley et al., in press). Again, it makes good clinical sense that patients who hide their true feelings and give their therapists what they want to hear would form weaker real relationships, and this is precisely what Kelley et al. (in press) found.

I should note the correlations found between the real relationship and the four other variables that have been noted are modest (rs ranging from .25 to .33). At the same time, one could not expect correlations much higher than this, because each of the variables is probably best understood as one piece of a very complex puzzle. In addition, the findings reported in this section have not yet been replicated, so they are best viewed as very tentative. Although, as I have mentioned, the findings certainly do fit with what would be expected clinically and enrich our understanding of the real relationship, further study of these interrelationships is needed.

WHAT DOES THE THERAPIST HAVE TO DO WITH IT?

Earlier in this chapter I discussed the weakening effect of therapists' attachment avoidance on the real relationship. Two other therapist factors have been studied in connection with the real relationship: (a) empathy and (b) self-disclosure. In the aforementioned Fuertes et al. (2007) study, 59 patients' ratings of their therapist empathy on a commonly used measure (Barrett-Lennard, 1962) were significantly related to their ratings of the strength of the real relationship ($r = .50$). Thus, the greater the empathy clients perceive from their therapists, the stronger they view their real relationship.

The question of how much therapists should self-disclose to their patients, as well as the kind of material that should be disclosed, has been the source of controversy over many years in psychotherapy and psychoanalysis (see Farber, 2006). When one integrates my previous discussion in this book of how such disclosure relates to the real relationship, one might conclude that there will be a modest relationship. The relationship would not be a very strong one because, as I have suggested, self-disclosure is only one road to a real relationship, and explicit self-revelations on the part of the therapist may well have more to do with making the real relationship salient than with strengthening it. It is certainly very conceivable that the material a therapist discloses will weaken the real relationship while simultaneously pushing it to the forefront of the overall relationship.

Knox, Hess, Peterson, and Hill (1997) conducted a qualitative study of 13 adult psychotherapy patients' experiences with helpful instances of therapist self-disclosure. Their findings seemed to suggest that such disclosures resulted in therapists being seen as more real and human and in patients being more open and honest. This implies that the genuineness component of the real relationship, in particular, is strengthened by helpful disclosures. But does disclosure on the whole aid the real relationship? The only study to date that has examined this question was Ain and Gelso's (2008) investigation of 94 graduate and undergraduate students who had terminated therapy within 3 years of the study and had received a median of 12 therapy sessions.

Ain and Gelso (2008) found that former patients' perceptions of the overall amount of their therapists' self-disclosures was positively related to the strength of the real relationship ($r = .33$); however, the relevance of therapists' self-disclosures to the patient and his or her needs was more strongly related to the real relationship ($r = .53, p < .05$). Furthermore, when the researchers used a simultaneous regression to examine the comparative importance of overall amount of self-disclosure versus the overall relevance of therapists' disclosures to the patient and his or her problems, only the latter uniquely predicted the strength of the real relationship. How might this finding be interpreted? It appears that *only the portion of overall therapist self-disclosure that is relevant to the patient and his or her problems matters in terms of strengthening the real relationship— and it does indeed matter. Thus, it is the relevance of therapists' self-disclosures, not the amount, that is likely to facilitate a strong real relationship in patients' eyes.*

Naturally, because Ain and Gelso's (2008) study relied on patients' retrospective reports, further research based on patients in treatment or only those who have recently ended treatment is in order.

THE UNFOLDING OF THE REAL RELATIONSHIP

At this point, there are no published data describing how the real relationship changes across psychotherapy sessions. However, my and my colleagues' research teams have conducted preliminary analyses on two studies that have been presented at national conferences (Fuertes et al., 2008; Spiegel et al., 2008). In the first of these studies, the real relationship was rated after every session of six brief therapies by both therapists and patients, and outcome was assessed through patient and therapist evaluations (Fuertes et al., 2008). The patients were college students (at the University of Maryland and Fordham University), and the therapists were both doctoral trainees and senior staff. In the second study, this same kind of tracking occurred for 28 therapist–patient dyads, which allowed for more sophisticated hierarchical linear modeling of the data. Again, the patients were university students (at James Madison University and University of Maryland), and the therapists were counseling center psychologists and advanced doctoral students.

In the study of 28 cases over the course of brief psychotherapy (an average of seven sessions), according to patients' ratings there was a significant linear increase in the strength of the real relationship over the course of therapy

(Spiegel et al., 2008). The real relationship was strong to begin with (the mean item score on our measure was 4.2 on a 5-point scale) and increased in strength linearly over the course of treatment, so that the mean item rating in the final session was 4.6, $t(188)$ for the change = 3.26, $p < .01$. The hierarchical linear modeling analysis also permitted us to examine quadratic and cubic trends. It is interesting to note that the researchers did find a significant quadratic effect, $t(188) = 2.27, p < .05$. Patients' ratings of the real relationship dropped slightly after the initial sessions but then increased beyond the initial level as treatment unfolded. The linear trend for therapist ratings of the real relationship did not quite attain significance and suggested some highly complex patterns that have not yet been fully analyzed.

The data from our study of six dyads (Fuertes et al., 2008) fully confirmed Spiegel et al.'s (2008) findings. In that study, patients again started out perceiving a strong real relationship (mean item score = 4.2 for the first quarter of treatment) and perceived a gradual increase in the next two quarters, followed by a leveling off during the last quarter (4.6 for each of the last two quarters). Four of the clients clearly appeared to have very positive outcomes, whereas two of the clients did not (from their perspectives and those of their therapists). These figures exactly parallel the study of client ratings in the study of 28 therapist–patient dyads reported in the preceding paragraph. Therapists' ratings in Fuertes et al.'s study also mirrored these findings, although, consistent with findings of numerous studies that have examined numerous variables, therapists' ratings were lower than patients' ratings. Therapists' ratings during the first quarter of treatment yielded a mean item score of 3.8 (on a 5-point scale) and increased to 4.2 on this same scale.

In sum, two studies from our program that used vastly different methodologies and statistical analyses yielded highly converging findings. *In patients' eyes, the real relationship tends to be strong from the beginning, but it strengthens further as the work progresses. In therapists' eyes, this same pattern seems to emerge, although therapists' ratings generally tend to be lower than those of patients.* I shall have more to say about the unfolding of the real relationship as I inspect the data that have been amassed on the relation of the real relationship to treatment outcome.

ROLE OF THE REAL RELATIONSHIP IN PSYCHOTHERAPY EFFECTIVENESS

We now arrive at what is perhaps the most fundamental question about the real relationship: Is it related to treatment outcome or effectiveness? To address this question, one may examine data from different perspectives gathered in a variety of ways. For example, evaluations of individual sessions and how these relate to the real relationship may be viewed as an indirect indication of treatment effectiveness. Patients' opinions about what helped them also bear on the question of outcome and effectiveness. Therapist opinions, too, are relevant to the general question at hand. Of course, the most direct indication of the role of the real relationship in treatment outcome and effectiveness is derived from quantitative studies that assess this relationship. To date, 13 studies that are part of the Maryland Psychotherapy Relationship Research Program and other programs have a bearing on this question. These studies may be divided into three categories: those focused on (a) session evaluations, (b) therapist and patient opinions, and (c) quantitative analyses of the relation of the real relationship to treatment outcome and effectiveness.

Session and Therapist Evaluation

In the earliest quantitative study of the real relationship, Eugster and Wampold (1996) surveyed 114 expert psychologists (diplomates of American Psychological Association) and 119 patients of these therapists. Participants completed measures of nine treatment process variables, of which the therapist and patient versions of their real-relationship measure were two. These were related to participants' evaluations of a therapy session, in which the session evaluation referred to whether the session was experienced as useful, valuable, or good versus worthless, insignificant, or bad. The researchers found that both the patient and therapist ratings of the therapist and patient real relationship (four ratings) were significantly related to patients' and therapists' evaluations of one of their sessions (rs ranged from .28 to .64, $Mdn = .56$). When regression analyses were used, some complex and perplexing findings emerged for the therapists' ratings of their real relationships with their patients. I do not explore these findings here, because it is unclear how they may aid our understanding of the role of the real relationship in session evaluations.

In a second study of the relation of session evaluations to the strength of the real relationship, Gelso et al. (2005) found that 88 therapists' evaluations of the strength of their real relationship with a given patient were significantly correlated with their ratings of the depth ($r = .36$) and smoothness ($r = .43$) of sessions. These significant relationships occurred for both the Genuineness and Realism subscales of the Real Relationship Inventory (RRI; Gelso et al., 2005; Kelley et al., 2009), as well as the total score.

Finally, Kelley, LeBeouf-Davis, and Weiss (2008) reported a study in which 174 patients who self-reported as lesbian, gay, or bisexual and were in ongoing psychotherapy rated their real relationships and their working alliances with their therapists, as well as the positive and negative psychotherapy practices of their therapists, and these therapists' expertness, attractiveness, and trustworthiness (EAT). These investigators found that the real relationship predicted patients' perceptions of their therapists' EAT better than did the working alliance. Both the real relationship and working alliance mediated the relation of positive and negative practices to perceptions of EAT. In other words, it may be that therapists' more and less effective practices may affect patients' perceptions of the strength of the real relationship and the working alliance, which in turn affect patients' perceptions of the therapists' effectiveness (i.e., EAT).

On the basis of these three studies it seems clear that *the strength of the real relationship is positively associated with patients' and therapists' evaluations of the quality and effectiveness of given sessions, as well as patients' perceptions of their therapists' EAT*. Although session and therapist evaluation may be viewed as proximal measures of treatment success, they are not the same thing as treatment success. Thus, it is important to also examine direct indexes of outcome.

Therapists' and Patients' Opinions

A second vehicle for studying the role of the real relationship in treatment success is through the opinions of therapy participants. In one of the studies emerging from the Maryland Psychotherapy Relationship Research Program, 11 psychodynamic psychotherapists each responded to telephone interviews by our research team, answering questions in depth about one successful long-term therapy case in which transference was an important part of treatment (Gelso et al., 1999). One of the key findings was that the resolution of transference in these cases, in the eyes of the therapists, was greatly dependent on strong real relationships. Thus, "virtually everything the therapists said implied that working alliances and real relationships (characterized especially by mutual liking) served essentially as buffers in allowing often very difficult transference feelings to come into the open and get resolved" (Gelso et al., 1999, p. 265). Because the resolution of transference issues was very fundamental to the success of these cases in the eyes of the therapists, it appears that working alliance and real relationship, in tandem, were key mediators of such success.

A study conducted by Curtis, Field, Knaan-Kostman, and Mannix (2004) provides further hints about the role of the real relationship in treatment success. These investigators examined the views of 75 psychoanalysts about their own experiences as analysands. The behavior that these analysts found most helpful coming from their analysts was genuineness, one of the two elements of my conception of the real relationship. Other items ranked among the most helpful that were highly pertinent to a strong real relationship were "was accepting," "showed warmth," and "was emotionally available." Similarly, when the researchers explored the behaviors of these psychoanalysts' analysts that were the most highly correlated with change, items pertinent to or reflective of the real relationship again emerged as significant.

Examples of such items were "tolerated feelings of anger between us," "tolerated sadness between us," "was genuine," "was accepting," and "explored my feelings about him/her." These behaviors appear, directly or indirectly, to be part of the key ingredients of strong real relationships: genuineness, realism, and their magnitude and valence. It appears that when psychoanalysts think back on the analyses they received, aspects of what I have theorized as a strong real relationship are extremely important.

In sum, *the two studies discussed in this section suggest that, in the opinions of therapists and patients, a good or strong real relationship is an important contributor to treatment success.* However, these are very "soft" data, and one is left wondering what more rigorous quantitative studies of the association of real relationship to treatment success might offer.

The Real Relationship, Psychotherapy Progress, and Treatment Outcome

Six studies have now been completed that relate assessments of the real relationship to the progress or outcome of psychotherapy. As of this writing, two of these studies have been published (Fuertes et al., 2007; Marmarosh et al., 2009), and four have been presented at professional conferences (Ain & Gelso, 2008; Fuertes et al., 2008; LoCoco et al., 2009; Spiegel et al., 2008). Each of the latter four studies is now in various stages of preparation for publication. In addition to examining the association of the real relationship to treatment progress or outcome, three of the studies sought to determine whether the real relationship predicts outcome above and beyond the variance accounted for by the working alliance. This question of incremental validity is very important to this line of research because of the very close theoretical relationship between the working alliance and the real relationship. If the real relationship does not predict relevant phenomena differently than the working alliance, then very serious questions may be raised about the meaning and value of the concept of the real relationship, as well as its measurement.

Fuertes et al. (2007) surveyed 59 therapist–patient dyads and found that both therapists' and patients' ratings of the strength of the real relationship were significantly associated with their evaluations of these patients' progress in behavior, feelings, self-understanding, and overall (r for patient ratings of the real relationship and progress = .36, $p < .001$; r for therapist ratings of real relationship and progress = .49, $p < .001$). Because each participant made ratings at a given point in time during ongoing treatment, these findings reflect progress instead of outcome, strictly speaking.

Marmarosh et al. (2009) studied a sample of 31 therapist–patient dyads at a university counseling center and actually assessed the association of the real relationship to treatment outcome. They examined each participant's rating of the strength of the real relationship after the third session of therapy as well as their ratings of psychiatric symptoms at the beginning and the end of treatment. Clients' ratings of the real relationship after the third session were not associated with symptom change, although the correlations did approach statistical significance (e.g., rs of real relationship total, realism, and genuineness with symptom change were .28, .18, and .35, respectively). However, it was found that therapists' ratings of the real relationship were significantly associated with symptom change (posttreatment symptoms, controlling for pretreatment symptoms). The partial correlation coefficients were substantial (rs: overall real relationship with symptom change = .58, $p < .01$; realism = .43, $p < .05$; and genuineness = .68, $p < .001$).

A third study is similar to Marmarosh et al.'s (2009) investigation but was conducted at the counseling center at the University of Palermo in Sicily, Italy (LoCoco et al., 2009). In this study, therapist–patient dyads completed measures of the real relationship after the third ($n = 50$) and eighth ($n = 18$) sessions. A measure of psychological distress and the Outcome Questionnaire–45.2 (Lambert et al., 1996), a highly validated measure of treatment outcome, were taken after the first session, and the Outcome Questionnaire–45.2 was again taken after the last session. Patients' ratings of the genuineness aspect of the real relationship after the third session was correlated with treatment outcome (with premeasures partialed out, $r = .26$, $p < .05$). Eighth-session real-relationship scores for patients (but not therapists) correlated even more highly with outcome ($rs = .50$ for genuineness, .51 for realism, and .52 for total).

An investigation by Spiegel et al. (2008) of 28 therapist–patient dyads at two university counseling centers yielded findings that are similar to those of LoCoco et al. (2009). In this study, patients' and therapists' ratings of the strength of the real relationship were measured after every session in brief therapy (eight sessions on average). Although therapists' and patients' ratings of the real relationship early in treatment were not found to relate to treatment outcome, the overall patient ratings of the real relationship after all sessions were substantially related to treatment outcome for patients ($r = .56, p < .001$). The correlation for therapists attained what would be considered a medium effect size, but because of the small sample only approached statistical significance ($r = .31, p < .06$).

Ain and Gelso (2008) used a very different method to assess students who had been in psychotherapy up to 3 years before being studied. Ninety-four former patients made retrospective ratings of, among other things, the strength of their real relationships with their therapists and the outcome of treatment. A strong relationship was found between recollections of the overall real relationship and outcome ($r = .70$) as well as for both genuineness ($r = .67$) and realism ($r = .69$) and outcome. Finally, when the authors tested the real relationship elements of genuineness and realism simultaneously with therapist self-disclosure they observed that the real relationship predicted outcome more effectively than did patient recollections of the relevance of their therapists' disclosures to their problems.

These five studies each point to the relevance of the real relationship and its two defining features (realism and genuineness) to treatment progress and outcome. None of the studies precisely corroborated the findings of any other study. For example, Marmarosh et al. (2009) found that therapists' ratings of the real relationship were most associated with outcome, whereas patients' ratings were not; LoCoco et al. (2009) found that patients' ratings of the real relationship were predictive of outcome, whereas therapists' ratings were not; and Fuertes et al. (2007) found that both therapists' and clients' ratings were predictive. Furthermore, whereas Marmarosh and her collaborators found that early real relationship predicted outcome, LoCoco et al. indicated that late ratings of the real relationship are more predictive than early ones, and Spiegel et al. (2008) added to this mix in finding that the overall real relationship (the sum of ratings after every session) instead of the early real relationship predicted outcome.

What may be concluded from this mix of findings? In all of the five studies, *the real relationship measured at one point or another from the vantage point of therapists and/or patients appears to be significantly related to treatment outcome. The relationship is especially pronounced when patients recall their therapies, but it also exists in prospective studies.*

The Real Relationship, the Working Alliance, and Treatment Outcome

As indicated earlier, one must ask whether the real relationship adds anything above and beyond the working alliance to the prediction of treatment outcome. Three studies bear directly on this topic. First, in Fuertes et al.'s (2007) study of 59 therapist–patient dyads, hierarchical regression analyses indicated that, for patients' ratings, the real relationship clearly and strongly predicted treatment progress above and beyond the variance accounted for by the working alliance (as well as patients' attachment to therapists and ratings of therapist empathy). Thus, despite the fact that both the patient-rated real relationship ($r = .49, p < .001$) and the working alliance ($r = .30, p < .05$) individually correlated with progress, the real relationship predicted progress after the variance accounted for by working alliance is already controlled. For therapist ratings, too, the real relationship predicted variance in progress beyond that accounted for by working alliance, although the 5% increase did not quite attain statistical significance ($p = .056$).

Marmarosh et al.'s (2009) study of 31 psychotherapy dyads yielded similar results. Using hierarchical liner modeling, they found that the therapist-rated real relationship after the third session of treatment predicted treatment outcome (in the form of symptom change), above and beyond the variance accounted for by the working alliance, which itself did not significantly predict outcome. When the subscales of the RRI were examined separately, it appeared that therapist-rated realism in the relationship was especially predictive of symptom change. When one looks at individual correlations one notices that the therapist-rated real relationship significantly correlated with symptom change ($r = .58, p < .01$), whereas the working alliance did not ($r = .36, p > .05$), perhaps because of the small sample size.

Whereas Fuertes et al. (2007) found patient ratings to be especially predictive of progress (above and beyond the alliance), Marmarosh and her collaborators (2009) did not. In fact, they found that neither the patient-rated real relationship ($r = .28$) nor working alliance ($r = .16$) significantly related to symptom change. The third study (LoCoco et al., 2009), like Fuertes et al.'s study, revealed that the patient-rated real relationship was especially predictive. When these investigators studied the ratings of 49 dyads after the third session, they found that the patient-rated real relationship accounted for substantial variance (29%) in symptom change above and beyond the variance accounted for by the working alliance. Therapist ratings of neither the real relationship nor the working alliance were predictive of symptom change at the end of treatment.

Whether the patient- or therapist-rated real relationship predicts patient outcome in the form of different indexes of change depends on which study one examines. However, it does appear that *in each study the real relationship outperformed the working alliance in predicting change, and in each study either the patient- or therapist-rated real relationship accounted for substantial variance above and beyond the variance accounted for by the working alliance*. This cluster of studies provides strong evidence for the real relationship adding to the power of the working alliance in accounting for patient change in psychotherapy.

THE UNFOLDING OF THE REAL RELATIONSHIP AND TREATMENT OUTCOME

A final question to address pertains to how the unfolding of the real relationship over the course of therapy relates to outcome. My colleagues and I have sought to gain a beginning understanding of what the curves of the real relationship over the course of treatment may look like for more and less successful cases. Two of our studies—Fuertes et al. (2008) and Spiegel et al. (2008)—bear on this topic. As noted earlier, Fuertes et al. examined six dyads, and Spiegel et al. examined 28 dyads.

TABLE 7.1
Client-Rated Real Relationship and Treatment Outcome
at the Beginning and End of Treatment

Outcome group	First session real relationship means	Last session real relationship means
Client-rated outcome: Moderate and high change	4.25	4.30
Client-rated outcome: Low change	4.15	3.96
Therapist-rated outcome: Moderate and high change	4.15	4.42
Therapist-rated outcome: Low change	4.20	4.13

Note. The real relationship was measured through ratings on the client version of the Real Relationship Inventory (Kelley et al., 2009). From "Unfolding of the Real Relationship and Its Connection to Outcome," by E. B. Spiegel, J. Busa-Knepp, E. Ma, R. D. Markin, S. Ain, A. Hummel, D. M. Kivlighan, and C. J. Gelso, 2008, paper presented at the 116th Annual Convention of the American Psychological Association, Boston, MA. Reprinted with permission of authors.

As one can see in Table 7.1, in Spiegel et al.'s (2008) investigation patients who changed in what we termed a *moderate* or *high* amount on outcome measures they completed after the first session begin treatment with a strong real relationship (mean rating of 4.25 on the 5-point Likert scale of the client version of the RRI [RRI-C]; see Chapter 6, this volume) and increased slightly to about a 4.30 during brief therapy. Conversely, clients who were in the low-change group had mean ratings on the RRI-C of 4.15 after the first session that then dipped slightly to 3.96 by the last session. When we examined therapists' ratings of their patients' outcome and these same patients' ratings of the real relationship, we observed a similar but more pronounced pattern. The moderate- and high-change group again began treatment with a strong real relationship (mean rating of 4.15 on the 5-point Likert scale of the RRI-C) and ended up at an even stronger level (M = 4.42). The low-change group started out at about the same level as the moderate- and high-change groups (M = 4.20 on the 5-point scale) but declined in their ratings of the strength of their real relationship with their therapists during treatment to 4.13 by the last session. When we combine these ratings it appears that the patients who did best in brief therapy began treatment with a strong real relationship, and this relationship strengthened further over the course of the work. By contrast, patients who did not do as well in treatment began with an equally strong real relationship but evidenced a weakening of the relationship during the course of the work. It should be noted that the patterns just described and presented in Table 7.1 were all statistically significant based on our hierarchical linear modeling analysis.

The analysis of six cases of brief therapy by Fuertes et al. (2008) yielded a very similar pattern. In analyses of Fuertes et al.'s data provided by Tamara Walden (personal communication, July 23, 2009), the four patients who improved substantially according to their and their therapists' ratings of outcome were compared with the two patients whose change was substantially less during treatment. The pattern of means on the RRI client and therapist forms combined is presented in Figure 7.1. As one can see, the high improvers began treatment with a mean RRI-C and RRI-T combined score of 4.08 for the first quarter of therapy and ended with a 4.55 during the last quarter. Their pattern of change was a linear increase in the strength of the real relationship over the four quarters of treatment. The low improvers, however, exhibited a very different pattern: They began with slightly weaker real relationships (M = 3.84 for the first quarter) and increased linearly during the next two quarters (to 4.19 for the fourth quarter). However, their real relationship ratings dropped during the last quarter to 4.08.

What may be concluded from these two studies? Before responding, I must underscore that these are preliminary analyses, and inferential statistical analyses have not been performed on the data from Tamara Walden (personal communication, July 23, 2009). Thus, a healthy amount of caution is warranted regarding the findings. With that in mind, the two studies taken together suggest that in brief therapy of approximately 6 to 20 sessions, it appears that *patients who do well in treatment typically form a strong real relationship very early in treatment. They probably click well with their therapists in the initial meeting. In addition, this initially strong real relationship gets even stronger throughout the course of treatment.* On the basis of the analyses my colleagues and I have done, it does not appear that there are any dips in the real relationship in these successful cases, as have been found in the working alliance (i.e., alliance ruptures, see Kivlighan & Shaughnessy, 2000; Stiles et al., 2004). *For patients who do not*

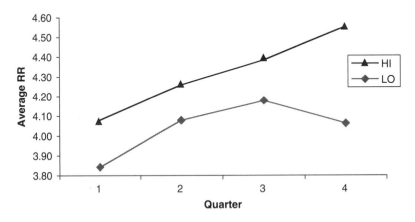

Figure 7.1. Combined therapist and patient real relationship (RR) mean item score by quarter for the high-outcome (HI) and low-outcome (LO) groups. Data from Fuertes et al. (2008).

do as well in brief treatment, however, a different pattern emerges. They begin treat-
ment with slightly weaker real relationships and then essentially stay the same or
decline in the strength of the real relationship toward the end of treatment. Again,
further analyses by our research teams, as well as replication of these patterns,
is needed before firm conclusions may be drawn about the unfolding of the
real relationship for patients who profit substantially from brief therapy as
compared with those who do not so profit.

FUTURE DIRECTIONS FOR RESEARCH

It bears repeating that empirical research on the real relationship is in
its very early stages; however, the studies that have been reported in this
chapter are highly promising. They begin to map out the nomonological network of associations between this variable and other clinically meaningful
patient and therapist variables as well as its connection to treatment outcome. So far, the findings are promising in the sense that they represent considerable convergent validity. The real-relationship variable, when studied
empirically, behaves as it theoretically should! For the most part, it correlates
in theoretically expectable ways with other variables, and it correlates with
treatment outcome. It also seems to perform at least as well as the working
alliance in predicting outcome, and generally better, adding substantially to
the working alliance in the variance in outcome for which it accounts. In this
sense, the real-relationship construct exhibits incremental validity.

In Chapter 6 I discussed future directions in the measurement of the real
relationship. In what directions should research on the real relationship
move? Given the early stage of this research, there are numerous possibilities
for empirical study. I should first point out that nearly all of the individual
findings reported in this chapter were derived from one or two studies. Thus,
as investigators address new questions it would be useful to incorporate one
or more of the questions already examined by the studies reported in this
chapter. Such studies would represent partial replications, which are more
viable than full replications because few investigators are willing to invest the
time and effort into simply duplicating an existing study.

A fertile area for research is that of how the real relationship may be differentiated from the working alliance. Theory-driven research that starts with
conceptually overlapping but distinct definitions of the two and then seeks
to understand empirically how they interplay during treatment would be
extremely valuable. *Working alliance* and *real relationship* may of course be integrated into one definition and studied with one measure of a global concept
of therapeutic relationship, but I believe that it is important to move beyond
such global conceptualizations in the area of the psychotherapy relationship.

Also in Chapter 6 I discussed the very high correlation between the Realism and Genuineness subscales of both the client and therapist forms of the RRI. Before concluding that such correlations imply that realism and genuineness amount to the same construct, it would be useful to determine whether the two subscales differentially relate to constructs that they theoretically should. Examples of differential prediction of realism and genuineness were provided in Chapter 6. An additional example that appeared in one of our studies (Marmarosh et al., 2009) was that the patient's attachment anxiety appeared to be better predicted by both therapist and patient ratings of realism than by genuineness. This makes theoretical sense, because high attachment anxiety may readily be seen as substantially misperceiving aspects of a relationship and the other person. The small sample size in Marmarosh et al.'s (2009) study may have prevented these differences from attaining statistical significance, so examining such relationships in larger samples could be quite useful.

Throughout this book I have referred to differences between the *salience* and *strength* of the real relationship; however, the measures that my colleagues and I have developed address only strength. It would be very useful to differentiate the two empirically and then study the correlates of strength versus salience, including their correlations with treatment success and failure.

A striking lack in our research program has been in the area of long-term therapy and psychoanalysis. Although the aforementioned Curtis et al. (2004) study of psychoanalysts' personal analyses certainly had implications for the real relationship, virtually all of the studies that have specifically examined the real relationship focused mainly or exclusively on brief treatments. It would be extremely useful to study how the real relationship unfolds and is associated with outcome in both psychoanalytic and nonanalytic longer term treatments.

At this point, it would be especially useful to study questions such as the following: What therapist–patient interactions (e.g., transference and countertransference reactions, specific therapist and patient response modes) occur in sessions marked by stronger versus weaker and more salient versus less salient real relationships? What therapist factors (personal and technical) and patient factors facilitate the development of strong real relationships? How do the real relationship (strength and salience) and its importance vary for therapists of different theoretical stances and for patients with differing personality types, degrees and types of psychopathology, and cultural backgrounds? Regarding this last question, it could be most fruitful to examine the real relationship and its association with outcome for treatment dyads of the same and different races, ethnicities, sexual orientations, and so on. An examination of the therapist's multicultural competence as a potential moderator could be illuminating. Kelley et al.'s (2008) study of the connection of gay, lesbian, and bisexual patients' ratings of the real relationship to their perceptions of their therapists' expertness, attractiveness, and trustworthiness is a beginning. In keeping with the internationalization of psychology and psychotherapy, it would also be illuminating to study the real relationship in countries other than the United States. LoCoco et al.'s (2009) study, which was done at the University of Palermo in Sicily, Italy, was a step in this direction.

A useful line of research might investigate whether the process and outcomes might differ for patients and therapists who have similar versus different perceptions of their relationship. Along these same lines, there is some evidence (LoCoco et al., 2009) that therapists and patients converge in their ratings of the real relationship as treatment progresses. This finding needs to be replicated and studied in relation to outcome. One might expect that convergence would lead to improved outcomes, especially when initial ratings are divergent.

CONCLUSION

My colleagues and I have learned quite a bit about the real relationship through recent empirical efforts, and I have sought to provide a nontechnical summary of the key findings in this chapter. These studies have tentatively answered some questions and raised many more. In fact, there are a very large number of questions that may be fruitfully studied at this point. Elsewhere (Gelso, 2009b), I used the words of Lewis Carroll's Walrus in stating that "the time has come." However, rather than it being the time "to talk of many things," I believe it is the time to dig in empirically and scrutinize the real relationship. It seems to me that we are at a point, unlike when Jean Carter and I theorized about the real relationship (Gelso & Carter, 1985, 1994), where research is quite viable. We have measures that, although very fallible, have sound psychometric features, and a wide array of questions await empirical scrutiny. Such vigorous empirical work will help us better know the place of the real relationship in the overall therapeutic relationship and in treatment success and failure. Research will also help us as therapists facilitate more effective real relationships and more efficacious psychotherapy and psychoanalysis.

8

CLOSING REFLECTIONS ON THE REAL RELATIONSHIP IN PSYCHOTHERAPY

In this concluding chapter I offer some summary points about the real relationship, its role in treatment, and how therapists may most effectively capitalize on this component of the therapeutic relationship. The chapter may be viewed as a short series of take-home messages, most of which are distilled from the earlier chapters. To focus attention on these take-home messages, I have italicized them throughout this chapter. I do want to reiterate, however, that any statements made about the real relationship must be provisional because of the early stage of sound clinical theory and research on this construct. Some statements will surely be confirmed by future clinical observation and empirical research, whereas others will likely be refuted as more is learned about this very old topic that is a very new area of scientific inquiry.

THE REAL RELATIONSHIP AND THE TOTAL RELATIONSHIP

It is important to keep in mind that the *personal or real relationship is not the entire therapeutic relationship. Neither is the working alliance, nor the transference and countertransference relationship. The real relationship is best seen as joining with these other key components to form the total relationship.* I have maintained in this book, and earlier writings (Gelso & Carter, 1985, 1994; Gelso & Hayes, 1998), that these components all exist to varying degrees in every treatment, regardless of duration or theoretical orientation, and I believe there is good empirical evidence to support such a claim.

As treatment progresses, each of these components moves back and forth from foreground to background in the relationship, and this movement occurs throughout the treatment. At one time the personal relationship is most salient, whereas at other times the transference or countertransference is figure and everything else is ground. When needed, the working alliance may come to center stage.

The therapist naturally has a great deal of influence in how often a given component is in the forefront. For example, in psychoanalysis the transferences (and countertransference) are much more often in the foreground. This is because most analysts view the analysis of transference as key to the resolution of core unconscious conflicts, which then results in successful outcomes. Thus, the analyst is on the lookout for transference, and his or her patient is likely to follow suit and thus produce more transference. For person-centered, process-experiential, gestalt, and interpersonal therapists, the here-and-now real relationship is more salient, and much of the work is done through this personal relationship. The therapist seeks to be genuine and to perceive the patient realistically, to grasp empathically the experiential world of the patient, in an ongoing fashion. These therapists also seek to foster genuineness and realism in their patients. Regarding the latter, most therapists of these persuasions aim to help their clients see who they (the therapists) are, instead of providing conditions for the development of transference, such as ambiguity.

For cognitive–behavioral therapists the relationship is not the be-all and end-all that it is in psychoanalysis and the humanistic/experiential therapies, but as cognitive–behavioral therapists have increasingly moved toward an awareness of the importance of the relationship the emphasis has been on a sound real relationship and a solid working alliance. The real relationship for these therapists seems to become more prominent when working with profoundly troubled persons, for example, borderline personalities, as is very clear in the work of Marsha Linehan (1993; see Chapter 4, this volume).

Not only is the personal or real relationship an important part of the overall therapeutic relationship in all therapies, but it also may be seen as a part of the therapist's and patient's individual responses to each other, especially those responses that are directly or indirectly about each other and their relationship. Thus, when patient or therapist speaks to the other about their relationship, shares his or her experience of the other and the relationship, asks questions of the other, makes allusions to their relationship, dreams about the other (even in disguise), thinks about the other, and so on, these individual responses carry with them one degree or another of the real relationship; that is, to one degree or another such responses have to do with the person-to-person relationship, even as they also have to do with the work relationship and the transference relationship. It should be helpful for therapists to pay attention to their own and their patients' responses and to consider the extent to which they represent these different but related components of the overall relationship. This does not mean that therapists ought to be obsessively concerned with the extent to which every one of their and their patient's responses to each other have loadings of transference, the real relationship, and the working alliance. However, keeping in mind the fact that these elements occur to some degree in individual responses and sessions, as well as in the total relationship, will aid the therapist in having a dynamic sense of just what is happening in his or her relationship with the patient and how to respond in helpful ways according to the dictates of his or her own personality and theory of therapy.

THE GOOD REAL RELATIONSHIP

Obviously, the good real relationship will entail high degrees of genuineness and realism on the part of patient and therapist. This has been the central topic of this book. Perhaps less obvious is that suggestion that *strong and effective real relationships require that patient and therapist have basically positive feelings toward the realistically perceived and experienced other*. Like any good personal relationship, the real relationship involves a mixture of feelings. However, if the real relationship is to be strong and effective, the valence of these feelings must be mostly positive. Therapist and patient must have good feelings toward one another as persons. These positive feelings may be termed *liking, caring, valuing, connection, respect, warmth,* or even a kind of loving. The kind of love experienced by both therapists and patients within the context of a real relationship might best be described as *agape,* a nonsexualized kind of loving that I believe occurs far more in effective psychotherapy and psychoanalysis than therapists lead each other to believe. These loving feelings make for powerful and helpful real relationships. Such deeper positive feelings generally occur more often in longer term psychotherapy because the persons in the dyad know more and more about each other within a healing context as treatment is extended, even though it is of course the patient whose life and conflicts are the center of the work. Knowing, and to an extent experiencing, the other's pain deeply in such a context or, from the patient's side, sharing one's pain, will tend to bring patient and therapist together in a more intimate personal relationship that is often marked by loving feelings.

It is not surprising that psychotherapists have shied away from more profound affects such as love (and hate) in their professional writing. The word itself makes professionals uncomfortable, even squeamish, because it does not bespeak a very "professional" relationship and because the word conjures up thoughts around sex and sexuality. However, agape is not sexual but instead reflects a very deep human caring, which is likely to have a healing effect in psychotherapy, often a powerful healing effect. Although psychotherapy is certainly a professional activity, it is important to stay mindful of the fact that it is also deeply personal. Shying away from this reality may make us therapists more comfortable, but it does not help our patients.

The view that feelings within the real relationship must be largely positive if the therapy is to be effective in no way means that all of the feelings must be positive, although idealizations may be needed transiently by some patients. A good real relationship instead actually allows or fosters the awareness and expression of negative affect by the patient toward the therapist, both negative affect based on transference and negative affect based on realistic perceptions. In Chapter 5 I presented case examples in which sound real relationships permitted the expression of negative affect on the part of patients based on their reality-based perceptions of their therapists. These genuine, reality-based bits of feedback from patients were both an expression of the real relationship and actually permitted by having a strong real relationship.

The role of the real relationship in resolving complex transference issues was evident in Gelso, Hill, Mohr, Rochlen, and Zack's (1999) qualitative study of successful long-term psychodynamically based psychotherapy. In that study, one of the questions posed to 11 therapists pertained to the role of the real relationship in the development and resolution of transference. These therapists typically viewed the real relationship as crucial in providing a safe place for the patient's transference-based feelings, negative as well as positive.

THE REAL RELATIONSHIP AND THE WORKING ALLIANCE

The early evidence presented in Chapter 7 very clearly supports the proposition that the strength of the real relationship is an important element of successful psychotherapy. However, *I do not believe that the real relationship works effectively alone; instead, it has its effect in combination with the working alliance or collaboration. The two ingredients together especially affect treatment success, positively when they are strong and adversely when they are weak.* At the same time, it is certainly possible for one of these components to be strong and the other moderate or weak. In such cases, I would expect the treatment to be less effective.

A personal example of the differential strength of the working alliance and the real relationship in two different psychotherapies I have experienced as a patient might help make the point. In the first, I experienced my therapist as highly competent technically. I trusted him to do his job with me, and indeed he did; I did, too. At the same time, I felt little person-to-person connection, and I suspect he did not feel this either. We seemed just so different, as if we were not in the same tribe, so to speak. I felt a sense of holding back aspects of my self, and I never had the sense of a depth of genuineness on my therapist's part. However, I believe both of us would rate the outcome as positive.

A second therapy evidenced a sound working alliance and a strong real relationship from both my side and my therapist's side. As with the first therapist, I felt I could count on him to do his job in a highly competent way. He knew his stuff, and I knew he would continue with me until we both felt the work was finished. Although we seemed quite different as persons in some ways, we clearly were on the same page in ways that mattered. I felt a liking and affection for this therapist, and I believe he did for me, too. We cared about each other. Because of this, I believe we went further and deeper (including the exploration of negative transference) in this second therapy than I was able to in the first treatment, even though that first therapy helped considerably.

Finally, consider a situation in which there is a strong personal or real relationship but a weak working alliance. Therapist and patient would likely very much enjoy being with one another, but the work of therapy would not get done. It is hard to imagine such a treatment having a strong impact on the patient.

In sum, both the real relationship and the working alliance matter substantially. Speaking empirically, up to now the evidence for the importance of the alliance is solid and consistent, if unremarkable in terms of the magnitude of the effect. The real relationship is the new kid on the block, but at this early stage it appears that it joins the working alliance in accounting for therapy success and failure.

SALIENCE, STRENGTH, AND FOSTERING THE GOOD REAL RELATIONSHIP

It is important for therapists to stay mindful of the fact that *the salience of the real relationship does not have a great deal to do with its strength, and it is strength that likely has the greater impact. Salience* means that the real relationship is in the forefront of the work. Clinically speaking, it seems that the real relationship is at center stage early on, when the therapy participants are getting to know each other; during the termination phase of treatment as therapist and patient prepare to part; during crises in the work, when patients have had a deep loss or a great success; and when the therapist has had major events occur in his or her life. In addition, the therapist can bring the real relationship to the fore deliberately through disclosures about his or her feelings and life and inquiries about the patient's feelings toward the therapist and their relationship.

One thing that seems clear when one combines research findings with clinical experience is that although self-disclosure on the part of the therapist magnifies the real relationship, in itself it does not strengthen the real relationship. I am reminded of one of the participants in Ain and Gelso's (2008) study who indicated that her therapist had self-disclosed too much during their therapy. She felt the work would have gone better had he disclosed less about his studies at Yale. I also recall a therapist trainee who tearfully expressed his sadness that his time-limited work of 12 sessions was coming to an end with his patient and who gave the patient an expensive gift in the last session as a token of his appreciation for the patient. This trainee had many issues around abandonment and had recently been left by his significant other. This therapist's disclosures did not serve to strengthen the real relationship but instead likely left the patient scratching his head as to what in the world was going on with his therapist. *The acting out of countertransference conflicts likely weakens the real relationship, even as it represents the therapist "playing with his cards face up"* (Renik, 1999).

On the basis of research findings on both self-disclosure and immediacy (e.g., Farber, 2006; Hill et al., 2008), I propose that *self-disclosures and immediacy (e.g., expressions in the moment of what the therapist is experiencing with the patient) have a healthy effect on the real relationship if they are highly relevant to the patient's needs, well timed, infrequent, and given in small doses. Here the patient's dynamics, the dynamics of the therapeutic relationship, and the patient's actual concerns are all crucial in determining whether a given self-disclosure or expression of immediacy has an impact. The best message for a practicing therapist is to think deeply and empathically about the patient and his or her needs, and to monitor your own needs and conflicts closely, when deciding what and how to share with the patient.*

Self-Disclosure, Genuineness, and the Real Relationship

As a therapist who is cautious about self-disclosure, and who is relatively nondisclosing, I have pondered for some time what allows for nondisclosing therapists to be experienced as genuine by their patients. I offer four factors that so enhance perceptions of genuineness of the therapist who discloses little.

1. *The therapist's nonverbal behavior is crucial.* Stated simply, some nonverbal behaviors just look more genuine than others. I strongly suspect that therapists who show their inner experience in their face and with other nonverbal behaviors exude a greater sense of genuineness than therapists who have a consistently bland, affectless, or ambiguous appearance.

2. *Congruence between what is said and how it is said is crucial.* There are few things that breed mistrust and a sense of the

other's disingenuousness as a discrepancy between verbal and nonverbal behavior.

3. *Consistency is crucial.* One of the key ingredients of effective therapy, especially long-term work, is the therapist's constancy. Patients need to trust that the therapist will be the same (or at least nearly so) from session to session, month to month, year to year. This constancy feeds the patient's sense that the therapist is being him- or herself and is trustworthy.

4. *Clarification of nondisclosures can help a great deal.* Telling a patient honestly why you cannot share your feelings, if the reason is good, will often foster the patient's sense of your genuineness, despite the nondisclosure. I am reminded of a particular patient I had seen in weekly sessions for about 6 months. I looked forward to our sessions, admired the patient's courage, her sense of humor, and who she fundamentally was. However, when this patient pulled at me, as she pulled at everyone close to her, to tell her I cared about her, I told her instead that I just did not think this would help her in any enduring way. What seemed most important, I said to her, was that we explore and work through why she so desperately needed that from everyone and why her getting such expressions of caring felt good for only a few seconds. Despite my nondisclosure of my feelings for this patient, I am certain she rightly perceived me as being quite genuine with her.

What Is a Therapist to Do?

This brings me to a question that psychotherapists must ask about the personal or real relationship and its strength: "What can I do to foster and maintain a good, strong real relationship?" I have always shied away from this question because it bespeaks a prescriptive approach that, I suggest, just cannot work in the area of the real relationship. Carl Rogers (e.g., 1957) had this same view about prescription in his many discussions of the therapist–patient relationship and the necessary and sufficient conditions of effective treatment. He talked about how these conditions (the therapist's empathic understanding, unconditional positive regard, and congruence) are best seen as attitudes instead of specific techniques. Alas, however, attitudes must be expressed in behavior if they are to matter. It is important not to get too prescriptive about the operationalization, and it is equally important to understand that by *behavior* one can refer to very subtle nonverbal behavior as well as to clear, readily observable, and measurable behavior.

With these caveats and considerations in mind, my answer to the question of fostering and maintaining a good real relationship is at once simple and extremely complex: *The good real relationship is fostered and maintained, first, by the therapist's being truly him- or herself with the patient, and the inverse, not being phony or maintaining an impersonal, so-called "professional" front.* Such genuineness implies both congruence between the therapist's inner experience and how it is consciously symbolized (being self-aware) and the therapist's stance with the patient. In this sense, I am suggesting that *being* genuine, instead of *acting* genuine or using genuineness techniques, is key. The latter often result in a caricature of genuineness. Earlier in this chapter I discussed the question of what the therapist does to seem genuine to the patient, but I need to underscore that the emphasis for the real relationship is to actually *be* genuine, to be oneself. With this in mind, the therapist's particular theoretical orientation matters little, if at all. Humanistic and experiential psychotherapists, for whom therapist genuineness has always been a key construct, certainly have not cornered the market on genuineness.

The second ingredient of the development and maintenance of a good real relationship on the therapist's part is the ongoing attempt to grasp empathically who the patient is and what is going on inside the patient. Part of this effort involves the therapist's management of his or her own internal countertransference. As I discussed in Chapter 3, this ingredient assumes that there is indeed an inner world or psyche of the patient to be grasped, a world that the patient brings with him or her to the therapy and that greatly transcends the co-constructions of therapist and patient. The real relationship is partly fostered and maintained by the therapist's continuing struggle to grasp that inner world, as free as possible from the distorting influences of his or her own conflicts. This struggle is in a certain sense doomed to failure, for the therapist can never fully grasp the patient's enormously complex inner world, but it is the effort, the nearly grasping, and the approximation that matter most.

As is the case with genuineness, the therapist's theoretical orientation has little if anything to do with how effectively he or she grasps the patient's inner world. I do not believe the specific constructs used by different theories matter at all. The therapist can seek to understand patients' irrational cognitions, their generalized anxiety, their core unconscious processes, or the incongruence between their organismic experiences and self-concept. These all represent different slants on the human psyche, the patient's inner world, and I seriously doubt that taking one position or another would affect the strength of the real relationship. Of course, an empiricist would recognize a few good research questions in this statement.

Warmed-Over Person-Centered Therapy?

The critical reader will by now have seen that my comments on the good real relationship and how to foster it are very close to Carl Rogers's (1957) necessary and sufficient conditions for successful treatment, to which I have referred at several points. The therapist seeks to be genuine, seeks to accurately and empathically grasp the patient's inner world, and possesses largely positive feelings for the patient. Despite the close connection of the real relationship as I have construed it, and the necessary and sufficient conditions, there are key differences. First, the theory of the real relationship assumes that there is indeed an "other" to be accurately understood, thus reflecting in part a philosophy of realism (or, more precisely, constructive realism, as I discussed in Chapter 3), whereas Rogers's theory, given its phenomenological and constructivist roots, does not make a distinction between reality and perception. Second, although positive feelings are important, in no way have I suggested the possibility of unconditional positive regard, one of Rogers's three key therapist-offered conditions. In fact, good relationships involve a great mixture of affects, and effective therapists possess a far greater range of affects toward their patients than is generally understood in the person-centered tradition, even as that tradition has moved toward a fuller appreciation of this range. Third, also at a philosophical level, there is no assumption in the theory of the real relationship that humans are fundamentally good and trustworthy, a view that has been a key tenet of humanism since it emerged during the Renaissance period. Humans are a great mixture of potentialities, for both good and evil, for being loving and hating; our fundamental nature reflects these varied potentialities.

A fourth difference is that when I have suggested that the good real relationship must be mostly positive, I am referring to positive feelings toward the realistically experienced and perceived other. Feelings for the projected other, which constitute the patient's and the therapist's transference and countertransference, are not part of a real relationship. Rogers (1957) did not make such a distinction.

Perhaps most important, the theory of the personal or real relationship offered in this book is different from Rogers's (1957) conditions theory in that the present notion is deeply bipersonal. Although I have focused in this section on what the therapist can do, the real relationship is indeed a relationship, one in which patient and therapist constantly participate and to which each contributes. A strong real or personal relationship cannot occur unless therapist and patient contribute to its strength. Also, the therapist's feelings within the real relationship depend greatly on the real relationship offered and permitted by the patient, and vice versa.

THE RIGHT AMOUNT OF REAL RELATIONSHIP

Is there an optimum amount of real relationship? Can there be too much of a real relationship? These are important questions for psychotherapists and researchers alike. The first question is easy to answer, although the answer involves great complexity: There is likely an optimum amount of real relationship in terms of its salience in the work, and this amount varies enormously according to the vulnerabilities, needs, and preferences of both the patient and therapist. A therapist who can realize this optimum amount may have any theoretical orientation but is likely a gifted psychotherapist.

With regard to the second question, whether there can be too much real relationship, my provisional answer is the always-dissatisfying "It depends." The answer depends on whether the reference is to the strength or the salience of the personal relationship. As for strength, generally speaking, I do not believe there can be too much, and I would suggest that, again generally, the stronger the better in terms of the effects on psychotherapy and psychoanalysis; that is, it seems unlikely that there can be too much genuineness, as I have defined it, and I doubt it there can be too much realism (as long as it is understood that realistic perceptions and experiences of the other can coexist with transference and that high realism does not imply that inner experiences are less emotional). The research studies my colleagues and I have conducted support this contention, because the relationships we have found between the strength of the personal relationship and indexes of proximal and distal outcome are linearly positive. We have not been able to detect any trend toward the highest levels of real relationship being connected to weaker outcomes.

The one caution to this assertion, and the reason that I have said "generally speaking," is that there probably can be feelings for the realistically experienced other (nontransference feelings) that are so positive that they disrupt the work. I hasten to add, however, that I have never seen or experienced this in my years as a psychotherapist and psychotherapy supervisor. It seems to be something, though, that we therapists worry about. However, it surely is true that transference feelings can be too positive, to the point that the work is disrupted or damaged, especially if those feelings are acted out.

Too Much Salience

Although I have claimed that the real relationship cannot be too strong, I would also suggest that it can indeed be too salient—too much in the forefront of the work, to the point that it serves as a threat to the patient and impedes the work. The real relationship can be too salient both in terms of the patient's contribution and the therapist's contribution. Two case examples may serve to make the point.

Sharing Too Much

In the first case, the patient was a 28-year-old man who had many schizoid qualities. He tended to be shy, fearful, withdrawn, and very quiet. His affect was very muted. He did develop relationships, but in these he withheld much of himself, and his romantic relationships didn't last beyond a few months. The therapist was also 28 years old, a doctoral student conducting weekly psychodynamically oriented psychotherapy under my supervision as part of an internship. Despite the patient's defenses, and partly because of the great sensitivity of the therapist, a working alliance formed, and the real relationship, too, seemed to develop and strengthen. The patient revealed more and more of himself, sharing heretofore-unspoken feelings, including some of his private writing. Still, by typical standards the patient was not sharing all that much. The therapist responded appreciatively to what was shared, and in supervision we at times commented on the surprisingly strengthening real relationship. However, after 18 sessions the patient suddenly stopped coming, without any clarification. After being contacted by his perplexed therapist, the patient came to a session late and claimed that he just did not have much to say, and then no-showed again. The therapist again pursued this further (at my suggestion, which is unusual for me), and when the patient finally responded to the therapist's e-mails and phone calls he did agree to come to a session. In response to the therapist's question about whether perhaps their relationship was getting too close and was thus too scary, the patient talked about how he has a limit on how close he will let people get to him. This interaction opened to door to an exploration of how the patient has closed off others, including former therapists. It marked a turning point in the successful treatment.

In this therapy the patient shared more of himself than he was ready for. I would not say he was too genuine but instead that his real relationship with his therapist came too much to the center of the stage in the sessions before he stopped coming. It was not that the therapist was making the real relationship too salient; instead, the patient allowed more of himself to be exposed than he was ready for. Had the therapist not pursued the patient repeatedly, the treatment no doubt would have ended, as had this lonely patient's other treatments (and romantic relationships).

Look At Me

Another case example of too much sharing was reported by one of the leading investigators of the real relationship, Cheri Marmarosh (2009), in her long-term psychodynamic psychotherapy with a patient, Laura, who had been diagnosed with borderline personality disorder. The real relationship with such patients can be extremely important in helping them differentiate between what is real and what is imagined as real. Marmarosh provided the following (partial) description of her work with Laura:

> The real relationship has evolved over time with Laura and is often at the foreground of my work with her. I am keenly aware of the impact that

I have on her, and I often struggle to maintain my own sense of real-ness when working with her. The intensity of the transference and lack of insight create a situation where Laura and I continually dance between the real, the projected, and the enacted. Our ability to lose the real relationship, experience the enactment of earlier relationship experiences, and then return to the real relationship allows us to understand what is real and what was real. It is the basic ingredient of the therapeutic change.

At one point in the work, Laura described aspects of her sexual life that were shameful to her, and she was sure that Marmarosh, too, was feeling crit-ical and judgmental. In fact, Marmarosh reported feeling closer to Laura and responded to her empathically as she described her feelings:

> I invited Laura to experience for herself how I was feeling by asking her to look at my face and tell me what she saw. I knew how I was feeling inside and trusted that she would experience my caring if she allowed herself to experience the real me. She immediately shook her head no and kept her face down. I recognized how hard it was for her and asked again . . . to look up at me. After a third attempt, she briefly looked up and into my face and eyes. I asked her what she saw and she said, "This is too hard for me." I acknowledged how difficult it was and asked her to try again. She stated, "I feel confused . . . I see you now and you look like you care." She paused, looked away and then said, "But I know you must think less of me." I invited her to stay with the first part, the part that sensed my caring. I asked her to keep looking into my face and to tell me how she felt the caring. As she was looking at me, her tears started to emerge, and she said "Guess I see it in your eyes. I just see it in the way you are looking at me." (Marmarosh, 2009)

After this moving session, Laura no-showed, and in response to her therapist's call offered that perhaps she needed a break from therapy. Because of Marmarosh's exquisitely sensitive handling of this crisis in the relationship, the patient did come back to treatment, and Marmarosh described further examples of the curative effects of the strong real relationship in their work together. However, the crisis was very close to destroying the therapeutic relationship because the real relationship, in this one dra-matic instance, was made too salient, given the patient's profound fears and vulnerabilities.

In sum, *although in general the real relationship cannot be too strong, it can become "too big" in the overall relationship, taking more space in the overall relation-ship than the patient is able to manage. This possibility is probably most pronounced with patients who have the greatest deficits and vulnerabilities. At the same time, these may well be the patients who will profit most from a strong real relationship that is sensitively offered by the therapist.*

CONCLUSIONS

Although the therapeutic relationship has been a central concern of psychotherapists and psychoanalysts from the beginnings of the talking cure, what may be termed the *real* or *personal relationship*, as I have conceptualized it in this book, has been a sadly neglected stepchild in clinical theory and empirical research. However, it has not been a stepchild in the actual work of psychotherapists. I believe that most practicing psychotherapists intuitively as well as theoretically grasp that their person-to-person connection with their patients, the real relationship, is deeply important to the work.

In this last chapter I have sought to distill what I view as a few key messages that I hope the reader will ponder and perhaps integrate into his or her work, either as a researcher or as a practitioner. As I have stated repeatedly throughout this book, despite the fact that the real relationship has been written about for a very long time, theoretical and empirical work on this construct is at a very early stage. The evolution of this concept in the years ahead will be exciting, as we come to understand its role in the overall therapeutic relationship and in effective psychotherapy of every theoretical persuasion. It will also be very meaningful to understand more, much more, about which patients will profit most from what kinds and degrees of the real relationship in their psychotherapy. In this venture, given the experience-near flavor of the real relationship, I hope that practicing psychotherapists, theorists, and empirical researchers learn a great deal from one another in coming to understand the role of the real relationship in the practice of psychotherapy.

REFERENCES

Ain, S., & Gelso, C. J. (2008, September). *Chipping away at the blank screen: Self-disclosure, the real relationship, and therapy outcome.* Poster presented at the annual convention of the North American Society for Psychotherapy Research, New Haven, CT.

Ainsworth, M. D. S., Blehar, M. C., Waters, E., & Wall, S. (1978). *Patterns of attachment: A psychological study of the strange situation.* Hillsdale, NJ: Erlbaum.

Aron, L. (1996). *A meeting of minds: Mutuality in psychoanalysis.* Hillsdale, NJ: Analytic Press.

Baehr, A. P. (2004). *Wounded hearers and relational experts: A grounded theory of experienced psychotherapists' management and use of countertransference.* (Unpublished doctoral dissertation). Pennsylvania State University, University Park.

Barrett-Lennard, G. T. (1962). Dimensions of therapist responses as causal factors in therapeutic personality change. *Psychological Monographs, 76*(43, Whole No. 562).

Barrett-Lennard, G. T. (1964). *The Relationship Inventory: Form OS-M-64, Form OS-F-64, Form MO-M-64 and MO-F-64.* Armidale, New South Wales, Australia: University of New England.

Barrett-Lennard, G. T. (1985). The helping relationship: Crisis and advance in theory and research. *The Counseling Psychologist, 13,* 279–294. doi:10.1177/0011000085132006

Bibring, E. (1937). On the theory of the therapeutic results of psycho-analysis. *International Journal of Psycho-Analysis, 18,* 170–189.

Bohart, A. C. (2005). Person-centered psychotherapy and related experiential approaches. In A. Gurman & S. Messer (Eds.), *Essential psychotherapies: Theory and practice* (2nd ed., pp. 107–148). New York, NY: Guilford Press.

Bohart, A. C., Elliott, R., Greenberg, L., & Watson, J. C. (2002). Empathy. In J. Norcross (Ed.), *Psychotherapy relationships that work* (pp. 89–108). New York, NY: Oxford University Press.

Bonitz, V. (2008). Use of physical touch in the "talking cure:" A journey to the outskirts of psychotherapy. *Psychotherapy, 45,* 391–404. doi:10.1037/a0013311

Bordin, E. S. (1979). The generalizability of the psychoanalytic concept of the working alliance. *Psychotherapy Theory, Research, Practice, Training, 16,* 252–260.

Bowlby, J. (1973). *Attachment and loss: Vol. 2. Separation, anxiety and anger.* New York, NY: Basic Books.

Bowlby, J. (1982). *Attachment and loss: Vol. 1. Attachment* (2nd ed.). New York, NY: Basic Books. (Original work published 1969)

Bowlby, J. (1988). *A secure base: Parent–child attachments and healthy human development.* New York, NY: Basic Books.

Bozarth, J. D. (1984). Beyond reflection: Emergent modes of empathy. In R. Levant & J. Shlien (Eds.), *Client-centered therapy and the person-centered approach* (pp. 59–75). New York, NY: Praeger.

Brennan, K. A., Clarke, C. L., & Shaver, P. R. (1998). Self-report measurement of adult attachment: An integrative overview. In J. A. Simpson & W. F. Rholes (Eds.), *Attachment theory and close relationships* (pp. 46–76). New York, NY: Guilford Press.

Busseri, M. A., & Tyler, J. D. (2003). Interchangeability of the Working Alliance Inventory and Working Alliance Inventory, Short Form. *Psychological Assessment, 15,* 193–197. doi:10.1037/1040-3590.15.2.193

Cassidy, J. (2000). Adult romantic attachments: A developmental perspective on individual differences. *Review of General Psychology, 4,* 111–131. doi:10.1037/1089-2680.4.2.111

Cassidy, J., & Shaver, P. R. (Eds.). (2008). *Handbook of attachment: Theory, research and clinical applications* (2nd ed.). New York, NY: Guilford Press.

Charman, D. P., & Graham, A. C. (2004). Ending therapy: Processes and outcomes. In D. P. Charman (Ed.), *Core processes in brief psychodynamic psychotherapy* (pp. 275–288). Mahwah, NJ: Erlbaum.

Clarke, A. R. (1996). *The development of a scale measuring the observing ego functions.* (Unpublished doctoral dissertation). Georgia State University, Atlanta.

Couch, A. S. (1999). The therapeutic functions of the real relationship in psychoanalysis. *The Psychoanalytic Study of the Child, 54,* 130–168.

Curtis, R., Field, C., Knaan-Kostman, I., & Mannix, K. (2004). What 75 psychoanalysts found helpful and hurtful in their own analyses. *Psychoanalytic Psychology, 21,* 183–202. doi:10.1037/0736-9735.21.2.183

Duquette, P. (1997). The role of the real relationship in long-term psychotherapy. *International Journal of Psychotherapy and Critical Thought, 4,* 11–20.

Eagle, M. N. (2000). A critical evaluation of current conceptions of transference and countertransference. *Psychoanalytic Psychology, 17,* 24–37. doi:10.1037/0736-9735.17.1.1.a

Eagle, M. N. (2003). The postmodern turn in psychoanalysis. *Psychoanalytic Psychology, 20,* 411–424. doi:10.1037/0736-9735.20.3.411

Eagle, M., Wolitzky, D. L., & Wakefield, J. (2001). The analyst's knowledge and authority: A critique of the "new view" in psychoanalysis. *Journal of the American Psychoanalytic Association, 4,* 457–488. doi:10.1177/00030651010490020301

Elliott, R., Greenberg, L. S., & Lietaer, G. (2004). Research on experiential psychotherapies. In M. J. Lambert (Ed.), *Handbook of psychotherapy and behavior change* (5th ed., pp. 493–539). New York, NY: Wiley.

Eugster, S. L. (1995). *Systematic effects of participant role on the evaluation of the psychotherapy session.* (Unpublished doctoral dissertation). University of Wisconsin–Madison.

Eugster, S. L., & Wampold, B. E. (1996). Systematic effects of participant role on evaluation of the psychotherapy session. *Journal of Consulting and Clinical Psychology, 64,* 1020–1028. doi:10.1037/0022-006X.64.5.1020

Farber, B. A. (2006). *Self-disclosure in psychotherapy*. New York, NY: Guilford Press.

Fauth, J., & Williams, E. N. (2005). The in-session self-awareness of therapist-trainees: Hindering or helpful? *Journal of Counseling Psychology, 52*, 443–447. doi:10.1037/0022-0167.52.3.443

Fenigstein, A., Scheier, M. F., & Buss, A. H. (1975). Public and private self-consciousness: Assessment and theory. *Journal of Consulting and Clinical Psychology, 43*, 522–527. doi:10.1037/h0076760

Frank, K. A. (2005). Toward a conceptualization of the personal relationship in therapeutic action: Beyond the "real relationship." *Psychoanalytic Perspectives, 3*, 15–56.

Freedman, S. R., & Enright, R. D. (1996). Forgiveness as an intervention goal with incest survivors. *Journal of Consulting and Clinical Psychology, 64*, 983–992. doi:10.1037/0022-006X.64.5.983

Freud, A. (1954). The widening scope for indications for psychoanalysis [Discussion]. *Journal of the American Psychoanalytic Association, 2*, 607–620. doi:10.1177/000306515400200404

Freud, S. (1953a). The dynamics of transference. In J. Strachey (Ed. & Trans.), *Standard edition of the complete psychological works of Sigmund Freud* (Vol. 12, pp. 97–108). London, England: Hogarth Press. (Original work published 1912)

Freud, S. (1953b). On psychotherapy. In J. Strachey (Ed. & Trans.), *Standard edition of the complete psychological works of Sigmund Freud* (Vol. 7, pp. 255–268). London, England: Hogarth Press. (Original work published 1905)

Freud, S. (1955). Lines of advance in psychoanalysis. In J. Strachey (Ed. & Trans.), *Standard edition of the complete psychological works of Sigmund Freud* (Vol. 17, pp. 135–144). London, England: Hogarth Press. (Original work published 1919)

Freud, S. (1957). Future prospects of psychoanalytic psychotherapy. In. J. Strachey (Ed. & Trans.), *Standard edition of the complete psychological works of Sigmund Freud* (Vol. 11, pp. 139–151). London, England: Hogarth Press. (Original work published 1910)

Freud, S. (1959a). Fragment of an analysis of a case of hysteria. In J. Riviere (Ed. & Trans.), *Collected papers of Sigmund Freud* (Vol. 3, pp. 13–146). London, England: Hogarth Press. (Original work published 1905)

Freud, S. (1959b). Recommendations for physicians on the psycho-analytic method of treatment. In J. Riviere (Ed. & Trans.), *Collected papers of Sigmund Freud* (Vol. 2, pp. 323–341). London, England: Hogarth Press. (Original work published 1912)

Freud, S. (1964). Analysis terminable and interminable. In J. Strachey (Ed. & Trans.), *Standard edition of the complete psychological works of Sigmund Freud* (Vol. 23, pp. 216–253). London, England: Hogarth Press. (Original work published 1937)

Fuertes, J. N., Gelso, C. J., Perolini, C., Walden, T., Kasnakian, C., & Parsons, J. (2008, August). *Development of the real relationship in time-limited therapy*. Paper presented at the 116th Annual Convention of the American Psychological Association, Boston, MA.

Fuertes, J. N., Mislowack, A., Brown, S., Gur-Arie, S., Wilkinson, S., & Gelso, C. J. (2007). Correlates of the real relationship in psychotherapy: A study of dyads. *Psychotherapy Research, 17*, 423–430. doi:10.1080/10503300600789189

Gardiner, M. (Ed.). (1971). *The Wolf-Man: The double story of Freud's most famous case*. New York, NY: Basic Books.

Geller, J. D. (2005). Style and its contribution to a patient-specific model of therapeutic technique. *Psychotherapy, 42*, 469–482. doi:10.1037/0033-3204.42.4.469

Gelso, C. J. (2002). The real relationship: The "something more" of psychotherapy. *Journal of Contemporary Psychotherapy, 32*, 35–40. doi:10.1023/A:1015531228504

Gelso, C. J. (Ed.). (2007). *Psychotherapy Theory, Research, Practice, Training, 44*(3).

Gelso, C. J. (2009a). The real relationship in a post-modern world: Theoretical and empirical explorations. *Psychotherapy Research, 19*, 253–264. doi:10.1080/10503300802389242

Gelso, C. J. (2009b). The time has come: The real relationship in psychotherapy research. *Psychotherapy Research, 19*, 278–282. doi:10.1080/10503300902777155

Gelso, C. J., & Carter, J. A. (1985). The relationship in counseling and psychotherapy. *The Counseling Psychologist, 13*, 155–243. doi:10.1177/0011000085132001

Gelso, C. J., & Carter, J. A. (1994). Components of the psychotherapy relationship: Their interaction and unfolding during treatment. *Journal of Counseling Psychology, 41*, 296–306. doi:10.1037/0022-0167.41.3.296

Gelso, C. J., & Harbin, J. (2007). Insight, action, and the therapeutic relationship. In L. G. Castonguay & C. E. Hill (Eds.), *Insight in psychotherapy* (pp. 293–311). Washington, DC: American Psychological Association. doi:10.1037/11532-014

Gelso, C. J., & Hayes, J. A. (1998). *The psychotherapy relationship: Theory, research, and practice*. New York, NY: Wiley.

Gelso, C. J., & Hayes, J. A. (2002). The management of countertransference. In J. Norcross (Ed.), *Psychotherapy relationships that work* (pp. 267–284). New York, NY: Oxford University Press.

Gelso, C. J., & Hayes, J. A. (2007). *Countertransference and the therapist's inner experience: Perils and possibilities*. New York, NY: Routledge.

Gelso, C. J., Hill, C. E., Mohr, J. J., Rochlen, A. B., & Zack, J. (1999). Describing the face of transference: Psychodynamic therapists' recollections about transference in cases of successful long-term therapy. *Journal of Counseling Psychology, 46*, 257–267. doi:10.1037/0022-0167.46.2.257

Gelso, C. J., & Johnson, D. H. (1983). *Explorations in time-limited counseling and psychotherapy*. New York, NY: Teachers College Press.

Gelso, C. J., Kelley, F. A., Fuertes, J. N., Marmarosh, C., Holmes, S. E., Costa, C., & Hancock, G. R. (2005). Measuring the real relationship in psychotherapy:

Initial validation of the therapist form. *Journal of Counseling Psychology, 52,* 640–649. doi:10.1037/0022-0167.52.4.640

Gelso, C. J., Kivlighan, D. M., Spiegel, E. B., Busa-Knepp, J., Ain, S., . . . , Ma, E. (2010). *The unfolding of therapists' and clients' perceptions of the real relationship and their association to psychotherapy outcome.* Manuscript submitted for publication.

Gelso, C. J., Kivlighan, D. M., Wine, B., Jones, A., & Friedman, S. (1997). Transference, insight, and the course of time-limited therapy. *Journal of Counseling Psychology, 44,* 209–217. doi:10.1037/0022-0167.44.2.209

Gelso, C. J., & Samstag, L. W. (2008). A tripartite model of the therapeutic relationship. In S. Brown & R. Lent (Eds.), *Handbook of counseling psychology* (pp. 267–283). New York, NY: Wiley.

Gelso, C. J., & Woodhouse, S. S. (2002). The termination of psychotherapy: What research tells us about the process of ending treatment. In G. S. Tryon (Ed.), *Counseling based on process research: Applying what we know* (pp. 344–369). Boston, MA: Allyn & Bacon.

Gitelson, M. (1952). The emotional position of the analyst in the psychoanalytic situation. *The International Journal of Psycho-Analysis, 33,* 1–10.

Gitelson, M. (1962). The curative factors in psychoanalysis: The first phase of psychoanalysis. *International Journal of Psycho-Analysis, 43,* 194–205.

Goldfried, M. R. (2007). What has psychotherapy inherited from Carl Rogers? *Psychotherapy, 44,* 249–252. doi:10.1037/0033-3204.44.3.249

Goldfried, M. R., & Davila, J. (2005). The role of relationships and technique in therapeutic change. *Psychotherapy, 42,* 421–430. doi:10.1037/0033-3204.42.4.421

Graff, H., & Luborsky, L. L. (1977). Long-term trends in transference and resistance: A report on a quantitative method applied to four psychoanalyses. *Journal of the American Psychoanalytic Association, 25,* 471–490. doi:10.1177/000306517702500210

Greenberg, L. (1994). What is real in the real relationship? *Journal of Counseling Psychology, 41,* 307–309. doi:10.1037/0022-0167.41.3.307

Greenberg, L. (2002). *Emotion-focused therapy: Coaching clients to work through their feelings.* Washington, DC: American Psychological Association. doi:10.1037/10447-000

Greenson, R. R. (1965). The working alliance and the transference neurosis. *Psychoanalytic Quarterly, 34,* 155–181.

Greenson, R. R. (1967). *The technique and practice of psychoanalysis* (Vol. 1). New York, NY: International Universities Press.

Greenson, R. R. (1971). The "real" relationship between the patient and the psychoanalyst. In M. Kanzer (Ed.), *The unconscious today: Essays on Max Schur* (pp. 213–232). New York, NY: International Universities Press.

Greenson, R. R. (1972). Beyond transference and interpretations. *International Journal of Psycho-Analysis, 53,* 213–217.

Greenson, R. R. (1974). Loving, hating, and indifference towards the patient. *International Review of Psycho-Analysis, 1,* 259–266.

Greenson, R. R. (1978). *Explorations in psychoanalysis.* New York, NY: International Universities Press.

Greenson, R. R., & Wexler, M. (1969). The non-transference relationship in the psychoanalytic situation. *International Journal of Psycho-Analysis, 50,* 27–39.

Hatcher, R. L. (2009). Considering the real relationship: Reaction to Gelso's "The Real Relationship in a Postmodern World: Theoretical and Empirical Explorations." *Psychotherapy Research, 19,* 269–272. doi:10.1080/10503300802527189

Hatcher, R. L., & Barends, A. W. (2006). How a return to theory could help alliance theory. *Psychotherapy, 43,* 292–299. doi:10.1037/0033-3204.43.3.292

Hatcher, R. L., & Gillaspy, J. A. (2006). Development and validation of a revised version of the Working Alliance Inventory. *Psychotherapy Research, 16,* 12–25. doi:10.1080/10503300500352500

Hayes, J. A., & Gelso, C. J. (2001). Clinical implications of research on countertransference: Science informing practice. *Journal of Clinical Psychology, 57,* 1041–1051.

Hayes, S. C., Strosahl, K. D., & Wilson, K. (1999). *Acceptance and commitment therapy: An experiential approach to behavior change.* New York, NY: Guilford Press.

Hill, C. E. (1989). *Therapist techniques and client outcome: Eight cases of brief psychotherapy.* Newbury Park, CA: Sage.

Hill, C. E. (1994). What is the therapeutic relationship? A reaction to Sexton and Whiston. *The Counseling Psychologist, 22,* 90–97. doi:10.1177/0011000094221005

Hill, C. E. (2004). *Helping skills: Facilitating exploration, insight, and action.* Washington, DC: American Psychological Association. doi:10.1037/10624-000

Hill, C. E. (2009). *Helping skills: Facilitating exploration, insight, and action* (3rd ed.). Washington, DC: American Psychological Association.

Hill, C. E., & Knox, S. (2002). Self-disclosure. In J. Norcross (Ed.), *Psychotherapy relationships that work* (pp. 249–259). Oxford, England: Oxford University Press.

Hill, C. E., Sim, W., Spangler, P., Stahl, J., Sullivan, C., & Teyber, E. (2008). Therapist immediacy in brief psychotherapy: Case Study II. *Psychotherapy, 45,* 298–315. doi:10.1037/a0013306

Holtforth, M. G., & Castonguay, L. G. (2005). Relationship and techniques in cognitive-behavioral therapy—A motivational approach. *Psychotherapy, 42,* 443–455. doi:10.1037/0033-3204.42.4.443

Horvath, A. O. (1982). *Users' manual of the Working Alliance Inventory* (Unpublished manuscript No. 82.2). Simon Fraser University, Burnaby, British Columbia, Canada.

Horvath, A. O. (2006). The alliance in context: Accomplishments, challenges, and future directions. *Psychotherapy, 43,* 258–263. doi:10.1037/0033-3204.43.3.258

Horvath, A. O., & Bedi, R. P. (2002). The alliance. In J. C. Norcross (Ed.), *Psychotherapy relationships that work* (pp. 37–70). New York, NY: Oxford University Press.

Horvath, A. O., & Greenberg, L. (1989). Development and validation of the Working Alliance Inventory. *Journal of Counseling Psychology, 36,* 223–233. doi:10.1037/0022-0167.36.2.223

Kahn, J. H., Achter, J. A., & Shambaugh, E. J. (2001). Client distress, disclosure characteristics at intake, and outcome in brief counseling. *Journal of Counseling Psychology, 48,* 203–211. doi:10.1037/0022-0167.48.2.203

Kasper, L., Hill, C. E., & Kivlighan, D. M. (2008). Therapist immediacy in brief psychotherapy: Case study I. *Psychotherapy, 45,* 281–297. doi:10.1037/a0013305

Kelley, F. A. (2002). *The Real Relationship Inventory: Development and validation of the client form* (Unpublished doctoral dissertation). University of Maryland, College Park.

Kelley, F., Gelso, C. Fuertes, J., Marmarosh, C., & Lanier, S. (in press). The Real Relationship Inventory: Development and psychometric investigation of the client form. *Psychotherapy Theory, Research, Practice, Training.*

Kelley, F. A., LeBeouf-Davis, D., & Weiss, B. (2008, August). *Psychotherapy practices with LGB clients: Relation to the real relationship, working alliance, and clients' ratings of their therapists.* Paper presented at the 116th Annual Convention of the American Psychological Association, Boston, MA.

Kiesler, D. J. (1988). *Therapeutic metacommunication: Therapist impact disclosure as feedback in psychotherapy.* Palo Alto, CA: Consulting Psychologists Press.

Kivlighan, D. M., & Shaughnessy, P. (2000). Patterns of working alliance development: A typology of clients' working alliance ratings. *Journal of Counseling Psychology, 47,* 362–371. doi:10.1037/0022-0167.47.3.362

Klein, M. H., Kolden, G. G., Michels, J. L., & Chisholm-Stockard, S. (2002). Congruence. In J. Norcross (Ed.), *Psychotherapy relationships that work* (pp. 195–216). London, England: Oxford University Press.

Knox, S., Hess, S. A., Peterson, D. A., & Hill, C. E. (1997). A qualitative analysis of client perceptions of the effects of helpful therapist self-disclosure in long-term therapy. *Journal of Counseling Psychology, 44,* 274–283. doi:10.1037/0022-0167.44.3.274

Kohlenberg, R. J., & Tsai, M. (1995). Functional analytic psychotherapy: A behavioral approach to intensive treatment. In W. T. O'Donohue & L. Krasner (Eds.), *Theories of behavior therapy: Exploring behavior change* (pp. 637–658). Washington, DC: American Psychological Association. doi:10.1037/10169-023

Kohut, H. (1977). *The restoration of the self.* New York, NY: International Universities Press.

Lambert, M. J., & Barley, D. E. (2002). Research summary on the therapeutic relationship and psychotherapy outcome. In J. C. Norcross (Ed.), *Psychotherapy relationships that work* (pp. 17–36). New York, NY: Oxford University Press.

Lambert, M. J., Hansen, N. B., Umphress, V., Lunnen, K., Okiishi, J., Burlingame, G., & Reisinger, C. W. (1996). *Administration and scoring manual for the Outcome Questionnaire (OQ 45.2).* Wilmington, DE: American Professional Credentialing Services.

Latts, M. G., & Gelso, C. J. (1995). Countertransference behavior and management with survivors of sexual assault. *Psychotherapy, 32*, 405–415. doi:10.1037/0033-3204.32.3.405

Lejuez, C. W., Hopko, D. R., Levine, S., Gholkar, R., & Collins, L. M. (2005). The therapeutic alliance in behavior therapy. *Psychotherapy, 42*, 456–468. doi:10.1037/0033-3204.42.4.456

Lietaer, G. (1993). Authenticity, congruence, and transparency. In D. Brazier (Ed.), *Beyond Carl Rogers* (pp. 17–46). London, England: Constable.

Linehan, M. M. (1993). *Cognitive–behavioral treatment of borderline personality disorder*. New York, NY: Guilford Press.

Lipton, S. D. (1977). The advantages of Freud's technique as shown in his analysis of the Rat Man. *International Journal of Psycho-Analysis, 58*, 255–273.

LoCoco, G., Prestano, C., Gullo, S., & Gelso, C. (2009). *Relation of the real relationship and the working alliance to symptom change in brief psychotherapy*. Manuscript submitted for publication.

Mallinckrodt, B. (2000). Attachment, social competencies, and interpersonal process in psychotherapy. *Psychotherapy Research, 10*, 239–266. doi:10.1093/ptr/10.3.239

Mallinckrodt, B., Gantt, D., & Coble, H. (1995). Attachment patterns in the psychotherapy relationship: Development of the Client Attachment to Therapist Scale. *Journal of Counseling Psychology, 42*, 307–317. doi:10.1037/0022-0167.42.3.307

Marmarosh, C. (2009, August). *Chipping away at the blank screen: Real relationship in practice*. Paper presented at the 117th Annual Convention of the American Psychological Association, Toronto, Ontario, Canada.

Marmarosh, C. L., Gelso, C. J., Markin, R. D., Majors, R., Mallery, C., & Choi, J. (2009). The real relationship in psychotherapy: Relationships to adult attachment, working alliance, negative transference, and therapy outcome. *Journal of Counseling Psychology, 56*, 337–350. doi:10.1037/a0015169

Masling, J. (2003). Stephen A. Mitchell, relational psychoanalysis, and empirical data. *Psychoanalytic Psychology, 20*, 587–608. doi:10.1037/0736-9735.20.4.587

McCullough, L. (2009). The challenge of distinguishing figure from ground: Reaction to Gelso's work on the real relationship. *Psychotherapy Research, 19*, 265–268. doi:10.1080/10503300802592498

Meissner, W. W. (1998). [Review of S. A. Mitchell's *Influence and Autonomy in Psychoanalysis*]. *Psychoanalytic Books, 94*, 419–423.

Meissner, W. W. (2000). The many faces of analytic interaction. *Psychoanalytic Psychology, 17*, 512–546. doi:10.1037/0736-9735.17.3.512

Meissner, W. W. (2006). The therapeutic alliance: A proteus in disguise. *Psychotherapy, 43*, 264–270. doi:10.1037/0033-3204.43.3.264

Menaker, E. (1942). The masochistic factor in the psychoanalytic situation. *Psychoanalytic Quarterly, 11*, 171–186.

Mitchell, S. A. (1993). *Hope and dread in psychoanalysis*. New York, NY: Basic Books.

Mitchell, S. A., & Eron, L. (Eds.). (1999). *Relational psychoanalysis: The emergence of a tradition*. Hillsdale, NJ: Analytic Press.

Moore, S., & Gelso, C. J. (2009, September). *Attachment in psychotherapy: Considerations of the real relationship*. Poster presented at the New England chapter of the Society for Psychotherapy Research, Williamstown, MA.

Neisser, U. (1967). *Cognitive psychology*. New York, NY: Appleton-Century-Crofts.

Norcross, J. (Ed.). (2002). *Psychotherapy relationships that work*. Oxford, England: Oxford University Press.

Ogden, T. (1982). *Projective identification and psychotherapeutic technique*. New York, NY: Jason Aronson.

Orange, D. M. (1995). *Emotional understanding: Studies in psychoanalytic epistemology*. New York, NY: Guilford Press.

Orange, D. M. (2003). Antidotes and alternatives: Perspectival realism and the new reductionisms. *Psychoanalytic Psychology, 20,* 472–486. doi:10.1037/0736-9735.20.3.472

Perls, F. (1969). *Gestalt therapy verbatim*. Lafeyette, CA: Real People Press.

Perls, F., Hefferline, R., & Goodman, P. (1951). *Gestalt therapy: Excitement and growth in the human personality*. New York, NY: Dell.

Ponterotto, J. G., & Ruckdeschel, D. E. (2007). An overview of coefficient alpha and a reliability matrix for estimating adequacy of internal consistency coefficients with psychological research measures. *Perceptual & Motor Skills, 105,* 997–1014. doi:10.2466/PMS.105.7.997-1014

Prochaska, J. O., & Norcross, J. C. (2007). *Systems of psychotherapy: A transtheoretical approach* (6th ed.). Belmont, CA: Brooks/Cole.

Psychological Films. (Producer). (1965). *Three approaches to psychotherapy* [DVD]. Available from http://www.psychedfilms.com

Rabin, H. M. (1995). The liberating effect on the analyst of the paradigm shift in psychoanalysis. *Psychoanalytic Psychology, 12,* 467–481. doi:10.1037/h0079691

Reich, A. (1951). On countertransference. *International Journal of Psycho-Analysis, 32,* 25–31.

Renik, O. (1999). Analytic interaction: Conceptualizing technique in light of the analyst's irreducible subjectivity. In S. Mitchell & L. Aron (Eds.), *Relational psychoanalysis: The emergence of a tradition* (pp. 407–424). Hillsdale, NJ: Analytic Press.

Reynolds, W. M. (1982). The development of reliable and valid short forms of the Marlowe–Crowne Social Desirability Scale. *Journal of Clinical Psychology, 38,* 119–125. doi:10.1002/1097-4679(198201)38:1<119::AID-JCLP2270380118>3.0.CO;2-I

Robbins, S. B., & Jolkovski, M. P. (1987). Managing countertransference feelings: An interactional model using awareness of feeling and theoretical framework. *Journal of Counseling Psychology, 34,* 276–282. doi:10.1037/0022-0167.34.3.276

Rogers, C. R. (1957). The necessary and sufficient conditions of therapeutic personality change. *Journal of Consulting Psychology, 21*, 95–103. doi:10.1037/h0045357

Rogers, C. R. (1959). A theory of therapy, personality, and interpersonal relationships as developed in the client-centered framework. In S. Koch (Ed.), *Psychology: A study of a science: Vol. 3. Formulations of the person and the social context*. New York, NY: McGraw-Hill.

Samstag, L. W. (2006). The working alliance in psychotherapy: An overview of the invited papers in the Special Section. *Psychotherapy, 43*, 300–307. doi:10.1037/0033-3204.43.3.300

Spiegel, E. B., Busa-Knepp, J., Ma, E., Markin, R. D., Ain, S., Hummel, A., . . . Gelso, C. J. (2008, August). *Unfolding of the real relationship and its connection to outcome*. Paper presented at the 116th Annual Convention of the American Psychological Association, Boston, MA.

Sterba, R. (1934). The fate of the ego in analytic therapy. *International Journal of Psycho-Analysis, 15*, 117–126.

Sterlin, R. A. (2006). Where relational theory and attachment theory intersect: The real relationship and a real attachment. *Clinical Social Work Journal, 34*, 161–174. doi:10.1007/s10615-005-0018-0

Stiles, W. B. (1995). Disclosure as a speech act: Is it psychotherapeutic to disclose? In J. W. Pennebaker (Ed.), *Emotion disclosure and health* (pp. 71–91). Washington, DC: American Psychological Association.

Stiles, W. B., Glick, M. J., Osatuke, K., Hardy, G. E., Shapiro, D. A., Agnew-Davies, R., . . . Barkham, M. (2004). Patterns of alliance development and the rupture-repair hypothesis: Are productive relationships U shaped or V shaped? *Journal of Counseling Psychology, 51*, 81–92. doi:10.1037/0022-0167.51.1.81

Stiles, W. B., & Snow, J. S. (1984). Counseling session impact as viewed by novice counselors and their clients. *Journal of Counseling Psychology, 31*, 3–12. doi:10.1037/0022-0167.31.1.3

Stolorow, R. D., Brandchaft, B., & Atwood, G. (1987). *Psychoanalytic treatment: An intersubjective approach*. Hillsdale, NJ: Analytic Press.

Stolorow, R. D., & Lachmann, F. (1984–1985). Transference: The future of an illusion. *Annual Review of Psychoanalysis, 12–13*, 19–37.

Stone, L. (1954). The widening scope of indications for psychoanalysis. *Journal of the American Psychoanalytic Association, 2*, 567–594. doi:10.1177/000306515400200402

Stone, L. (1961). *The psychoanalytic situation*. New York, NY: International Universities Press.

Teyber, E. (2006). *Interpersonal process in psychotherapy: A relational approach* (5th ed.). Pacific Grove, CA: Brooks/Cole.

Tracey, T. J., & Kokotovic, A. M. (1989). Factor structure of the Working Alliance Inventory. *Psychological Assessment, 1*, 207–210. doi:10.1037/1040-3590.1.3.207

Van Wagoner, S. L., Gelso, C. J., Hayes, J. A., & Diemer, R. (1991). Counter-transference and the reputedly excellent therapist. *Psychotherapy, 28*, 411–421. doi:10.1037/0033-3204.28.3.411

Viederman, M. (1991). The real person of the analyst and his role in the process of psychoanalytic cure. *Journal of the American Psychoanalytic Association, 39*, 451–489. doi:10.1177/000306519103900208

Wachtel, P. L. (1980). Transference, schema, and assimilation: The relevance of Piaget to the psychoanalytic theory of transference. *Annual Review of Psychoanalysis, 8*, 59–76.

Wachtel, P. L. (2006). The ambiguities of the "real" in psychoanalysis. *Psychoanalytic Perspectives, 3*, 17–26.

Wallin, D. J. (2007). *Attachment in psychotherapy*. New York, NY: Guilford Press.

Woldt, A. S., & Toman, S. M. (2005). *Gestalt therapy: History, theory, practice*. Newbury Park, CA: Sage.

Woodhouse, S. S., Schlosser, L. Z., Ligiero, D. P., Crook, R. E., & Gelso, C. J. (2003). Client attachment to therapist: Relations to transference and client recollection of parental caregiving. *Journal of Counseling Psychology, 50*, 395–408. doi:10.1037/0022-0167.50.4.395

Yalom, I. D. (2002). *The gift of therapy: An open letter to a new generation of therapists and their patients*. New York, NY: HarperCollins.

Zetzel, E. R. (1956). Current concepts of transference. *International Journal of Psycho-Analysis, 37*, 369–375.

INDEX

ABOUT THE AUTHOR

Charles J. Gelso, PhD, has been a professor of psychology in the Department of Psychology at the University of Maryland, College Park, since 1970. He has published widely on the topic of the therapeutic relationship, including both empirical and theoretical articles and books. His work has focused on the real relationship, therapist countertransference, patient transference, the therapist–patient working alliance, and the interplay of these key concepts. He has also been the editor of major journals, including his most recent editorship of *Psychotherapy Theory, Research, Practice, & Training*. He has maintained a practice in psychotherapy throughout his career.

Dr. Gelso has received many honors and awards, including the Leona Tyler Award (from the Society of Counseling Psychology of the American Psychological Association [APA]), which is the top award in counseling psychology given for outstanding contributions to the field; the Distinguished Psychologist Award from APA Division 29 (Psychotherapy); and a grant in his name awarded annually by APA Division 29. Among his previous books are *The Psychotherapy Relationship: Theory, Research, and Practice* (1998) and *Countertransference and the Therapist's Inner Experience: Perils and Possibilities* (2007).